The MLA's Trusted Guide Goes Digital

With *MLA Handbook Plus*, students and instructors can access the ninth edition of the handbook online. New to the platform are two of our best-selling companion titles—the *MLA Guide to Digital Literacy* and the *MLA Guide to Undergraduate Research in Literature*—as well as a video course on MLA style.

MLA Handbook Plus is

Trusted
The only authorized subscription-based digital resource featuring the *MLA Handbook* is available for unlimited simultaneous users.

Dynamic
Features an easy-to-search interface, cross-linking of related material, and a split view that lets students see illustrations while reading corresponding content.

Evolving
Get the same content as the print edition, plus seamless annual updates and additional resources such as videos and companion titles.

Flexible
Whether on campus, at home, or in a coffee shop, students can access the platform from anywhere—perfect for remote or hybrid learning environments.

Accessible
Meets WCAG 2.1 accessibility standards—ensuring that learning MLA style is available to all.

Affordable
Tiered pricing model based on full-time undergraduate enrollments.

mlahandbookplus.org

2021 *Composition Studies* Reviewers

Richard Colby
Dominic DelliCarpini
Kara Poe Alexander
Ira Allen
Chris Anson
Hadi Banat
Christopher Ryan Basgier
Heather Bastian
Mark Blaauw-Hara
Beth Boquet
Lauren Bowen
Casey Boyle
Katherine Bridgman
Kevin Brock
Robert Brooke
Felicita Arzu Carmichael
Beth Brunk-Chavez
Carolyn Calhoon-Dillahunt
Christina Cedillo
Caroline Dadas
Sidney I. Dobrin
Dylan Dryer
Michele Eodice
Michael Faris
Robert Fuchs
Chris Gallagher
Romeo Garcia
TJ Geiger
Greg Giberson
Jackie Grutsch McKinney
Leigh Gruwell
Holly Hassel
Lavinia Hirsu

Amy Hodges Hamilton
Charlotte Hogg
Drew Holladay
Florianne Jimenez
Alison Knoblauch
Carmen Kynard
Christina LaVecchia
Donna LeCourt
Ben McCorkle
Cruz Nicholas Medina
Kelly Anne Myers
Jeff Naftzinger
Bernice Olivas
Enrique Paz
Carolina Pelaez-Morales
Stacey Pigg
Jim Ridolfo
Jeffrey Ringer
Todd Ruecker
David Seitz
Jennifer Sheppard
Rebekah Sims
Ryan Skinnell
Natalie Szymanski
Howard Tinberg
Elizabeth Vander Lei
Xiqiao Wang
Elizabeth Wardle
Scott Warnock
Joanna Wolfe
Erin Workman
Hui Wu

composition STUDIES

Volume 50, Number 1
Spring 2022

Editors
Matthew Davis
Kara Taczak

Book Review Editor
Jason Chew Kit Tham

Managing Editor
Megan Busch

Content Editors
Cydney Alexis
Jaclyn Fiscus-Cannady
Mike Haen
Callie Kostelich
Emma Kostopoulos
Rhiannon Scharnhorst
Roberto Sebastian Leon

Blog Editors
Ben Hojem
Jada Patchagondla

Social Media Editors
Mikala Jones
Annmarie Steffes

Editorial Consultant
Cydney Alexis

Former Editors
Gary Tate
Bob Mayberry
Christina Murphy
Peter Vandenberg
Ann George
Carrie Leverenz
Brad E. Lucas
Jennifer Clary-Lemon
Laura R. Micciche

Advisory Board
Sheila Carter-Tod
Virginia Tech University

Chen Chen
Utah State University

David Green
Howard University

Christina LaVecchia

Michael McCamley
University of Delaware

Cruz Medina
Santa Clara University

Jessica Nastal-Dema
Prairie State College

Melissa Berry Pearson
Northeastern University

Annette Harris Powell
Bellarmine University

Margaret Price
The Ohio State University

Nathalie Singh-Corcoran
West Virginia University

Darci Thoune
University of Wisconsin-La Crosse

SUBSCRIPTIONS

Composition Studies is published twice each year (May and November). Annual subscription rates: Individuals $25 (Domestic), $30 (International), and $15 (Students). To subscribe online, please visit https://compstudiesjournal.com/subscriptions/.

BACK ISSUES

Back issues, five years prior to the present, are freely accessible on our website: https://compstudiesjournal.com/archive/. If you don't see what you're looking for, contact us. Also, recent back issues are now available through Amazon.com. To find issues, use the advanced search feature and search on "Composition Studies" (title) and "Parlor Press" (publisher).

BOOK REVIEWS

Assignments are made from a file of potential book reviewers. If you are interested in writing a review, please contact our Book Review editor at Jason.Tham@ttu.edu.

JOURNAL SCOPE

The oldest independent periodical in the field, *Composition Studies* publishes original articles relevant to rhetoric and composition, including those that address teaching college writing; theorizing rhetoric and composing; administering writing programs; and, among other topics, preparing the field's future teacher-scholars. All perspectives and topics of general interest to the profession are welcome. We also publish Course Designs, which contextualize, theorize, and reflect on the content and pedagogy of a course. CFPs, announcements, and letters to the editor are most welcome. *Composition Studies* does not consider previously published manuscripts, unrevised conference papers, or unrevised dissertation chapters.

SUBMISSIONS

For submission information and guidelines, see https://compstudiesjournal.com/submissions/.

Direct all correspondence to:

> Matthew Davis, Co-Editor
> Department of English
> UMass Boston
> 100 Morrissey Blvd
> Boston MA 02125–3393
> compstudiesjournal@gmail.com

Composition Studies is grateful for the support of the University of Massachusetts Boston and the University of Denver.

© 2022 by Matthew Davis and Kara Taczak, Co-Editors

Production and distribution is managed by Parlor Press, www.parlorpress.com.

ISSN 1534–9322.

Cover art by Megan Busch.

https://compstudiesjournal.com/

composition STUDIES

Volume 50, Number 1
Spring 2022

Contents

2021 *Composition Studies* Reviewers   4
From the Editors: A Critical Encomium to Pasts, Presents, and Futures   9

At a Glance

By the Numbers: A Citation Analysis   29
    Doug Eyman

Articulations   31
    Dale Jacobs and Jay Dolmage

Familia's Digital Garden   35
    Ronisha Browdy, Esther Milu, Victor Del Hierro, and Laura Gonzales

Reflections

AI-Based Text Generation and the Social Construction of "Fraudulent Authorship": A Revisitation   37
    Chris M. Anson

Collaborative Writing, Collage, and Cooking: From Humanist to Post-Humanist Assemblages   47
    Anis Bawarshi and Mary Jo Reiff

Differences within Difference: Everyday Praxis from Latinx Lived Experiences   55
    Yvette Chairez, Victoria Ramirez Gentry, and Sue Hum

Rhetoric 2050: In Honor of Richard M. Coe's "Rhetoric 2001"   62
    Sidney I. Dobrin

The Democratization of Writing and the Role of Cheating   67
    Peter Elbow

Creating Space for Emotion in the *Composition Studies* Archive   73
    Alexis Sabryn Walston and Jessica Enoch

Embodying Mentorship and Friendship: A Love Letter to Villanueva's "Tradition and Change"   79
    Alexandra Hidalgo

Critical Distance in *Composition Studies*   84
    Rebecca Lorimer Leonard

The Catharsis for Poison: A Counterstory Retrospective on *Composition Studies'* 50th Anniversary   90
    Aja Y. Martinez

Composing in the Discomfort of Institutional Violence *Cruz Medina*	95
Composition Studies at 50: The New Work of Writing Instruction as a Way Forward *Staci Perryman-Clark*	100
Generation(al) Matters: Story, Lens, and Tone *Louise Wetherbee Phelps*	106
Renewing Commitments to Minoritized Writers *Ray Rosas and Cheryl Glenn*	127
In Search of the Sentence *Hannah J. Rule*	135

Where We Are: What's Next for (Publishing in) Composition & Rhetoric?

Pushing Through: Moving Beyond Revision to Achieve Substantive Change *Sheila Carter-Tod*	141
Speculative Middles and *Composition Studies* at 50 *Jennifer Clary-Lemon*	146
Anti-Racist Futures for Publishing in Rhetoric and Composition *Christina M. LaVecchia*	149
On the Future of Writing about Teaching *Carrie S. Leverenz*	153
Where We've Been and Where We Might Go *Bob Mayberry*	158
Fragile Material *Laura R. Micciche*	163

Book Reviews

Self+Culture+Writing: Autoethnography for/as Writing Studies, edited by Rebecca L. Jackson and Jackie Grutsch McKinney Reviewed by Bryna Siegel Finer	167
Working in the Archives: Practical Research Methods for Rhetoric and Composition, edited by Alexis E. Ramsey, Wendy B Sharer, Barbara L'Eplattenier, and Lisa Mastrangelo Reviewed by Lynée Lewis Gaillet	170
Postprocess Postmortem, by Kristopher Lotier Reviewed by Jason Tham	174
Contributors	179

From the Editors: A Critical Encomium to Pasts, Presents, and Futures

2022 is the 50th anniversary of *Composition Studies*–the field's oldest independent, peer-reviewed journal. To celebrate this milestone, we have invited contributions from a number of previous and current editors, authors, and board members from *CS*'s history. Specifically, we invited them to revisit the journal's past–whether their own contributions or or those of others–in the spirit of a critical encomium. In invoking this phrase, we hoped to draw on the genre's ancient roots–to draw forth praise for the journal (it is our birthday, after all!)–but also to welcome criticism, honest examination, and exhortations for improvement. We're very excited about how our 35 contributors interpreted this task, and we're excited to use this editorial introduction to join them in reflecting upon the previous half-century in order to understand the present moment of the journal and the future of our field.

The Past: Views of a Future to Come

We've heard it said that everything old is new again, an apt idiom for this issue of *Composition Studies*. As we perused the archives to see where it all began (at Texas Christian University! on typewriters!), we noticed how much carries forth from decades past.

***

Matt: In the very first article of issue 1.1, reprinted in full at the end of this introduction, Richard Larson writes about the changes in the content of composition, including the inclusion of public texts and student writing as content.

Kara: Well, we took this and ran with it, huh? Certainly using student texts to teach with and making public writing part of our courses, assignments, and sometimes even assessments, has become more popular. And the way conversations about the content of composition have taken center stage in recent years. Even the content of non-first year composition courses in a variety of curricular locations for writing classes. And we now have the writing major, the writing minor, MA and PhDs in rhetoric and composition–all of which are locations for thinking about writing-as-content.

Matt: Funny you should mention that. He also writes about a wide variety of approaches to course content, from theme courses, to speaking and writing, to those focusing on the "personal life," and on the identities of students. This certainly hasn't gone away! It is a bit more complicated than we have time for here, but these approaches have been generative of so many disciplinary conversations and debates over the last 50 years.

> Kara: So, did you see the part about "multiplying abundance" of offerings for what we might call "Freshman English" and what we might do to make some changes? Among those changes, he suggests: new, cheaper, and more usable textbooks. And we've definitely got plenty to choose from! Textbook production, cost, and availability is a constant concern for teachers. We've got more and more open-source textbooks– and open-access teacher resources–offering viable solutions. But! He also writes about how language itself "helps one to know and to organize one's knowledge."

Matt: Ha! Reflection, meta-cognition, key terms, transfer, threshold concepts– it's like the seedlings of all of that are right there. Much of the work in our journals in the intervening five decades has further explored how language and knowledge within first year writing can (or should?) be taught and explored.

And not just language. Get this–Larson also writes about how a "multiplication of forms" that includes "all modes of communication, print, non-print verbal, and non-verbal" as the hallmark of humanistic study. This is almost a full 25 years before the New London Group and multiliteracies!

> Kara: Exactly! Multimodality. Widely used and explored in many first year writing courses, writing across the curriculum programs, and writing center contexts. He even incorporates it into his piece. Look at this diagram–he focuses on studying students' "processes of thought and ways to increase the power of thinking" and–

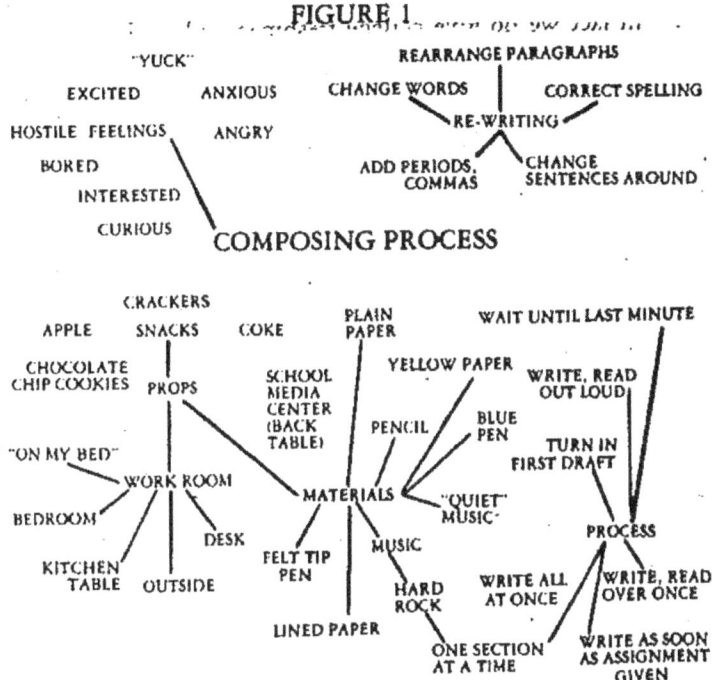

FIGURE 1.

Matt: The writing process!

Kara: Right?! One of our most transformative and enduring disciplinary concepts. And now we understand the power (and limits!) of it and its importance to students thinking critically about their own writing.

Matt: Not to mention the way the diagram anticipates attention to materiality (snacks, the kitchen table!), the affective turn ("yuck"!), and work in spatial rhetorics (there's the kitchen table from the extracurriculum!). He's got a bit about the goals of composition in there, too: "helping students achieve genuine rhetorical effectiveness in their writing"–which he specifically juxtaposes to the enforcement of correctness norms–and "helping human beings to make the most of themselves" as individuals, citizens, and inhabitors of a shared world.

Kara: Rhetorical effectiveness and making-meaning for oneself and others might be the most common course goal out there. And there's a lot to love and appreciate about this last statement: "helping human beings to make the most of themselves" as individuals, citizens, and inhabitors of a shared world. It's something most of us still strive for today.

***

Everything old really is new again! Fifty years ago, Larson's piece prefigured a lot of what we'd be researching, arguing about, and implementing in the writing classroom. On the one hand, it reads as if we've come full circle, writing about similar things over and over. On the other hand, those issues, questions, and concerns have been so generative– for revising, reinventing, remixing, transforming. Half a century later, this stuff really has staying power. Writing, and the teaching of it, transcends time. Why?

To consider the "why" question, we wonder about what issues have staying power in composition studies. And, if we just consider some of what was written about in the first pages of *Composition Studies*, these issues emerge clearly:

- Arguments about the content of composition
- Teaching writing across institutional contexts (especially two-year colleges)
- Articulating disciplinarity while valuing variety, reflection, and metacognition
- Understanding multimodality and changes that come with modalities
- Writing across the curriculum and the vertical curriculum
- Advocating for students, especially their rights to their own languages

Naming these issues helps us look at current movements and toward possibilities of what our future might be. And while there are parts of our past that–like most (maybe all?) histories–have things we wish could be undone, we remain hopeful about building a new way forward.

***

Events & Fun Facts in the History of CS

Among the many events in the pages of *CS*, we've selected a few we thought readers might enjoy (with issue numbers in parentheses):

- Announcement of the revival of the Rhetoric Society of America (1.1)

> *Freshman English News* is published three times a year at Texas Christian University. Subscription price for one year is $2.00. All news items, articles, books for review, and queries should be sent to the editor.
>
> Editor . . . . .Gary Tate
> Texas Christian Univ.

- Announcement of the beginning of *Teaching English in the Two-Year College* (3.2)
- Announcement of first forum on Freshman English at MLA (4.2)
- First Special Issue: A Forum on Doctoral Pedagogy (23.2)
- First international author contribution: Thomas from Soong Sil University, we think! (25.2)
- First issue typeset on a computer: spring 2003 (31.1)
- Special Issue: Composition in the Small College (32.2)
- First "Polylog" on Writing Center Directors and Writing Program Administrators (34.2)
- Special Issue: Growing Pains - The Writing Major in Rhetoric and Composition (35.1)
- Special Issue: Wo/men's Ways of Making it in Writing Studies (39.1)
- Special Issue: Comics, Multimodality, and Composition (43.1)
- Special Issue: Composition's Global Turn (44.1)
- Special Issue: Corequisite Writing Courses: Equity and Access (48.2)
- Special Issue: Diversity is Not Justice: Working Towards Radical Transformation and Racial Equity in the Discipline (49.2)

***

The Present: Reconsidering a Past

CS has long been conscious of and responsive to issues of equality, equity, and linguistic justice—even as we have sought to correct our mistakes, right past wrongs, and do better. In staging a critical encomium, this issue continues that tradition.

For instance, the At A Glance pieces (Eyman; Jacobs & Dolmage; Milu et al.) in this issue resulted from invitations to authors of some of our most-cited publications. We asked authors to to revisit their previous work and create visual representations of those pieces. These texts make that previous work comprehensible in news ways and also push at the limitations of their previous publications.

In lieu of articles for the issue, we invited a selection of previous *CS* authors to reflet on either their own contribution to the journal or on the work of others. What resulted is a fantastic array of interpretations of that invitation: some folks revisited specific pieces, ideas, or eras (Anson; Dobrin; Lorimer Leonard; Martinez; Rule), while others created specific encomia of individualized praise (Hidalgo;

CORRECTION

In the Winter issue, Richard Welna, English Editor for Scott, Foresman was quoted (p. 2. col. 1) as saying "Textbooks seem to be in a decline." What Mr. Welna said was "Textbookese seems to be in a decline." He still believes in textbooks! Our apologies.

Medina). Some took historical approaches to the tasks that were by turns personal, scholarly, and fun (Bawarshi & Reiff; Martinez; Phelps), and yet others cast new understandings of the past as possible future (Elbow; Enoch & Walston; Perryman-Clark). Finally, several contributors read the past through the lens of current thinking on race and ethnicity (Chairez et al.; Rosas & Glenn), thereby offering critiques for improvement and possible ways forward.

Similarly, we invited previous journal Editors and current Advisory Board members to contribute to a Where We Are focused on the question: "What's next for (publishing in) rhetoric & composition?" The resulting texts include deep microhistorical accounts (Clary-Lemon; Micciche), specific visions of futures contiguous with the journal's past (Leverenz; Mayberry), and critical accounts oriented to progressive futures (Carter-Tod; LaVecchia).

We also invited current and previous Book Reviewer Editors to review any book of their choosing. We think the results are a lot of fun: postprocess postmortem, autoethnography in writing studies, and a revisitation of the archives make for a tripartite exploration of major turns in the field's previous two decades (Gaillet; Siegel Finer; Tham). This issue doesn't contain any course designs, though fret not: those will continue again in the next issue!

Although not everyone we invited was inclined or able to take us up on the invitation, we're very grateful to the 35 contributors who were able to make it work during a very busy and difficult time.

At this particular present moment, the *CS* staff is also changing, so we want to thank the folks who are rotating off of our editorial staff. We're incredibly grateful to the following people, each of whom has been with us the past year and has helped immensely with editing the journal, growing our social presence, and leading *FEN Blog's* incredibly successful first year!

- *FEN Blog* Editors: Lauren Fusilier and Megan von Bergen
- Social Media Editor: Nitya Pandey
- Content Editors: Alex McAdams and Clare Sully-Stendahl
- Editorial Assistant: Anna Aldrich

We are incredibly grateful for your hardwork and dedication to the journal and wish you well in the next leg of your journey.

The Future: Where Do We Go Next?

Thankfully, the future of *CS* is also in its people, and we are thrilled to welcome a some new editors onto the team:

- *FEN Blog* Editors: Ben Hojem (Univ of Cincinnati) and Jada Patchagondla (UCLA)
- Social Media Editor: Mikala Jones (Young Harris College)

- Content Editors: Cydney Alexis (Kansas State Univ), Jaclyn Fiscus-Cannady (Florida State Univ), Rhiannon Scharnhorst (Univ of Cincinnati), and Roberto Sebastian Leon (Univ of Maryland)

They join our fabulous returning team members: Megan Busch, Mike Haen, Callie Kostelich, Emma Kostopoulos, Annmarie Steffes, and Jason Chew Kit Tham. One thing is clear: wherever we go next, it will be together.

Another question is how we get to where we are going. In our summer 2021 editorial introduction, we mentioned that we've been building a Heuristic Guide for Anti-Racist Editorial Practices. It's been reviewed by our Advisory Board and our editorial team, both of which have offered helpful feedback and revision suggestions. We piloted an initial version in the Community Guidelines and Review Guidelines documents for *FEN Blog*–we're proud to have this part of the journal, run by graduate student editors, lead the way forward. The updated document, which will guide future editorial practices at the journal, is now live on our website. We will ask future authors and reviewers to review it and join us in using it as a set of guiding principles.

> The editor reserves the right to edit essays so that their usage conforms with the *Guidelines for Non-sexist Use of Language in NCTE Publications.*

Trying to predict the future–disciplinary, educational, and otherwise–is a risky endeavor, as the past two years have shown very clearly. Nonetheless, at this moment we wonder: what does the future hold for *Composition Studies*?

We see a number of vibrant areas of inquiry in the discipline, and we look forward to publishing more work of the kind that has made the last 50 years so productive. At the same time, there are transformational changes in the world of linguistic technologies (as Chris Anson's contribution to this issue makes clear), in education, politics, climate, and other domains of life that, we think, deserve more of our attention.

So, as we look forward, we want to encourage authors to send us their research articles. Publishing research is something we were committed to when we began our collaborative editorship of the journal, and it's something we want as a continued focus. Though the discipline has moved a bit away from research in recent years, it's something we've continued to believe in. And we don't mean a specific call for a narrow conception of empirical work (though we certainly welcome empirical work!). This vision is one where research offers writers and teachers of writing systematic, ethical accounts of what happens within and outside the walls of our classrooms and results in robust constructions of knowledge that presents us viable ways to improve practice. Research can help us be/come better researchers, teachers, administrators, mentors, and citizens because it helps us form dialogical, reciprocal relationships between inquiry, praxis, understanding, and knowledge. As researchers and teachers of writing, we have the opportunity to offer students–and each other–something incredibly meaningful: knowledge that results in powerful meaning-making practices, a voice with which to share them, and ways of making and remaking the world with it.

Those are some of the reasons why, 50 years later, we believe the researching and teaching writing has such staying power.

Kt and MD
Denver and Boston
May 2022

Freshman English News

Volume 1, Number 1   March, 1972

FROM THE EDITOR

The primary aim of *Freshman English News* will be to provide a continuing report on the status of Freshman English throughout the country. Such a report seems desirable because of a tendency in the academic world to make decisions on the basis of "what is going on at all the other schools." If this tendency is widespread, if we do look to others and are influenced by others when making our decisions, then it behooves us to know as precisely as possible what others are actually doing. I am afraid that we often make decisions on the basis of rumors rather than on the basis of hard facts. Providing these "hard facts" will be one of the goals of this newsletter.

Although the dispelling of rumors is, I suspect, a worthwhile endeavor, there are nobler goals toward which a newsletter such as this might strive. A broadening of our sense of what is possible, an extension of our vision, might well occur when we know how others have tried and succeeded, how still others have tried and failed. *What* has been tried and *how* it has been tried will be the central concerns of the newsletter.

The following topics strike me as significant (and I invite news items and accounts which deal with all of these and the many others which remain unnamed): changing requirements, the nature of the "course," the training of TA's, the success of experimental programs, the role of the director of Freshman English, the use of writing labs, the establishing of standards in composition, the use of media, the success and failure of honors programs, etc., etc.

I should emphasize that this first issue of the newsletter is not typical of what we hope to publish in the future. There are more articles than items of news and information. Because I wished to publish the first issue this spring, I asked acquaintances to contribute material. Mr. Pritchard, the two-year college editor, did the same. The results are pleasing, but this issue should probably be viewed not as an actual newsletter but as an announcement of a newsletter. It is in this spirit that we are distributing it.

I should like to take this opportunity to thank publicly the Texas Christian University Research Foundation and its director, E. Leigh Secrest, for providing the funds that made possible the publication and free distribution of this issue.

G. T.

FRESHMAN ENGLISH IN THE 1970's

Richard L. Larson
University of Hawaii

If there ever was a program one could call "freshman English," it is fast disappearing, if it has not already vanished. If, that is, one could ever talk of a program in "English" that was more or less the same for most freshmen from campus to campus around the country, and be reasonably confident that one's words referred to something real rather than hypothetical, one can't do so any more. Even the common elements one thought one could count on—the collection of essays, the rhetoric-handbook, the weekly theme, the insistence on thesis sentences and on unity in the standard expository paragraph—are disappearing. And few teachers or students are lamenting their departure.

If one doubts the change, talk to textbook publishers, editors, and field representatives, who try in vain to learn where their once lucrative market is going, so that they can sign books to publish when the demand for them develops, two or three years hence. Watch the profusion of books, many of them short, most of them paperbound, almost all of them highly diverse in content, plan, and cover design, that are replacing (for many publishers at least) thick rhetoric texts and rhetoric-readers among the review copies that cross one's desk. There are exceptions, of course—an important one is William Irmscher's *Holt Guide to English*—but texts today are typically shorter, their materials more current (a more precise adjective might be "modish"), than when I went to the University of Hawaii in 1963. And teachers are replacing the classic essays with pieces from today's newspaper or this month's magazine, not to mention the much more important substitute—the writing of students themselves, mimeographed, dittoed, or xeroxed, which is made increasingly the focus of attention—often the exclusive focus—in classroom after classroom.

But such evidence is unnecessarily indirect. Catalogues and syllabi testify to the increased diversity of the "English" that is offered to students (and "offered to," rather than "required of," is increasingly the correct phrase) in their freshman year—if indeed the course is offered exclusively in the freshman year, rather than being deferred to the senior year, spread over two or three of the undergraduate years, or made available to the student for his election in any one of his four years. Courses focusing on film as rhetoric (as at the University of Illinois); courses studying mass media; courses offered in short modules, of which all students take one and then choose two others (as at Fort Hays Kansas State College); programs offering the student a choice of a semester of written or a semester of oral composition, and then a choice among several courses in writing or speaking, including courses in imaginative writing (as at the University of Massachusetts at Amherst); programs offering the student a choice of as many as eight courses—including Narration and Description; Autobiography; The Study of the Past; Language and the Visual Media (as in our program at the University of Hawaii)—these instances can only hint at the multiplying abundance of guises in which what we once knew as "Freshman English" is appearing. And the multiplication of forms promises to continue.

I think that this multiplication of forms is all to the good, and not just because it gives the student one more chance to decide what he wants in his education, while giving teachers the chance to teach from their interests and their strengths—as the teachers I interview are doing increasingly anyway, ignoring standard syllabi or voting such syllabi out of existence. For diversity breeds experimentation, and experimentation, at least in "freshman English," is humanizing. Not only the study of literature, but the study of all modes of communication, print, non-print verbal, and non-verbal are the proper concerns of the Humanities (indeed of rhetoric itself, as the participants in the National Developmental Project on Rhetoric argued); freshman English, like possibly no other part of the curriculum in English, has the opportunity to involve students in these humanistic studies. "Invention," rather a latecomer to the freshman syllabus, has led teachers to study processes of thought and ways to increase the power of thinking—a concern expressed in courses on problem-solving and in books like Young, Becker, and Pike's *Rhetoric: Discovery and Change*. Some experimental courses focus on the personal life of the student and help him understand, by his writing, what sort of person he is and how he came to be that way; I think of Taylor Stoehr's course at the State University of New York at Buffalo (recently described in *College English*), and of the work of John Butler at Wichita State University and now at Drexel. In the hands of some teachers, the writing course becomes an intensive exploration of how language helps one to know and to organize one's knowledge, as in the teaching of William E. Coles (formerly at Case Western, now also at Drexel).

I think—I hope—that this kind of humanizing experimentation shows where we are headed as teachers of composition. I think we are going to enrich our efforts at helping students to achieve genuine rhetorical effectiveness in their writing (as distinguished from enforcing the observance of conventions and formulae) by leading them to see how language, and indeed all communication potentially, can help them learn about their world, their neighbors on this planet, their fellow citizens, their problems, their choices, and themselves. Since we are working to help human beings make the most of themselves, this kind of dual emphasis, on rhetorical effectiveness and on knowing oneself and one's kind, seems to me a healthy and encouraging prospect to look forward to.

FRESHMAN ENGLISH IN TEXAS
Richard Fulkerson
East Texas State University

In August of 1971, the East Texas State University Freshman English Committee conducted a survey of a broad group of freshman English programs in Texas. Questionnaires were sent to directors of freshman English at thirty-five colleges and universities. Twenty-seven schools (counting ETSU itself) replied, ranging from small private institutions such as Abilene Christian College and Southwestern University to large public ones like the University of Texas at Austin and Texas Tech. The survey showed that although freshman English in Texas shows considerable variety, it does so mainly within quite traditional limits.

Twenty-three of the respondents require six semester hours of freshman English, and contrary to national trends, only two (Austin College and McMurry) indicated that they were considering reducing their freshman requirement. Ten schools restrict their freshman courses almost exclusively to composition; the others use literature extensively: five devote the freshman course almost wholly to literature. Writing requirements range from the University of Texas at Arlington's recommendation that each student write twenty 200-word paragraphs each semester to Sul Ross's demand of ten themes of 1200-1500 words. In six schools almost all writing is done out of class; in seven it is almost all in class; in the others both types are done about equally.

Three new programs are somewhat unusual. At Prairie View A and M, where students meet in classes of 200, all writing is done in class and graded immediately, as either acceptable or unacceptable, by graduate assistants; to pass, the student must produce a minimum number of acceptable impromptu papers. McMurry College emphasizes "creative writing techniques for purposes of inspiration and originality." And Tarleton State allots equal time in the second semester to three media: print, television, and motion pictures. Even these programs apparently differ from the traditional ones described above more in implementation than in either goals or theory.

Greater variety than the responses imply may actually exist since most of the schools allow the teacher considerable freedom to design his own course. Only six of the respondents attempt to insure uniformity among sections by using detailed prescriptive syllabi. But an important restriction on course design is the careful control twenty-one schools exercise over textbook selection. The great majority of the prescribed textbooks are standard handbooks, rhetorics, or anthologies, such as McCrimmon's *Writing with a Purpose*, Baker's *The Complete Stylist*, Perrine's *Structure, Sound, and Sense*, and Brooks, Purser, and Warren's *An Approach to Literature*. A few schools provide the teacher with several options, but only six give him nearly complete freedom to select his own books.

Thus the Texas college freshman stands a very good chance of being required to study a combination of literature and composition, of using standard textbooks, of writing six to ten 500-1000 word papers each semester and of having a teacher who is free to conduct the class pretty much as he wishes within these limitations.

EVOLUTION IN FRESHMAN PROGRAMS AT THE UNIVERSITY OF WISCONSIN — MADISON
William T. Lenehan
Director of Introductory Courses

The editor of *Freshman English News* asked that I contribute a brief statement on recent changes in the Freshman English programs at UW-Madison in order to verify or refute some of the rumors in current circulation. My knowledge of human nature convinces me that interesting rumor will triumph over tedious fact regardless of equal availability; however, I will state my version of the facts.

It is a fact that at the end of the 1968-69 academic year, the English Department ceased to offer a required composition course to most of the entering freshmen. I view this act as a logical step in an evolutionary process — not a radical reaction to a particular set of problems. The process began in the late 50's with the dropping of remedial composition programs; it continued at Wisconsin in the fall of 1968 with the replacement of the two-semester composition requirement for most students with a pattern of one semester of composition and one semester of introductory literature, both courses taught primarily by teaching assistants. The next step was that instituted in 1970: we returned to a small remedial composition program for those students who proved on their placement exams clearly deficient in language skills and instituted a writing laboratory to help students at any level who found themselves deficient in compositional skills. We continue to use teaching assistants in the introductory literature course, the writing laboratory, remedial composition, and discussion sections of large lecture courses, but the TA staff has been reduced in size, a necessity considering the job market.

What made this evolution possible and desirable was the changing nature of the entering students. Admission requirements and student self-selectivity gradually reduced the number of entering freshmen having very limited writing skills: most of our freshmen could create clear expository prose. It is a truism that writing is a skill that can always be improved, but to move from clear prose to effective prose requires motivation on the part of the students. After following the well trodden experimental path in search of motivating subject matter — relevant readers, short stories, novels, etc. — we concluded that our required composition course was not sufficiently successful in attaining its end — to improve the writing of the students — to justify its existence. We therefore quit offering the course.

Other circumstances, of course, entered into the debate before the Departmental action. It is a fact that some of our teaching assistants agreed with and even encouraged their students in the belief that composition courses were useless; it is also true that the period was one of student activism. Other pressures emerged on questions of college requirements, faculty attitudes outside the department, curricular patterns, and administrative procedures. But these were circumstances, not causes, and interesting though they may be, they do not belong in this report.

Although reactions are mixed, the general results after three semesters without a large composition program are encouraging. The Letters and Science College faculty has ruled that each department must certify its majors as competent writers before graduation. Required writing is appearing in all kinds of unlikely courses; faculty members in all departments are learning to comment on form as well as content on papers and reports. The ideal world has not arrived, but a major step has been taken; the responsibility for the writing ability of all our students has been distributed to a university faculty, not relegated to a sub-sub-group of an English Department; students, perceiving the fact that improved writing proficiency is an on-going process rather than a one or two course repetition in the freshman year of principles they were exposed to in high school, will, I firmly believe, be the major beneficiaries of this evolutionary process.

SUBSCRIPTION BLANK ON PAGE 11

COMPARING STIPENDS OF TEACHING ASSISTANTS

Richard Braddock
University of Iowa

Needing some data on the stipends of teaching assistants in order to do the best I could for my crew with the dean, last spring I wrote for that information to the directors of freshman English at a number of comparable universities in the Midwest. (I discovered that the information in the CCCC *Directory of Assistantships* is sometimes erroneous.) As I tried to reduce the data to comparable form, it became apparent that several other factors deserved consideration as well as the stipend —tuition expense, number of class hours taught per week, and size of class. Consequently, I computed a "student-hour stipend," reported here in case it may be useful to others.

The "student-hour stipend" is computed by subtracting from the nine-month stipend the amount the teaching assistant usually pays in tuition and fees for the academic year. That remainder is then divided by the product of (1) the total number of classes (sections) the assistant teaches during the academic year (adjusted, if necessary, to a semester system), (2) the number of "hours" which one class meets during one week, and (3) the average number of students in such classes. Several examples of such computations are offered in the accompanying table.

The advantages of computing a "student-hour stipend" are obvious. The results are comparable from one institution to another, and they give weight to a consideration like class size which otherwise may be overlooked. The disadvantages are that the "student-hour stipend" itself does not seem quite as meaningful in the real world as the stipend itself, even though the stipend itself is less meaningful than some realize when they ignore tuition and teaching load. Furthermore, the "student-hour stipend" ignores such qualitative matters as the nature of the graduate program and the nature of any in-service preparation for teaching offered at the institution. In addition, the "student-hour stipend" does not take into account the number of papers expected from students or the possibility that a teaching assistant may have more than one preparation in the number of classes taught. Some institutions offer higher stipends for assistants with more teaching experience than others, but this can be accounted for by computing the "student-hour stipend" for such people at the higher stipend figure.

Despite its shortcomings as an index of a teaching assistant's entire financial and educational prospects, the "student-hour stipend" strikes me as an index useful in comparing from one institution to another the stipend offered for work expected.

SOME STUDENT-HOUR STIPENDS
for 1970-71

	1	2	2-1	3	4	5	3 x 4 x 5	2-1 / 3 x 4 x 5
Institution	Basic* Stipend	Tuition** and Fees	Net Stipend	No. Classes Taught***	No. Hours in 1 Class/Week	Average Class Size	Student Hours per week	Student Hour Stipend
A	$3866+	—	$3866	4	3	19	228	$17
B	$1000+	$144	$ 856	3	2	25	150	$ 9
C	$3450+	$710	$2740	3	4	18	216	$13
D	$3000+	$520	$2480	3	3	22	198	$13
E	$2800+	$270	$2530	2	3	23	138	$18
F	$4836+	$561	$4275	4	3	25	300	$14
G	$2300	—	$2300	2	3	25	150	$15
H	$3600+	—	$3600	4	3	28	336	$11
I	$2800+	$120	$2680	4	2	20	160	$17

* Note that these figures may, with just as much meaning, apply to what others would call a two-thirds, half, or one-third appointment. Note also that when an institution's stipend is followed by a plus sign (+), higher stipends are given for TA's who fulfill certain criteria.

** This figure is the sum that a teaching assistant usually pays in an academic year. Where no sum is given, tuition is waived.

*** This figure represents the total number of classes (i.e., sections) taught during an academic year, adjusted to a semester system. For example, Institution G has offered figures for an assistant teaching one class during each of three quarters, adjusted here to the equivalent of one class during each of two semesters.

Freshman English News is published three times a year at Texas Christian University. Subscription price for one year is $2.00. All subscriptions, books for review, and news items about four-year college programs should be sent to the editor. News items about two-year colleges should be sent to the two-year college editor. The editors are interested in facts and news about Freshman English only. Theoretical and speculative articles should not be submitted.
Editor .... Gary Tate
Dept. of English
Texas Christian Univ.
Fort Worth, TX 76129
Associate Editor ...... Priscilla Glenn
Texas Christian Univ.
Two-Year College
Editor .... Arthur Pritchard
Tarrant County Junior
College (South Campus)
Fort Worth, TX 76119

I LIKE THESE
Jim W. Corder
Texas Christian University

Booth, Wayne C. *Now Don't Try to Reason With Me.* 1971.

Corbett, E. P. J., "The Rhetoric of the Open Hand and the Rhetoric of the Closed Fist," *College Composition and Communication,* XX (December, 1969), 288-296.

Kinneavy, James E., "The Basic Aims of Discourse," *College Composition and Communication,* XX (December, 1969), 297-304.

Harrington, David, "Teaching Students the Art of Discovery," *College Composition and Communication,* XIX (February, 1968), 7-14.

Ohmann, Richard, "In Lieu of a New Rhetoric," *College English,* XXVI (October, 1964), 16-22.

Ong, Walter J. *The Presence of the Word.* 1967.

Scott, Robert L. and Donald K. Smith, "The Rhetoric of Confrontation," *Quarterly Journal of Speech,* LV (February 1969), 1-8.

Tibbetts, A. M., "To Encourage Reason on Campus: A Proposal for a New College Course in Thinking and Writing," *AAUP Bulletin,* LIV (December, 1968), 466-472.

Walter, Otis, "Toward an Analysis of Ethos," *Pennsylvania Speech Annual,* XXI (1964), 37-45.

Weaver, Richard. *The Ethics of Rhetoric.* 1953.

Wilder, Amos. *The New Voice.* 1969.

THE TREND TOWARDS FRESHMAN SEMINARS

Thomas W. Wilcox
University of Connecticut

The term "Freshman Seminar" seems to have been coined at Dartmouth in 1958, when the English Department there revised its freshman program to include as its second-term offering a battery of innovative courses, each of which would be devoted to a specific theme, body of literature, or critical concern. The seminars bore such titles as "The Education of the Young Man in Literature," "James and Conrad," and "Worlds within Worlds" (a study of fantasies), and their common purpose was to allow each student to explore a limited topic in considerable depth. A stipulated amount of writing (c. 6,000 words) was required in each ten-week seminar. The Department thought it could best help its students to improve their writing by giving them something substantial to write about; it also hoped to demonstrate that study in depth inevitably leads to consideration of fundamental problems and principles, that specialization is the best route to general education. Dartmouth's freshman seminars proved enormously popular — so popular that other departments asked to participate and by 1962 a college-wide program had evolved. Similar multi-discipline programs have since been instituted at Cornell, Boston University, Brown, and elsewhere. Courses of the seminar type are now being offered to freshmen at Mills, the University of Washington, Buffalo, Ohio University, and many other two and four-year colleges. It seems likely that the number will grow as the multiple advantages of the seminar plan become apparent to more and more departments.

Those advantages may be illustrated by our experience at the University of Connecticut. For many years we required most of our freshmen to take one semester of composition and one semester of literature. In 1968, inspired by the seminar programs at Dartmouth and Cornell, we inaugurated a pilot program which consisted of a term of literature followed by a term of seminars. We liked our new plan so well that we installed it across the board last year. This year we also reduced the freshman English requirement to one course — the introduction to literature (in which students write about nine papers). Our seminars have thus become optional, but they are so popular that we are offering some 27 this spring and have enrolled about 70% of the students eligible to elect them. The seminars are popular with the staff as well, because they afford opportunities to experiment with new courses in topics of special interest to the instructors. Each member of the staff — and 80% of them are Teaching Assistants — submits a detailed prospectus of the seminar he proposes. These are reviewed by a faculty committee, and a slate of topics is submitted to the students (all 1,600 of them) for their opinions and suggestions. Some seminars are dropped, others added in response to our analysis of the students' preferences; we try to place each student who elects the course in a seminar he prefers. The results of this laborious procedure are gratifying: most instructors are teaching subjects which engross them, most students are taking courses which engage them. This term we have seminars in *Humor in Literature*, in *Legend and Fantasy*, in *Modern Afro-American Literature*, in *The Woman as Hero*, and in a host of other intriguing topics. Morale is high, freshman English at the University of Connecticut was never easier to defend, never more fun to teach.

[Professor Wilcox offers to answer queries about the planning and administration of freshman seminar programs. His address is U-25, University of Connecticut, Storrs, Conn. 06268.]

WORDS OF CAUTION

Ronald E. Freeman
UCLA

Even though some present elective systems in secondary schools avoid the teaching and experience of writing, I am skeptical that colleges will again try to make up deficiencies in preparation. Yet as many four-year colleges and universities abridge and abandon freshman English programs, it is not difficult to foresee further decline in the present sorry state of writing competence of college students. The junior colleges with their almost impossible variety of abilities and preparation provide too often a stop-gap operation. They also tend to work from the tightly structured (often prescriptive) to the impossibly loose—films, media, communication—with writing on the side. Still the most creative teaching and experiments may well be coming from these varied colleges. Such different approaches to composition and the experiments with sophomore and junior composition courses, sometimes with content more immediately related to students' interests and studies, may well provide some new methods for improving writing effectiveness.

I am assuming that two current approaches 1) theme or issue-oriented courses with widely ranging contents and 2) literature—composition courses will continue, perhaps proliferate. But I am not sanguine about these courses that appear to be so grounded in the immediate—specific issues, problems, themes of the day, probably overly content-oriented. Such courses may incite discussion and even motivate writing (often polemical), but do such courses *teach* writing skills and the effectiveness of prose? Similarly, can we assume that the study of literature will necessarily lead to effective writing by students? It too may stimulate and interest, and models have proven their value for centuries, but again without some *teaching* of writing *per se*, I think too often that technical form, literary criticism, ideas and themes may be emphasized and then the knowledge gained not transferred to students' practice of the art of composition.

I believe, however, that the clear move towards more imaginative literature in the composition courses across the country reflects the attempt by English departments to combine basic responsibilities. In their desire to do two things, I hope that they will focus on patterns of ordering ideas, use of details and various kinds of evidence along with concern for how and why language works in poems and stories, and the strategies employed for particular purposes and effects in order to relate the literature to the study of writing. I hope, too, that writing a critical analysis is not the only offspring of this marriage.

Clearly, I am still hopeful the composition course will continue to emphasize rhetoric and persuasion—occasion, audience, reception, strategies, stylistic variety, evidence; language study—semantics, nuances of words, dialects, literary and indirect, even devious, uses of language, polemical language, analytical and persuasive uses, etc.; and a variety of personal and reading experiences as sources for more direct and personal handling of themes and ideas. In fact, I believe that the study of rhetoric and language can easily be combined with any subject, especially literature, so that method might be wedded to content, providing some specific ways of showing students how to compose. The caution necessary in the use of any of these contents is that the art and skill of writing itself should always be the focus as well as the goal and not, I think, ideas alone.

RHETORIC SOCIETY REVIVED

Under the leadership of Richard Larson, Edward P. J. Corbett, Ross Winterowd, Richard Young, and others, the faltering Rhetoric Society of America has recently been revived, a constitution drawn and approved, and an 11-member Board of Directors elected. An Executive Secretary and an editor for the Society's newsletter will be chosen within a short time. The purpose of the RSA, according to its constitution, "shall be to gather from all relevant fields of study, and to disseminate among its members, current knowledge of rhetoric, broadly construed; to identify new areas within the subject of rhetoric in which research is especially needed, and to stimulate such research; to encourage experimentation in the teaching of rhetoric; to facilitate professional cooperation among its members; to organize meetings at which members may exchange findings and ideas; and to sponsor the publication of newsletters and reports concerning all aspects of rhetoric." For further information, write to Winterowd (USC), Corbett (Ohio State) or Larson (Hawaii).

New and recent titles for—and about—Freshman English...

APOCALYPSE
Dominant Contemporary Forms

JOE DAVID BELLAMY, *Mansfield State College*

An issues-oriented reader which emphasizes and explores the nature of existing contemporary forms of the essay.
400 Pages/Paperbound/1972/About $4.95

INSIGHT
A Rhetoric Reader

EMIL HURTIK, *San Diego Mesa College*

Includes material from an unusually wide range of traditional and contemporary sources. Arranged rhetorically.
480 Pages/Paperbound/1970/$4.95

COUNTERPOINT
Dialogue for the 70s

CONN McAULIFFE, *San Diego Mesa College*

Essays have been chosen for their lucidity and their potential for involving the student in the issues of the 70s.
462 Pages/Paperbound/1970/$4.95

AMERICAN MIX
The Minority Experience in America

MORRIS FREEDMAN and
CAROLYN BANKS, *University of Maryland*

Selections in this highly original anthology include short memoirs, essays, dialogues, a full length play, poems and short stories.
450 Pages/Paperbound/1972/About $4.95

SUNSHINE AND SMOKE
American Writers and the American Environment

DAVID D. ANDERSON, *Michigan State University*

This collection of essays, stories and poems exposes the historical and literary roots of the ecological crisis.
535 Pages/1971/Paperbound/$5.50

POETRY AND A PRINCIPLE

GENE MONTAGUE, *University of Detroit*

The student is quickly involved in the reading of poetry, then led through a progression of poems to discover the permutations and practical applications of theory.
280 Pages/Paperbound/1972/About $3.50

INSCAPE
Stories, Plays and Poems

MURIEL DAVIS, *San Diego Mesa College*

A truly original collection of stories, plays and poems rich with diversity and contrast.
632 Pages/Paperbound/1971/$5.95

A NATIVE SONS READER

EDWARD MARGOLIES, *Staten Island Community College*

A brief collection of literary works by black writers. Arranged topically.
361 Pages/Paperbound/1970/$3.25

COURSE X
A Left Field Guide to Freshman English

LEONARD A. GREENBAUM and
RUDOLF B. SCHMERL

The authors expose the minor indignities and major failures of freshman English, but also offer the student a strategy for survival and success.
224 Pages/Paperbound/1970/$2.45

USES OF RHETORIC

JIM W. CORDER, *Texas Christian University*

Using an outline of classical rhetoric as a springboard, the author explores and delineates the *uses* of rhetoric.
230 Pages/1971/$5.95

Lippincott College Department, East Washington Square, Philadelphia, Pa. 19105

PRE-PUBLICATION REVIEW OF THE HOLT GUIDE TO ENGLISH

"...Bill Irmscher's erudition is so solid, his coverage so extensive, his treatment so sound and sensible, his style so lucid and graceful... I don't think I'm indulging in superlatives when I say that there isn't a handbook/rhetoric now on the market that can match [The Holt Guide to English] for extensiveness and variety of coverage, for soundness of treatment, for practicality, for depth of knowledge about how language works.

"...Some unusual or particularly well-done sections:
- the structural definitions of grammatical terms
- good transformational test for the dangling verbal
- lucid exposition on the main principles of transformational grammar
- use of Burke's Pentad for generating ideas, illustrated by showing how the pentad might be used on a topic like the student-activist movement
- the arguments and counter-arguments on the subject of grades set up in parallel columns (a form of self-dialogue useful in the invention process)
- apt selection of paragraphs to illustrate ways of developing paragraphs, with analyses in the margins of what is happening in the paragraphs
- description of the six major styles, classified according to function or occasion (novel and exceedingly well done)
- good section on revision--passages in parallel columns, with analyses and advice about revising
- good section on patterns in misspellings (only treatment I've seen that was really useful)
- good section revealing the distinguishing features of the major literary genres, using a skeletal form of the genre
- twenty assignments that a number of instructors made on Dennis Jasudowicz's play *Blood Money* (teachers, who are desperate for ideas about *kinds* of assignments to make, especially on literary texts are going to love this section)
- the whole section presenting student themes on literature, accompanied by comments on the student's performance
- glossary [of additional linguistic, literary and rhetorical terms]. Here is certainly 'God's plenty.' The best I have seen in any handbook. You can't match it unless you go to something like Fowler or Thrall and Hibbard. Some of the longer entries, like those on courtly love, free verse, epic, romance, tragedy, are valuable little essays on their own. I would suspect that some students, especially those who were going to be English majors, would retain the book simply for the reference value of this section.

"I could find something commendable to say about almost every section of the book, but I singled these sections out for special mention. But let me single out one section for special, special comment. The chapter 'Writing on Literary Topics' is superb. The best I've seen anywhere..."

Edward P. J. Corbett, Director of Freshman English, The Ohio State University

WILLIAM F. IRMSCHER'S

January | 660 pages | $6.50
Examination copies are available now. Write to Mary Ann Rice, Dept. FEN3, Holt, Rinehart and Winston, Inc., 383 Madison Avenue, New York 10017 for your copy.

In a quandary?

Up to your neck in unsolicited examination copies that all look alike?

Scribners continues to publish a wide variety of textual and supplemental material. We have established six regional information centers. If you are planning a new course syllabus, call collect to the office nearest you. Outline your needs, the direction your course will take, the level of difficulty you expect your students to be prepared for. Let us suggest titles from our list for your further examination.

JOHN AHRENS
Mid-West
(419) 882-7618

NEAL WHEELER
Southeast
(201) 464-5042

ROGER BILLINGS
East
(201) 635-7179

CHRISTOPHER KENWOOD
Northwest & West
(212) 486-4010

PETER GIVLER
Southwest & West
(213) 660-9543

J. WILLIAM MOFFETT
Northeast
(607) 546-6738

CHARLES SCRIBNER'S SONS
597 Fifth Avenue
New York, New York

REVERSE ENGLISH
or
IT'S NICE TO HAVE SOMETHING ON THE BALL EVEN IF IT'S JUST A SPIN

Robert D. Hoeft
Blue Mountain Community College (Oregon)

There are, perhaps, a dozen of us in the room. Male and females are we, some still hatchlings, some so old we could draw the face of Coolidge from memory. Problems range from how to cover pimples to the insufficiency of the Social Security check. But we don't talk about those things; they are beyond the reach of our twenty-gauge text. What we are here for is simple; we will bleach all grammar errors from these students by dipping them for an hour three times a week into the Purex of Basic English.

This we do repeatedly until the "Ain't got none's" and the "Him and me's" become fainter, fainter still, and eventually fade completely away. (Well, not completely, to be perfectly honest. There are some who are fade-resistant.) But for most, the errors become fewer, the writing becomes better.

How? The students do exercises in a workbook, but we do more than that. We discuss the reasons why a change of word will alter the meaning of a sentence. For example we try to learn about precision by looking at the Christmas song, *It Came Upon a Midnight Clear,* and seeing what happens when we substitute prepositions in the line:

Angels bending near the earth to touch their harps *of* gold. By substituting "with" we can change the meaning to imply that the angels are using a guitar pick (gold, of course) to produce their music. Or (not gold, alas) we substitute "for" and find that now the angels have become a celestial combo working their way through heaven. Or (not even pyrite, I'm afraid) we slip in "into" and show that now the angels have an advanced case of King Midas Disease. We all chuckle about this, but the point has been made; any change of word changes meaning. Once students know this on the conscious level they are ready to utilize it in their writing.

To make sure, we do the same type of thing with verbs.

She *walked* into the room.

That verb just lies there and whimpers. And we say no. Then comes a trickle of suggestions. "Jumped?" Nifty. She's so eager she pounces in there like a pesky lion. "Tiptoes!" Peachy. The timid little thing is either practicing up on her ballet or is getting ready to pull a Lizzy Borden on some poor chap in the room. "Slithers!" Bulls eye. With a rose in her teeth and seduction on her mind. Keep a goin'! "Limps." Sure. Listen to the sound she makes: THUMP-thump, THUMP-thump. "Explodes." Run for the fallout shelter! We have reached critical mass and Miss Atomic Bomb is HERE!

We do this sort of thing with all of the parts of speech: (limped HOW? painfully, defiantly, pathetically?) A dog? I can't see him (a lop-eared, short-tailed, belly-dragging, one-eyed, splay-footed, tongue-lolling, curly-haired, black and brown, feisty little runt.) Now I can see him. But I can't hear him or smell him or . . . And they lambaste us with sensory information. "He smells like a skunk somebody neglected to refrigerate." "He barks like a mortar." "He sounds like he's trying to chew through a tank with a buzz saw." Etc.

And the "etc's" are delightful. Once the student knows what words do, how flexible, exact or vague they can be, he is on his way towards liking the process of writing. Once he accomplishes this he might even write when he doesn't have to. At that point learning begins to change into education.

The most rewarding class for observable progress is Basic English. We say hello to caterpillars and wave good-by to butterflies.

AN AUTHENTIC MULTI-MEDIA FRESHMAN COMPOSITION PROGRAM

Otto Lewis Pfeiff
Arapahoe Community College (Colorado)

Self-evident truths bear repeating now and then lest we lose sight of them. For instance, one communication (Old or New) can do some thing better than another medium: a slide projector conveys a visual image better than the human voice can. Arapahoe Community College English instructors understand this principle well and, working as a team, have created a year-long, multi-media freshman composition program. (This program has been seen at conventions and by individual English departments throughout the midwestern and western states.)

The results have been encouraging. Our students, nourished from childhood by mechanical toys, radios, cameras, movies and television, respond enthusiastically to our multi-media presentation designed to *compete* with the familiar entertainment media. Importantly, our students are writing better, on the average, than any students in our memory. (The twelve members of our department represent, collectively, over a hundred years' teaching experience.)

Over the five-and-a-half years of our college's existence, the department's one constant has been a quest for the most effective teaching methods possible within the limits of our resources. Working as a cooperative team and operating on the premise that each instructor has strengths that should be exploited, the staff has evolved its three-part method of instruction.

1. Multi-Media Lectures

Information distribution being one part of education, it makes sense to distribute to as many students at one time as possible. On a Wednesday, for example, a student in our second quarter composition program selects which of two (9:00 a.m. or 2:00 p.m.) presentations he will attend. One instructor makes both presentations, thus freeing the other eleven members of the department to grade, plan, counsel students, or to do whatever else they need to do.

Let's look in on one presentation. On this day, as the student enters the lecture hall, he hears the familiar sounds of John Hartford singing (on tape over the P.A.), "Like Unto a Mockingbird," a song that satirizes the "follow the crowd" theme. (The presentations serve two functions — informational and motivational.) A real live professor with a personally-adapted script begins the presentation as the music ends. Today's lecture is called, "On Using and Being Used," and deals with ten common propaganda devices. Smoothly blended with the lecturer's words, slides on a large screen, center-front, show spicy advertisements from magazines and newspapers that illustrate each propaganda device. On the second screen high over the lecturer's shoulder, definitions and verbal examples of the propaganda devices are projected. The 30-minute presentation (our lectures range from 20 to 60 minutes) ends with taped examples from radio (used with permission of the sponsors) of the same propaganda devices.

Each of the three quarters of our program—personal narrative, argument, and literary criticism—is built around a series of multi-media presentations using combinations of live voice, slides, transparencies, super-8, audio-tapes, and video-tapes. The student has an accompanying student manual containing student and professional writing models, pictures, cartoons, quips, and pages especially designed for the student to record notes from the media presentations as he writes his own rhetoric.

One instructor is appointed annually to oversee the continued development of each quarter's program. This instructor has the primary responsibility for refining media presentations and upgrading the student manual. His normal 12-hour load is reduced for one quarter to 9 as he works on the program. Arapahoe's Instructional Resource Center provides the expert technical assistance needed to avoid overly-amateurish production work. Some twenty publishers provide varying degrees of advice on the development of our composition programs.

2. Discussion Groups

Ideally, the two one-hour discussion sessions per week would be limited to 20 students. Political and economic realities have forced us to increase these sections to 25. In these, the instructor and students review the lecture content, study writing models, do related exercises, or whatever the instructor in each section decides to do to make the best use of the lecture content.

Each English instructor at Arapahoe handles three composition sections and one literature section with 30 students.

3. Individual and Small Group Conferences

The Arapahoe instructors feel that, while each part of the method is essential, the small group (3 to 5 students sharing in critiquing each other's writing) or individual conference is the heart of the method. After each of four theme writing assignments during the quarter, the student signs up for a specified time to meet with the instructor to evaluate his work. The small group conferences typically last about an hour, while individual conferences range from 15 to 30 minutes.

Student response to this intimate approach to learning about writing is consistently enthusiastic. While each part of our method is given enthusiastic student response, especially by transfer students to Arapahoe, the individual or small group conference is graded highest by students.

ASSESSMENT TECHNIQUES

Both formal (written) and informal (word of mouth) student *and* teacher feedback (as well as evaluation of our product, the students' writings and understanding of the course content) help determine what changes to make from year to year.

In addition to these measures, Arapahoe instructors, working in a merit pay system, are required to undergo a peer group evaluation (the group comprised by the department chairman, a person selected by the Humanities Division, and a person chosen by the instructor being evaluated) every fourth year. Instructor evaluations are done annually by students and the department chairman, as well as by the instructor himself.

The department is currently working through the Research Division of Higher Education of Colorado University to explore the possibility of setting up a three-way teacher-program exchange with Community colleges of Denver and Metropolitan State College to make a comparative study of the three colleges' effectiveness in teaching composition. Our motive in exploring this type exchange is to learn how we can do our job better.

For now, we have reason to feel good about what we're up to. Our students enjoy writing, and more astonishing still, our instructors enjoy teaching it.

APPROACHING A COHERENT ENGLISH PROGRAM

Donald G. Bass
College of the Mainland (Texas)

Since its inception in 1967 the College of the Mainland English staff (eight members) has believed that [1] English is something one does; [2] English is not something one observes; [3] English is reading, listening, talking, seeing *and* writing. This may sound like a very dry beginning, but such purposes are like *Ben Hur* compared with the *biddyism*, "I think I'll start with adverbs next year."

AN APPROACH

English instruction as an activity fits this college's purposes, especially the aim to help young people become independent. Last spring the English staff and four students sat down to identify capabilities which they desired students to possess after a four semester sequence of instruction. Before that time individual instructors had employed the instructional system; however, the more immediate problem involved making the program coherent. The staff wanted one program because it would allow optimum use of resources; thus they developed the capability requirements.

There were seventy-four capabilities selected for the following categories: Process, Thinking and Logic, Speaking and Listening, Writing, Literature, Film, Creative Writing, and Communication Theory. From these capabilities instructors, in teams, designed environments they felt would produce the best learning opportunities for students. How many of these capabilities are achieved is at present a matter of close evaluation.

STUDENT CHARACTERISTICS

If these capabilities are desirable, one must look at the characteristics of our entering students. Here are some interesting ones:

1. 30% of the students work 40 or more hours a week;
2. 18%, black, 4% brown;
3. many are blue collar youths;
4. 70% want grades very strongly; no pass-fail stuff;
5. about the same number want the traditional classroom, are socially rigid;
6. 20% take reading improvement;
7. the composite ACT score for the student body is 16.7;
8. they tend to be the first from their families to go beyond high school.

DOING ENGLISH

The question becomes, "How do we design an instructional situation for students with these characteristics?" It is not possible to describe all of the English instructional terrain, but there are some facts on English 131, the first of the four semester sequence:

1. English 131 is designed in a format of large groups (stimuli for 280 students) — small groups (application for 23 students).
2. All students, including technical-vocational (40% of the student body), take this course. 450 are in the course now.
3. Students who are assessed remedial (variants: developmental, directed, guided, "bluebird" students) take a writing course and a reading course in addition to this course.
Sixty percent of these students have received credit in English 131 in the past.
4. Large group stimuli in the Fall '71 semester cover the four broad topics of: Communication Theory, Education, Conservation, and the Future. Some of the specific sessions have included these films: *The Communication Explosion, Sixteen in Webster Groves, Population Ecology, Say Goodbye, The Futurists, The Mystery of Life*. Members of Zero Population Growth and Sierra Club and concerned public have visited with slide presentations. There has been mediated instruction on organization, development and non-verbal communications, and there were two sessions produced by students.
5. Students contract for grades; some of the *activities* for C, B, and A grades are:
   a. evaluating the course,
   b. panel discussion activities,
   c. reporting on books and periodicals,
   d. writing congressmen,
   e. creating visual displays—tape-slide presentations, bulletin board,
   f. reviewing films,
   g. editing a community resource handbook,
   h. creating a proposal,
   i. reporting on a college event,
   j. tutoring,
   k. building a bibliography,
   l. planning a future and presenting it in the large group,
   m. and many others, including any negotiated activity that involves using the English language heavily.

These activities are indicative of the design of the other three courses in the sequence.

EVALUATION

This team applies the research design suggested by Arthur Cohen in *Is Anyone Learning to Write* (ERIC), and it has improved upon the criteria for grading composition that Cohen suggested. The research design has revealed a twenty-five percent improvement (pre-post-test) in those stated criteria. The design identifies areas the team should improve. Evaluation points out that the instructional sequence is headed in a direction which is desirable.

One important element of the design is the operation of the writing laboratory where students may "walk-in" for help at anytime during their college stay; the lab utilizes independent study units.

MONEY

The cost of the College of the Mainland program amounts to professional salaries and a program budget of $4,500.00 (visuals, films, instructional material, etc.)

Annually, the program serves approximately 1300 students ($3 a student).

Inquiries about this instructional sequence are invited.

The editors are interested in publishing descriptions of successful Writing Lab programs in two-year colleges. Please submit specific, brief descriptions (emphasizing *why* the Lab is successful) to:

Arthur Pritchard
Dept. of English
Tarrant County Junior College
(South Campus)
Fort Worth, Texas 76119

Book Reviews

Uses of Rhetoric. By Jim W. Corder. J. B. Lippincott Company, 1971. 280 pp.

Among a recent spate of noteworthy books on rhetoric, Jim W. Corder's *Uses of Rhetoric* stands out for a variety of reasons, not the least of which is its readability; it is written by a humane rhetorician who obviously values clarity and who has "style." Foregrounded against some of the murkier tomes that have appeared recently, *Uses of Rhetoric* glitters.

Corder's book also performs a real service to the field of knowledge that the author writes about. This long essay does concern the relevance of rhetoric, rhetoric's place in the here and now. And Corder does succeed in making the point that, it seems to me, so badly needs to be made: either modern society will learn accommodation, or it will confront, and the best tool of accommodation is rhetoric.

Some books attempt to advance new theory, and others attempt to interpret accepted doctrine in the light of the present. Corder's task is predominantly the latter.

Chapter titles give some notion of the range of inquiry in the book: "Urgencies and Possibilities in Rhetorical Study, with Some Account of Its Range"; "Shapes and Direction in Rhetorical Study"; "On the Preservation and Extension of Rhetoric"; "Rhetoric in the Classroom"; "Rhetoric in the Curriculum"; "Rhetoric at Large"; and "Certain Maxims and Questions, with No Conclusion to be Found." The heart of the book, however, is the third chapter, "On the Preservation and Extension of Rhetoric," which releates rhetoric to what's going on in the world today. Corder argues that "We have come at last to think ourselves good without question, our native wit sufficient without learning, our feelings right without deliberation." We have come, in short, to the point where discussion is impossible and shouting is a show of rightness and righteousness. We have come, that is, to an age in which the notion of adjusting ideas to audiences and audiences to ideas does not, at many crucial junctures, prevail. Or to state this point another way: many have abandoned the art of invention. The New Left, for example, is often totally uninventive, as are the McLuhanites:

> The claim shared by media-men is that when we loose the bonds of linearity in favor of simultandeity, then we have freed ourselves. This I take to be but another manifestation of the claim I have been talking about for some time, that we are free once we have escaped the tedium of imposed knowledge and the deliberations of invention for the greener slopes of the happening, the spontaneous finding.

To repeat: *Uses of Rhetoric* is an essay that intelligently *does* demonstrate the uses of rhetoric at the present time.

And yet, one speculates about the audience for this excellent book. It is clearly not a text (though it does contain a good introduction to the problems of rhetoric), and it is just as clearly not a major attempt to advance knowledge in the field significantly; rather it falls into that class of works that characteristically have "defense" in their titles: defense of reason or of poetry or religion. *Uses of Rhetoric* is model of its kind.

All of which is not to say that the book contains no new concepts; indeed, it is filled with them, but newness is not the main thrust. Any rhetorician who doubts that Corder has a good deal to teach should look, for instance, at the concept of "multiple invention," developed in the first chapter. *Uses of Rhetoric* is a useful book, one that every student in the field will profit from and enjoy reading.

W. Ross Winterowd
University of Southern California

The Holt Guide to English: A Contemporary Handbook of Rhetoric, Language, and Literature. By William F. Irmscher. Holt, Rinehart and Winston, Inc., 1972. 646 pp.

William Irmscher has put together what may well be the definitive English handbook for the 1970's. In *The Holt Guide to English*, Professor Irmscher brings together—coherently and with reasonable economy—much of the current wisdom in the fields of rhetoric, language, and literature and has produced an "English department complete" within the covers of a single book. Attempting to deal with all aspects of the English discipline, Professor Irmscher has generally succeeded in mapping, usefully and expeditiously, the terrain of English studies.

Actually few books have ever attempted so much: "to provide a complete and flexible text" giving "full attention to rhetoric, language, literature, criticism, and composition." Yet the attempt needed to be made, and in this excellent volume we begin to see a synthesis of all our concerns, begin to see how everything that we do in an English department can fit together, how a general concern with language brings all our disparate interests and skills together. The rhetorician, the linguistics specialist, the critic of literature—each will find his area of study acknowledged and included in the wholeness of English as Professor Irmscher analyzes and describes our discipline.

Professor Irmscher is well qualified to write this book, of course. Who else in the nation has read so many papers, articles, and essays—publishable and unpublishable—dealing with every aspect of English as has the editor of *College Composition and Communication*? Such editorial over-view has obviously given Professor Irmscher the sense of balance and proportion that prevails in this book and has obviously provided much of the insight into "latest trends" that helps make this book timely in the best sense of the word.

Professor Irmscher begins his book by surveying "The Elements of Rhetoric": he deals with the traditional matters of writer, audience, subject, structure, logic, paragraphing, the rhetoric of the sentence, style, and revision. In this section—as in others—he up-dates a good deal of our terminology, cuts through a lot of meaningless complexities, and makes rhetoric relevant for the student by identifying it "as a force against oppression, as a wedge against closed structures, as a force for freedom against tyranny." He suggests—in such terms as "the *drama* of thinking," "the *continuing* audience," "the essay as a *developing* form"—a dynamic approach to the use of language.

The second section of the book deals with "Special Kinds of Writing"—writing on literary topics and writing a reference paper. In this section, Professor Irmscher offers one of the most comprehensive—and certainly one of the "neatest"—expositions of literary studies I have ever read. "The Nature of Literature," pp. 191-283, is a monograph unto itself that will prove valuable to every English major in the country.

The third section deals with "The English Language: Origins, Growth, and Changes"; here we find a discussion of Indo-European, the sources of words, how words change in meaning and value—along with an analysis of grammar (acquainting the student with segmentals, suprasegmentals, and the like), and going on to "Usage," getting into the matter of dialects and various sociolinguistic patterns. The section ends with a glossary of usage and an informative discussion of the dictionary.

The fourth section, "Reference Resources," presents a microgrammar, along with a fairly detailed study of the parts of speech and a study of phrases, clauses and sentences (with transformational analysis explained and illustrated). This section also includes information about the preparation of manuscripts (punctuation, capitalization, italics, numbers, spelling, and the mechanics of letter forms) and a glossary of additional linguistic, literary, and rhetorical terms that gives definitions for terms ranging from *ablaut* and *allophone* to *trivium, trope*, and *Verner's law*.

In making such a rich survey of the entire English field, Professor Irmscher has provided a reference book par excellence. It is a compendium of valuable observations, with abundant illustrations, many effectively taken from student writing. Without venturing into areas of experimentation and for the most part ignoring "creative writing," the book—quite understandably—turns out to be a volume of current orthodoxies and present-day established views of what language is socially and culturally all about and how language can be used for general written communication.

None of us will agree, of course, with every single observation presented in the book, and I did find myself "taking exception" here and there—most frequently it seemed in Chapter 10: "Toward Better Writing: Revision." In this chapter, Professor Irmscher wrestles with the old problem of giving "advice" without becoming "prescriptive," and though he is well aware of the problem—"Attempts to define good writing are," he says, "for the most part futile because once the definition has been completed it may cover good writing of one variety, but fail to take in account numerous other kinds"—he nevertheless does proceed to give advice that at times seems to me to be somewhat restrictive. For instance, he tells students that—in general—they should "keep a firm and confident tone without seeming dogmatic," ignoring the fact that a dogmatic tone is just as much a part of a writer's repertoire as anything else while a "firm and confident one" may not be the most rhetorically effective one on certain occasions. At another point, Professor Irmscher lauds "honesty" as a rhetorical virtue, telling the student to "use personal experiences and firsthand observations whenever possible; don't invent hypothetical characters and situations. Above all, be natural in the expression of feeling." Such advice, I feel, drastically limits the student to one kind of writing, one rhetorical posture, excluding the entire area of imaginative, creative, fanciful expression, the rhetoric of the absurd, the communication that evolves from make-believe, and the like.

My exceptions aside, however, I think Professor Irmscher's book has a great future among us—primarily as a description and record of "what is." Though I'm not sure that Professor Irmscher's very thorough instructor's manual entitled "What Do You Do to Teach Composition" solves all the problems of converting a handbook into a systematic "how to" writing text, I suspect a good many teachers will find their various uses for the book—using one part in one course, another part in another, always recommending the volume as a major resource book belonging in every English major's library.

The book has been handsomely designed and produced by Holt, Rinehart and Winston, with good type, good illustrations, good arrangement of material. The book certainly represents a great deal of productive and successful work on the part of a knowledgeable and articulate author. It should be a great success.

Winston Weathers
University of Tulsa

BOOK REVIEW POLICY

The editors will attempt to have reviewed only those books which will be of interest to freshman English instructors. Normally we shall not carry reviews of handbooks, standard readers, and the like. We are especially anxious to review books which might not otherwise come to the attention of many teachers.

NEW AND FORTHCOMING

James E. Miller, Jr. *Word, Self, Reality: The Rhetoric of Imagination.* Dodd, Mead and Co., 1972.

Lloyd F. Bitzer and Edwin Black (eds.). *The Prospect of Rhetoric.* Prentice-Hall, 1971.

Walter J. Ong, S. J. *Rhetoric, Romance, and Technology.* Cornell University Press, 1971.

Juanita V. Williamson and Virginia M. Burke (eds.). *A Various Language: Perspectives on American Dialects.* Holt, Rinehart, Winston, 1971.

Richard L. Johannesen (ed.). *Contemporary Theories of Rhetoric.* Harper & Row, 1972.

Robert Scholes and Carl H. Klaus. *Elements of Writing.* Oxford, 1972.

Jacqueline Berke. *Twenty Questions for the Writer.* Harcourt Brace Jovanovich, 1972.

Ray Kytle. *Prewriting: Strategies for Exploration and Discovery.* Random House, 1972.

J. J. Lamberts. *A Short Introduction to English Usage.* McGraw-Hill, 1972.

SUBSCRIBE NOW ....

Enclosed is my check for $2.00 (payable to Freshman English News) for a one-year subscription to **Freshman English News**. Send this form to:

    Gary Tate
    Dept. of English
    Texas Christian Univ.
    Fort Worth, TX 76129

NAME_____(Please print)

ADDRESS_____

_____

_____(Zip)

A Theory of Discourse: The Aims of Discourse. By James L. Kinneavy. Prentice-Hall, Inc. 1971. 478 pp.

As the subtitle indicates, this volume of *A Theory of Discourse* deals with the *aims* of discourse—or, to use synonymous terms, the *uses*, the *functions*, the *purposes*, of discourse. A projected second volume will deal with the *modes* of discourse. "Classification of kinds of realities referred to by full texts," Kinneavy says (p. 35), "constitute 'modes' of discourse." This classification is based on a consideration of *what* is being talked about, whereas the aims of discourse are classified on the basis of *why* a thing is being talked about. The modes of discourse that Kinneavy will deal with in Volume II are narration, classification, evaluation, and description—a slight reshuffling of Alexander Bain's "forms of discourse," narration, exposition, argumentation, and description.

To derive his classification of the aims of discourse, Kinneavy uses the four elements in the Communication Triangle:

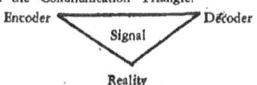

The aims of discourse are distinguished according to which element in this four-part interrelationship receives the predominant emphasis. If the emphasis is on the encoder (the speaker or writer), we get Expressive Discourse. If the emphasis is on the decoder (the audience), we get Persuasive Discourse. If the emphasis is on the signal (the work, the message, the artifact, the product), we get Literary Discourse. If the emphasis is on the reality (the universe, "the world out there"), we get Reference Discourse. (Those familiar with *The Mirror and the Lamp* will recall that M. H. Abrams, using the four elements in the communication triangle, arrived at his classification of the four main schools of literary criticism—the Expressive, the Pragmatic, the Objective, and the Mimetic. In *Teaching the Universe of Discourse*, James Moffett also used the communication triangle to distinguish kinds of discourse.) Reference Discourse in turn has three distinct species:
(A) Informative—"If the reality is conceived as known and the facts about it are simply relayed to the decoder, there is an informative use of language."
(B) Scientific—"If the information is systematized and accompanied by demonstrative proof of its validity, there is scientific use of language."
(C) Exploratory—"If the reality is not known but being sought, there is an exploratory use of language" (p. 39).

Each of these aims of discourse or uses of language, Kinneavy claims and convincingly demonstrates, has its own system of logic, its own organizational structure, and its own stylistic characteristics. After an Introductory chapter in which he argues the need for a theory of discourse, gives a brief historical sketch of discourse education, and proposes that the "field of English" be defined in relation to the communication triangle, Kinneavy devotes a chapter to each of the four aims of discourse. Each of these chapters follows the same pattern: definition of key terminology, discussion of the nature of the kind of discourse being dealt with in that chapter, consideration of the distinctive logic, organization, and style of that kind of discourse, a detailed analysis of a particular example of that kind of discourse, some study questions and assignments, and a bibliography. Here is a listing of the number of pages devoted to a discussion of each aim of discourse, the title of the specific example that is minutely analyzed, and the number of pages of bibliography:
Reference Discourse: 129 pages; "The Effective Use of Statistics"; Bibliography, 9 pages (177 items).
Persuasive Discourse: 91 pages; Franklin Delano Roosevelt's "First Inaugural Address"; Bibliography, 5 pages (101 items).
Literary Discourse: 79 pages; Gerard Manley Hopkins's "That Nature is a Heraclitean Fire and of the Comfort of the Resurrection"; Bibliography, 7 pages (130 items).
Expressive Discourse: 55 pages; "The Declaration of Independence"; Bibliography, 2 pages (35 items).

There is no other book in print quite like *A Theory of Discourse*—certainly none written by an English teacher for English teachers. The erudition exhibited so modestly and unpedantically in this book is staggering. Kinneavy alludes to or quotes from not only the full range of classical and modern rhetoricians but a wide range of literary critics, historians, sociologists, anthropologists, philosophers, semanticists, linguists, psychologists, logicians, and communications theorists. Kinneavy has come a long way in a relatively short time from his *A Study of Three Contemporary Theories of Lyric Poetry* published in 1956. Yet with all the learning displayed in this book, Kinneavy's style is admirably lucid and free from jargon.

Despite its price, this book should become a staple text in upper-division and graduate courses in rhetoric, in training courses for teaching assistants and prospective teachers, and in summer institutes and in-service courses for veteran teachers. After reading this book, Directors of Freshman English would be able to design more purposeful programs, and all of us should be able to teach composition more effectively.

Edward P. J. Corbett
Ohio State University

Freshman English News
TEXAS CHRISTIAN UNIVERSITY
FORT WORTH, TEXAS 76129

At a Glance

By the Numbers: A Citation Analysis

Doug Eyman

Anderson, Daniel, Atkins, Anthony, Ball, Cheryl E., Homicz Millar, Krista, Selfe, Cynthia, and Selfe, Richard. "Integrating Multimodality in Composition Curricula: Survey Methodology and Results from a CCCC Research Initiative Grant." *Composition Studies*, vol. 34, no. 2, 2006, pp. 59–84.

8 Themes

Multimodality & Praxis
Assessment of MM Work
Teaching Resources
Technology Resources

Pedagogy & Tech Training
Assessment of Training
Scholarship & T/P
Individuals & Programs

45 Respondents

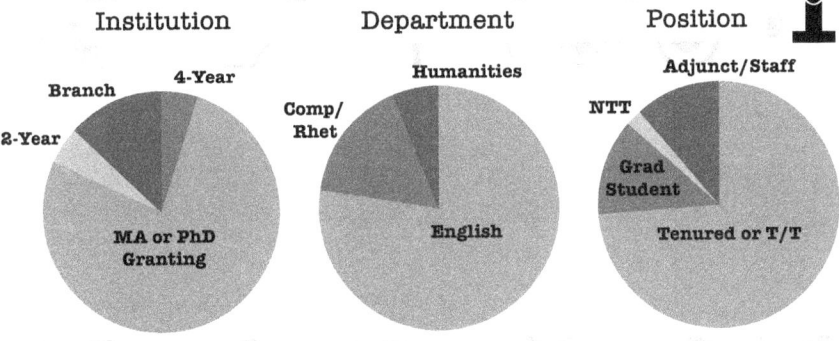

6 Findings

- primary instructional focus for multimodal assignments: visual images and photographs
- students expected to compose in university computer labs or at home
- digital media and multimodal composition PD lacking; teachers relied on colleagues and self-teaching
- teachers reported needing professional development beyond specific tool use
- teachers reported that they need better instructional materials
- scholars who compose multimodal texts uncertain whether such work will count towards tenure or promotion

120 Citations

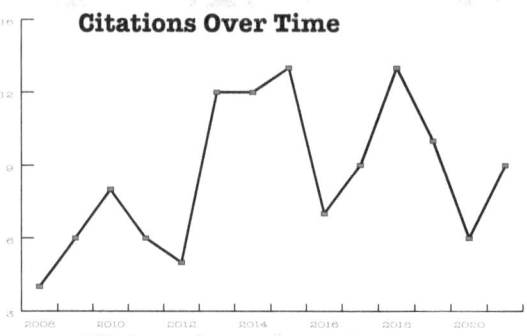

See Yancey (2019) for a classroom assignment using the data set

See Johnston (2021) for an update of the original survey

Themes

Assessment.........9
Survey...................9
PD..........................8
Grad Training.....7
Online Teaching..3
T & P.....................4

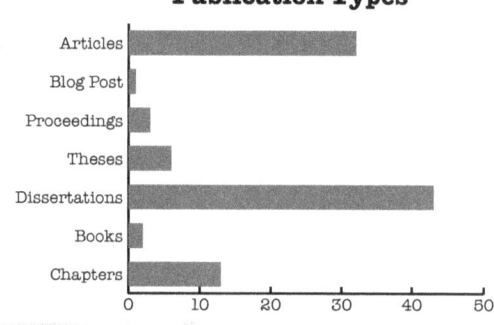

39% of articles appeared in *Computers & Composition*

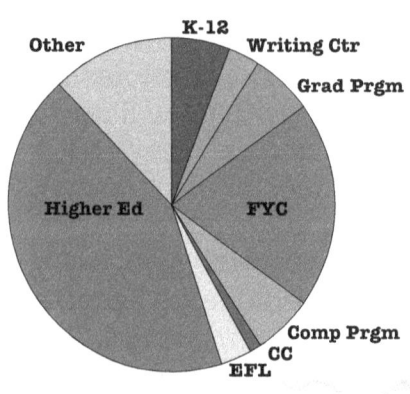

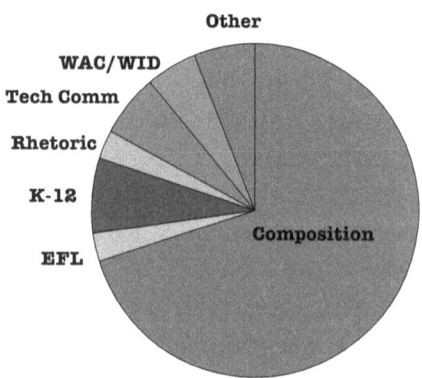

Articulations

Dale Jacobs and Jay Dolmage

Reflections on "Comics, Multimodality, and Composition" (special issue 43.1)

Articulations represents our collaboration about comics, rhetoric, and disability studies, a collaboration that began with our 2012 essay, "Difficult Articulations: Comics Autobiography, Trauma, and Disability" (on David Small's *Stitches*) and carried through to "Mutable Articulations" (on Georgia Webber's *Dumb*) and "Accessible Articulations: Comics and Disability Rhetorics in *Hawkeye* #19." These three essays encapsulate our ongoing consideration of comics and disability rhetorics.

We view comics as both a space for negotiating the meanings around bodies/minds and as an embodied form of expression. In doing so, we have tried to build on disability studies work that calls for attention to how meaning is attached to disability, and also that views the knowledge and meaning that disability generates; we want to move beyond policing negative portrayals of disability to recognizing disability as an engine of innovation and rhetorical invention. In this way, we see the potential of comics to go beyond the use of disability as narrative prosthesis—a kind of multimodal, narrative shorthand—and to *become a form of prosthesis themselves*, an additional tool in making meaning accessible and for intervening in and interrogating disability as a representational system.

What follows is an example from Georgia Webber's *Dumb* to show how we have attempted to put comics theory into productive dialogue with disability theory to interrogate and develop a disability rhetoric for the comic form. *Dumb* is, in Webber's words, "a comics series about my prolonged voice loss, and the slow crawl of recovery" (np). The first issue, in which Georgia's persistent throat pain is diagnosed as a result of her overuse of her vocal chords, sets the stage for the chronicle of voice loss in the subsequent issues.

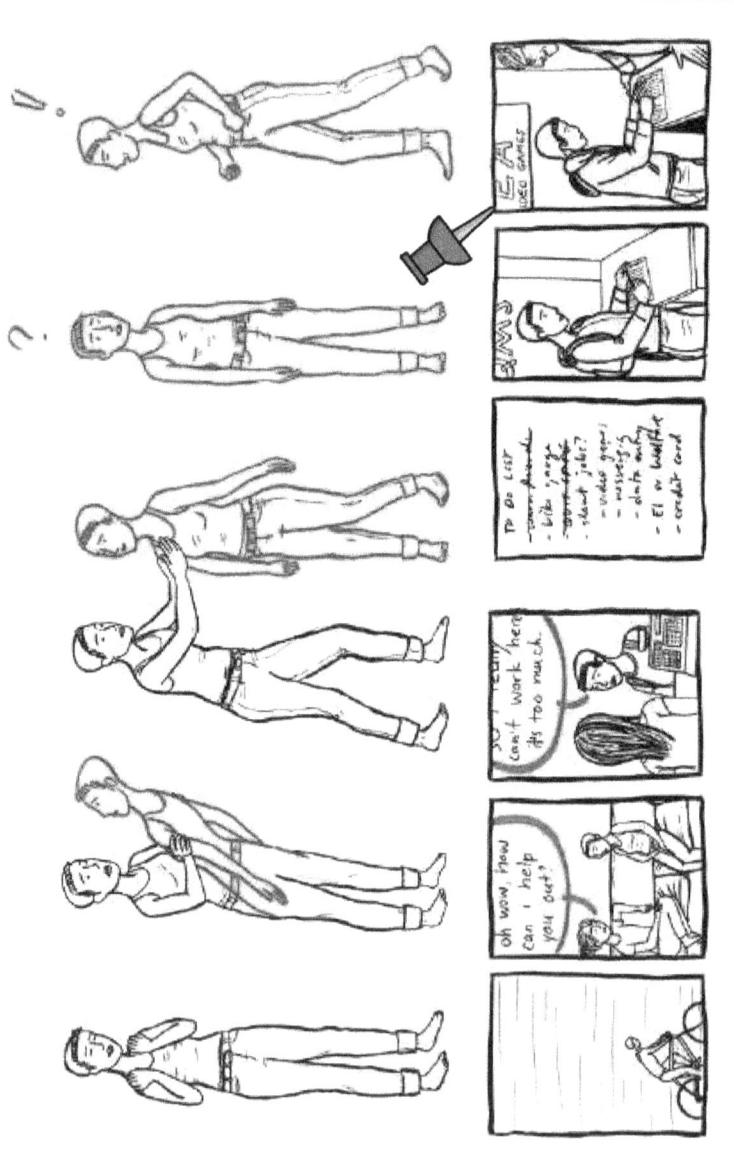

1. In this sequence—what we have come to call the "splitting" section—Webber begins her attempt to deconstruct disability by "demonstrating the pathology and psychic impairment within the seemingly productive art of comic book writing" (Squier 88). The red-penciled Georgia is but one articulation of self and in "splitting," Webber endeavors to come to terms with how she is to manage these multiple selves.

2. In "splitting," Webber takes advantage of the possibility in the comics medium of articulating multiple narratives simultaneously. Along the bottom of the eleven pages that make up this section, Webber utilizes three panels per page to tell the story of the tasks she must perform in order to best engage her new situation: quitting her job at the café, telling friends, applying for other jobs, etc. As Webber shows through these thirty-three panels, the process is clearly exhausting, but does end with a panel that shows a hand attaching a note to the wall next to her computer which reads, "it's going to be okay."

3. Parallel to the narrative at the bottom of the page, the upper two-thirds of each page is taken up with a series of unbordered panels in which Georgia is shown to be wrestling with her divided self. We see the initial process of separation in which the red-penciled version of Georgia is shown to emerge from the drawing of Georgia done in black, a representation in keeping with the way she has been drawn throughout the comic to this point. Readers are pushed to see the ensuing conflict between these two versions of Georgia in terms of silence (her new normal) versus sound (the voice that fights to be released, even though such release would be detrimental to physical recovery).

4. The parallel narratives force readers to think about the relationship between them. When the fight ends in an image of the black-penciled version of Georgia helping up the red-penciled version, the image is accompanied by "it's going to be okay," the words that appear in the final panel of the other narrative. Despite this image and these words, however, it is an uneasy peace, an articulation of selves that is stable only for the moment and subject to further reinterpretations as Webber moves through her story.

Squier, Susan M. "So Long as They Grow Out of It: Comics, the Discourse of Developmental Normalcy, and Disability." *Journal of Medical Humanities*, vol. 29, no. 2, pp. 71-88.

Familia's Digital Garden

A memorial to honor those we've lost, and those who help us grow.

Ronisha Browdy, Esther Milu, Victor Del Hierro, and Laura Gonzales

This text is an extension of our collaborative article, "From Cohort to Family: Coalitional Stories of Love and Survivance," published in *Composition Studies* 49.1 in 2021. In that article, we traced our experiences building and sustaining our familia—our community of support inside and outside of academia. We shared stories of some of the challenges we've experienced as scholars of color, highlighting how our different positionalities, and our commitment to supporting each other, helped us build a family and succeed. When we were invited to reflect on the process of collaborative research for this special issue of *Composition Studies*, we were unsure of how we could represent collaboration in a way that honored our individual relationships with each other, our collective relationship as a familia, and the individual experiences and orientations that we bring to these collaborations.

We created our digital garden, a space that can give us hope and healing at a time when we most need it. The images above represent our digital garden, a collection of flowers and offerings that represent someone we love, including those we have lost. These flowers are a memorial to honor these beautiful souls who remain with us. As the world continues grieving and processing so much loss, we invite readers to engage with our garden by navigating to the QR code or going to this URL: https://arcg.is/zCrCm.

Please read our stories, and then share your own garden offerings on social media using #familiasgarden. We hope this approach to collaboration showcases the importance of reflection, of building together, and of opening space for participation and dialogue. Collaboration is never just about those who are present, but is also about those who have shaped us and made us who we are.

Reflections

AI-Based Text Generation and the Social Construction of "Fraudulent Authorship": A Revisitation

Chris M. Anson

Student plagiarism has challenged educators for decades, with heightened paranoia following the advent of the Internet in the 1980's and ready access to easily copied text. But plagiarism will look like child's play next to new developments in AI-based natural-language processing (NLP) systems that increasingly appear to "write" as effectively as humans. How we theorize and contextualize these developments will guide the way we meet their challenges in all courses where writing is assigned and evaluated

Here, I first revisit an article I wrote for *Composition Studies* in 2011, "Fraudulent Practices: Academic Misrepresentations of Plagiarism in the Name of Good Pedagogy." In that article, I argued that what counts as plagiarism in some contexts occurs with impunity across a wide range of published material. This is because definitions of plagiarism are socially constructed and tied to context-sensitive cycles of reward for the production—and therefore the ownership—of certain kinds of texts. Helping students to understand plagiarism means showing them these contextually-specific constructs of text ownership, rather than assuming that any unattributed text, published anywhere, in any form, constitutes plagiarism. I then turn to AI-based NLP systems. Teachers who learn what these systems can do usually respond with the same hand-wringing and defensive posture triggered by concerns about student plagiarism. But a social-practices interpretation again breaks open the systems' perceived threats and reveals a more nuanced and contextual approach to their challenges—and their potential acceptance and use—alongside writing produced by humans.

Digging Critically into Plagiarism: A Return to 2011

At the time I wrote "Fraudulent Practices," I was keenly interested in the social construction of plagiarism, partly because plagiarism occupies so much attention across most educational contexts and needs deeper levels of analysis. In that piece, I used Internet research to show that beyond academia, plagiarism is rampant but often accepted. For example, information published by Federal agencies concerning the safe handling of meat or what to do when a tornado approaches is liberally copied verbatim at dozens of sites (including official state and municipal sites) without attribution. The need to circulate the material for the public good outweighs the need for authorial credit (even if a specific author, rather than a bureaucratic entity, can be found). Car dealerships replicate material from automobile insurance agencies—which replicate each other's material—about how to steer out of a skid, sometimes verbatim and sometimes patched into other text, again without any indication of authorship, to the point where the original source is unrecoverable. Hotel booking companies use property descriptions commissioned and published by the corporation that owns the properties but with no trace of the texts' origin—a process that, because the replicated text benefits both the booking agents and the hotel corporation, I dubbed "cooperative competition." This practice is also common across vast numbers of sites that broker the sale of products whose descriptions are extensively copied without indication of the original source (presumably commissioned or written by the manufacturer). Another piece I co-authored with an experienced military officer, "The Army and the Academy as Textual Communities," documented the widespread copying and reuse of text, either verbatim or repurposed, across the United States Army without acknowledgement of its original author(s) (Anson and Neeley).

In these and other cases, I drew on the New Literacy Studies (Gee; Russell; Street) to argue that what would count as plagiarism in some contexts is tolerated or even encouraged in others. Most importantly, the view that it is plagiarism to use someone else's text without attribution is perpetuated in contexts such as academia where authors accrue "credit and credibility" from their texts: publishing under one's name earns credit; as credit accumulates, so does greater credibility, which opens up further opportunities for more credit in a kind of cycle (see Latour and Woolgar). In this system of rewards, text ownership and attribution are sacrosanct, and "theft" is forbidden. But if little or no credit is associated with text, its authors have no concerns about it being co-opted and used by others: many scholars, myself included, urge colleagues to take material from their syllabi, assignments, and other teaching-related documents without worry about attribution, which the borrowers want to avoid as well so as not to appear lazy or unable to produce it on their own. "Credit" for original text, especially at research-extensive institutions, comes more strongly from peer-reviewed publications than teaching or administrative materials.

"Fraudulent Practices" ends with a call to deepen our discussion of plagiarism with students and to represent it more accurately based on communities of practice and their norms:

> [A]mong all aspects of rhetoric and written communication, representations of plagiarism often suffer the most from a kind of pedagogical myopia, and it is curious that we would deliberately conceal

the truth about how sources are or are not attributed in the world of discourse in order to compel students to believe in a specific perspective, even if just for the time being. When we show students the range of textual and discursive practices used in various contexts, and help them to understand the relationship between these practices and their underlying social and ideological sources, students begin to see plagiarism not as "rules" to be memorized uncritically and without regard to situation, but as socially constructed practices of utmost importance to the academic community they have joined. (p. 40)

When we consider the possibility that students could generate entire authentic-looking essays from a small input into an NLP program, will teachers represent the systems myopically and conceal the truth about their affordances? What would it look like to "show the range of textual and discursive practices used in various contexts" that such programs can enable?

The New "Threat": AI-Based Text Production

Recent advances in the production of natural language—text that mirrors the characteristics of writing by humans—now represent the next big perceived threat to teachers of writing. These deep-learning systems work by mining billions of existing, human-produced texts and, through a process akin to the creation of neural networks, generate new text based on highly complex predictive machine analysis. A system being widely tested and refined is GPT-3, the third iteration of OpenAI's "generative pretrained transformer." GPT-3 operates with 1.3 billion parameters, a technical term for the range of values the system can have for appropriate predictability. For an example of a primitive version of GPT-3 also developed by OpenAI, consider Gmail's Smart Compose function. When activated, Smart Compose suggests further words as the user types. Drawing on millions of other texts, the app predicts the writer's thoughts on a simple level. For example, at the end of an email response to a student's query about an assignment, I wrote the letters "Ple . . ." and based on the content of my email, Smart Compose offered "Please let me know if you have any questions." The text was appropriate, so I hit the tab key, and it was instantly added to my email.

 As a machine-learning program, Smart Compose continues to get better from its mistakes. But GPT-3 is a far more complex and robust system; it is capable not just of filling in words at the start of email sentences but generating entire texts or adding text that's completely coherent with existing text (for a stunning example of an essay about these programs, with text generated by

GPT-2 interspersed into the author's, see Seabrook). GPT-4 will be available in 2023, and Google is working on a similar system with 1.6 trillion parameters.

To consider how GPT-3 (or GPT-4, or Google's system) might subvert students' authentically composed writing, let's experiment with an essay topic of current interest in the context of the Covid pandemic: *vaccine hesitancy*. Using my access to GPT-3's playground, I typed "Write an essay about vaccine hesitancy" into a text box. In about four seconds, the system generated the following text.

> Vaccine hesitancy is a complex and multi-faceted problem. On the one hand, there is a clear public health benefit to vaccinating as many people as possible. Vaccines are one of the most effective ways to prevent the spread of disease. They have been responsible for saving millions of lives and eradicating devastating diseases like smallpox. On the other hand, there is a legitimate concern about the safety of vaccines. Vaccines are made from viruses or bacteria that have been weakened or killed. They are then injected into people, which causes the body to develop immunity to the disease. However, there is always a risk that the vaccine could cause serious side effects, including allergic reactions, fever, and even death.
>
> The problem of vaccine hesitancy is compounded by the fact that vaccines are not 100% effective. They may not work for everyone, and even when they do work, they may not provide complete protection from the disease. This means that even people who are vaccinated can still contract the disease and spread it to others.
>
> The best way to address vaccine hesitancy is to educate people about the risks and benefits of vaccination. It is important to dispel the myths and misinformation that circulate about vaccines. It is also important to encourage people to speak to their healthcare providers about their concerns and to get accurate information from credible sources.

Cutting and pasting all or part of this auto-generated text into a new text box can continue to prompt further content. The material is not plagiarized from existing sources but freshly composed. For this reason, it usually evades plagiarism-detection programs like Turnitin.[1]

GPT-3 is also capable of adding to already produced material, including fiction. In an attempt to do so, OpenAI has collaborated with the "think-of-an-idea-and-we'll-finish-it" website Inklewriter. Using GPT-3, Inklewriter's computer program can now write the next few paragraphs of a story and generate plots with a range of possibilities. (The last two sentences of this paragraph were written by GPT-3 after I gave it the first sentence—but for you, no doubt undetectably.)

Although imperfect, these examples show that even at this stage of development—with sweeping improvements on the near horizon—GPT-3 can serve as an effective "writing assistant." With a few minor revisions, some fact-checking, and a bit of editorial work, students can easily pass off what it generates as their own original compositions.

A Social Practices View of AI-Based Text Generation

Let's imagine that a student generates the content of an essay using a "robo-writer" like GPT-3 and submits the results as their own original composition. By most academic standards, this would not technically be a case of plagiarism—until or unless computers are considered authors—but instead would represent "contract cheating" (Curtis and Clare; Lancaster and Clarke), a violation of student codes of conduct similar to submitting a customized paper written by someone else. However, when we consider contexts beyond teaching and learning, NLP-written texts may not look like ethical violations, in much the way that vast amounts of replicated and unattributed text do not constitute plagiarism. Consider boilerplate—text or bits of text used repeatedly in forms, letters, emails, and legal documents. At base, boilerplate is text "auto-generated" for subsequent texts. Once written, it behaves as if a machine has produced it, easily spliced into new texts or simply sent or submitted verbatim, with perhaps different addressees and subject headings. Text-expanders like aText facilitate the use of boilerplate by allowing prewritten text to be inserted into new text with the use of a simple command. The rules and conventions of discourse in many contexts not only tolerate but encourage this repeated use of the same textual material for work efficiency. (For example, I sometimes use aText to splice frequently repeated advice into students' papers, with their knowledge.)

Boilerplate is the reuse by a human of existing text written by a human. But AI-based NLP systems create new, original text each time they are activated. When I asked GPT-3 to "write a tagline for a writing center," it offered these suggestions:

> The Writing Center: Your words, our passion
>
> The Writing Center: Where great writers are born
>
> Need help with your writing? We're here for you!
>
> The Writing Center: Your Home for Writing Help

At the least, these auto-generated examples might spark some new human-generated ideas—or perhaps one of them would be sufficient. In this sense, NLP systems can serve as invention prompts, or as text generators whose outputs are either revised or used verbatim. Like the acceptable use of unattributed text, this range of writing processes widens our conception of what is or is not permissible or ethical about NLP-based text production. Instead of darkly subverting the human invention and writing process, how might NLP systems support the disparate goals and activity systems of different contexts?

Among hundreds of examples (some at OpenAI's site), here are a few:

- Translation of legalese
  GPT-3 will take the input of complex legal language—the kind most people simply "accept" without reading when they download and activate an app—and make it understandable. Inputting several paragraphs of Verizon's Disclaimer of Warranties, which includes lines such as "Verizon hereby disclaims any and all representations, warranties, and guaranties regarding S & P, whether express, implied, or statutory . . . ," yields a one-sentence explanation: "This is a disclaimer of warranties. It basically says that the company is not responsible if something goes wrong with the product or service."

- Extraction of keywords
  Inputting the contents of this article produced a list of nineteen keywords that included *plagiarism, authorship, pedagogy, deep learning, GPT-3,* and *contract cheating*—from which, if required, I could select four or five for publication.

- Product name generator
  Inputting my made-up product description ("an app that tells you when to stop eating") yielded the product names *Overeater's Helper, Full Stop, Bite Counter,* and *Eat-o-Meter.*

- Abstract creation
  After finishing a draft of this essay, I pasted it into GPT-3 with the request to create an abstract, and it offered me the following: "This essay revisits the idea that plagiarism is a social construct, and explores how AI-based text generators fit into that construct. It argues that instead of trying to prevent students from using these tools, we should instead teach them how to use them responsibly."

Although I might add that the article revisits a previous article published in *Composition Studies*, the gist of the summary is accurate and provides the basis for a slightly tweaked or expanded version.

Some applications of NLP systems may seem acceptable for mundane and repetitive tasks, especially in a work context. But where does acceptability end? In my graduate course in writing studies, students must interview a scholar about their work. Imagine that a student asks GPT-3 to create a list of possible questions for an interview with writing-studies and plagiarism expert Rebecca Moore Howard. When I gave GPT-3 this task ("Write a list of questions for an interview with Rebecca Moore Howard"), it created questions such as "What inspired you to write your book on plagiarism?" and "What do you think are the best ways to prevent plagiarism?"

Auto-generated interview questions may be acceptable to some teachers, but what about a brief biography spliced into the start of the interview paper? Or imagine that a student (or scholar) asks GPT-3 to write the methods section of an article based on phrasal inputs. When I gave GPT-3 ten fragments from an imagined study of middle-school students about their reading habits, it produced a coherent methods description that began as follows:

> The present study sought to understand middle school students' reading habits. A total of 180 surveys were distributed to middle school students at a public, urban school located in the Southeast, with 146 surveys being usable. The survey had 15 questions and asked students about where they most often read, how often they read, and what types of books they most enjoyed reading.

In this case, I provided the information, but who lays claim to the expression of that information in a coherent string of sentences?

Many researchers in STEM fields might find auto-written methods sections acceptable, just as many STEM editors and researchers find the verbatim replication of methods sections in different published articles acceptable in a process my co-researchers and I have called "text recycling" (see Anson, Hall, Pemberton, and Moskovitz; Pemberton, Hall, Moskovitz, and Anson; and Anson, Moskovitz, and Anson). But in other contexts, such as when an author, in an article for *PMLA*, replicates three paragraphs from their previous article in *Shakespeare Quarterly* describing the methods used in interpreting the theme of resentment in select Shakespeare plays, both text recycling and NLP-generated text might be disallowed. In a college biology course, an instructor might accept an NLP-generated lab report as long as the student conducted the lab and entered all the correct information, while another instructor might refer the student to the Office of Student Conduct. In the first case, the learning goal might focus mainly on the experimental processes (the procedures and results), while in the second the goal might focus more strongly on the writing process (assembling the procedures and results in coherent prose). If these situations yield mixed opinions in academic settings, it is not difficult to imagine many other contexts where automatic text generation will be welcomed—or conflicted.

Sharing AI-Generated Text Production Systems with Students

Instructional responses to the prospect of student access to NLP-based text generation systems often focus, like plagiarism, on detection and prevention. Solutions include having students write at computers that block access to the Internet, write by hand in class, include references to discussions in class (to which AI systems don't have access), keep a process log of everything done to write a paper, and build the paper from a series of scaffolded writing activities (see Anson, "Cops"; "Defining"; Vie) But because automated writing systems are here to stay and will only improve over time, a more sensible approach could involve embracing the technology, showing students what it can and can't do, and asking them to experiment with it. As I argued in "Fraudulent Practices," doing so is supported by the "writing about writing" approach to first-year composition (see Downs and Wardle):

> In such a course, students could learn about or even study contexts for writing in order to deepen their understanding of the assumptions, processes, tools, values, discursive histories, and social practices that entail there. The resulting metaconsciousness would be far preferable for students who move into and among different activity systems than sets of isolated skills, such as learning how to write topic sentences. (p. 40)

For example, the process of exploring GPT technology is artfully demonstrated in an assignment developed by Paul Fyfe and shared in "How to Cheat on your Final Paper: Assigning AI for Student Writing." Fyfe asked undergraduates in his course to "harvest content from an installation of GPT-2" and then incorporate the material into their final essay. However, the students were required to highlight which content was theirs and which was auto-generated and then reflect on the results. Their reflections focused on the ethics of AI assistance, what the program did to extend their own perspectives, and how the material might or might not be considered plagiarism. The shared insights of the students are impressive and point to the broader goal of teaching discourse in all its complexities and contextual variations.

In addition, students need to learn the sinister side of NLP systems. Because they generate text based on what humans have already produced, the systems are prone to mirroring discriminatory and racist language and perpetuating stereotypes (such as assuming that roles like "flight attendant" or "nurse" are always performed by women). As Hutson points out, the systems can also support the insidious work of extremist communities, "produc[ing] polemics parroting Nazis, conspiracy theorists and white supremacists" (24). Helping students to navigate the ethics of use can only prepare them to make wise decisions about their own writing and the writing of others, including machines.

As David Russell has put it, "because writing…is a matter of learning to participate in some historically situated human activity that requires some kind(s) of writing, it cannot be learned apart from the problems, the habits, the activities—the subject matter—of some group that found the need to write in that way to solve a problem or carry on its activities" (194). With this bit from Russell, GPT-3 relieved me of composing a conclusion: In other words, we need to help students understand that the act of writing is always situated within a complex system of rules, assumptions, and values. AI-based text generation systems are just one more element in that system, and one that is likely to become more commonplace in the years to come. As such, it is important that we help students to understand how such systems work and how to use them responsibly.

Notes

1. Because AI-based systems scrape existing digital text to assemble new text, there is a small possibility that a string of words could get flagged by a plagiarism-detection system, but as Dehouche suggests, it is unlikely: "Our medieval concept of plagiarism (Sadeghi 2019) ('presenting the work of others as one's own') appears rather inadequate when the 'others' in question consist in an astronomical number of authors, whose work was combined and reformulated in unique ways by a 175-billion-parameter algorithm" (21).

Works Cited

Anson, Chris M. "We Never Wanted to Be Cops: Plagiarism, Institutional Paranoia, and Shared Responsibility." *Pluralizing Plagiarism: Identities, Contexts, Pedagogies.* Ed. Rebecca Moore Howard and Amy E. Robillard. Boynton/Cook-Heinemann, 2008, pp. 140-157.

—. "Fraudulent Practices: Academic Misrepresentations of Plagiarism in the Name of Good Pedagogy." *Composition Studies*, vol. 39, no. 2, 2011, pp. 29-43.

Anson, Ian G., Cary Moskovitz, and Chris M. Anson. "A Text-Analytic Method for Identifying Text Recycling in STEM Research Reports." *Journal of Writing Analytics*, vol. 3, 2019, pp. 125-150.

Anson, Chris M., Susanne Hall, Michael Pemberton, and Cary Moskovitz. "Reuse in STEM Research Writing: Rhetorical and Practical Considerations and Challenges." *AILA Review*, vol. 33, 2020, pp. 120-135.

Anson, Chris M., and Shawn Neely. "The Army and the Academy as Textual Communities: Exploring Mismatches in the Concepts of Attribution, Appropriation, and Shared Goals." *Kairos*, vol. 14, no. 3, 2010, n. pag. Web.

Curtis, Guy J., and Joseph Clare. "How Prevalent is Contract Cheating and to What Extent are Students Repeat Offenders? *Academic Ethics*, Vol. 15, 2017, pp. 115–124. DOI 10.1007/s10805-017-9278-x

Dehouche, Nassim. "Plagiarism in the Age of Massive Generative Pre-trained Transformers (GPT-3)." *Ethics in Science and Environmental Politics*. Vol. 21, 2021, pp. 17-23. DOI 10.3354/esep00195

"Defining and Avoiding Plagiarism: The WPA Statement on Best Practices. Council of Writing Program Administrators. 2019. https://wpacouncil.org/aws/CWPA/pt/sd/news_article/272555/_PARENT/layout_details/false

Downs, Douglas, and Elizabeth Wardle. "Teaching About Writing, Righting Misconceptions: (Re)Envisioning 'First Year Composition' as 'Introduction to Writing Studies.'" *College Composition and Communication*, vol. 58, no. 4, 2007, pp. 552-84.

Fyfe, Paul. "How to Cheat on your Final Paper: Assigning AI for Student Writing. *AI & Society*, Feb. 2022. https://doi.org/10.1007/s00146-022-01397-z

Gee, James Paul. "The New Literacy Studies." *The Routledge Handbook of Literacy Studies*. Ed. Jennifer Rowsell and Kate Pahl. Taylor and Francis, 2015.

Hutson, Matthew. "Robo-Writers: The Rise and Risks of Language-Generating AI. *Nature*, vol., 591, no. 7848, 2021, pp. 22-25.

Lancaster, Thomas, and Robert Clarke. "Contract Cheating: The Outsourcing of Assessed Student Work. *Handbook of Academic Integrity*. Ed. Tracey Bretag. Springer, 2015. 639-654.

Latour, Bruno, and Stephen Woolgar. *Laboratory Life: The Construction of Scientific Facts*. Princeton UP, 1979.

Pemberton, Michael, Susanne Hall, Cary Moskovitz, and Chris M. Anson. "Journal Editors' Views on Text Recycling: An Interview-Based Study." *Learned Publishing*, vol. 32, no. 4, 2019, pp. 355-366.

Russell, David R. "Vygotsky, Dewey, and Externalism." *JAC: The Journal of Advanced Composition*, vol. 13, no. 1 (1993): 173-197.

Sadeghi, Ramin. "The Attitude of Scholars Has Not Changed Towards Plagiarism Since the Medieval Period." *Research Ethics*, Vol. 15, 2019, pp. 1–3.

Seabrook, John. "The New Word: Where Will Predictive Text Take Us? *The New Yorker*, 14 Oct., 2019. https://www.newyorker.com/magazine/2019/10/14/can-a-machine-learn-to-write-for-the-new-yorker

Street, Brian. *Social Literacies: Critical Approaches to Literacy in Development, Ethnography, and Education*. Longman, 1995.

Vie, Stephanie. "A Pedagogy of Resistance Toward Plagiarism Detection Technologies." *Computers and Composition*, vol. 30, no. 1 (2013): 3-15.

Collaborative Writing, Collage, and Cooking: From Humanist to Post-Humanist Assemblages

Anis Bawarshi and Mary Jo Reiff

The term "collage" was originally applied to visual art, but most of us are familiar with written collages: single texts that consist of multiple and somewhat disconnected fragments.

—Peter Elbow, "Using the Collage for Collaborative Writing"

An assemblage is a collection of things—bodies, passions, words, ideas, objects—that aid and constrain the actions that transpire within it.

—William Duffy, *Beyond Conversation: Collaboration and the Production of Writing*

In the spring 1999 lead article of *Composition Studies*, titled "Using the Collage for Collaborative Writing," Peter Elbow offers collage as a method as well as a form for encouraging writers to compose/think/reflect in conversation with each other. Like much scholarship on collaboration at this time, Elbow locates his understanding of collaboration in the social turn and a conception of collaborative writing as dialogic—as an interaction or conversation between individual human subjects. We were drawn to this article because the two of us, a career-long collaborative team, have been thinking a lot recently about the nature of our writing together, both in terms of the productive "tension and energy" that Elbow describes as arising from multiple perspectives (10), and more recently, in terms of the more complex discursive and material ecologies of our collaborations–especially in terms of how our writing together has on many occasions been marked by time spent cooking together. What, we have been wondering, has been the relationship between the material act of writing together and the material act of cooking together? How have these collaborative practices informed one another, and how does their relationship help us engage recent scholarship in the field that focuses on relationality, materiality, and a post-humanist perspective on agency as distributed across human and other-than-human agents (Bennett; Boyle; Clary-Lemon; Cooper; Hawk; Shivers-McNair)? In addition, how does this help us think about (and rethink) Elbow's ideas about collage and collaborative writing from a post-humanist perspective?

***

If we were to make a collage of our cooking collaborations, it might look something like the image below (Figure 1), depicting the intra-action of text, material objects, and human and other-than-human actants.

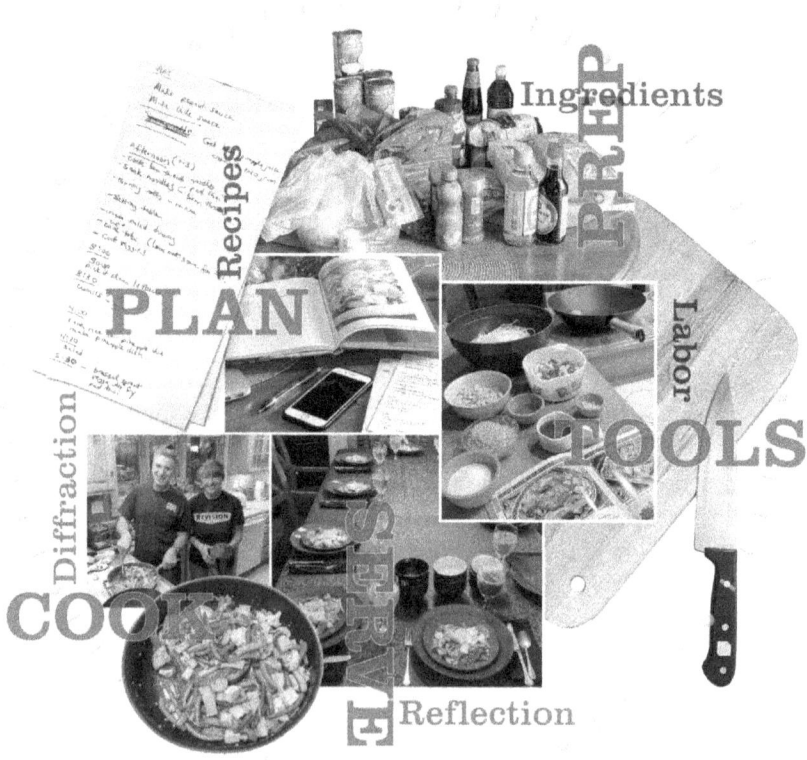

Figure 1: A collage of our collaborative cooking depicting the intra-action of texts (recipes, lists), material objects/tools (knives, plates, forks, ingredients), humans and non-human actants (the coauthors in the kitchen, at the stove), and technologies (pen and paper, smart phone).

Thinking about this image, a collage of our cooking collaborations, in relation to Elbow's method of collage enables us to reimagine collaboration. In what follows, we explore collaboration as post-humanist assemblage by drawing on Elbow's concept of collage—in which the development and organization of texts is "intuitive and associative" with "add[ed] fragments of writing by others" (8)—and by presenting our own collage of quotations, thoughts, and ideas about cooking and writing together.

***

"How to conjure up the togetherness of those early days: sitting in the library—or on a lush riverbank—trading stories of family and friends, experimenting with our first gardens, and spending lots of time cooking and eating together" (Lunsford and Ede 3).

"It is 6:00 p.m., 9 December 1988. We have been writing and talking and cooking and reading and listening and writing and talking and cooking and reading steadily for seven days now" (Lunsford and Ede 147).

***

The well-known collaborative team of Lisa Ede and Andrea Lunsford have reflected on the seamlessness and recursiveness of activities like writing and talking together and "cooking and eating together," which piqued our interest because, as collaborators ourselves for over 25 years, our writing collaborations have always included cooking collaborations. Our first co-authored piece, an interview with a major scholar in rhetoric and composition, took place in their home, followed by making lunch together in their kitchen. This would begin, for us, a continuation—over the next two decades of collaboration—of organizing our work of writing together around another kind of making together, cooking—with our creative brainstorming/drafting of projects, usually over a long weekend, merging with our creative ventures into making different cuisines. It would also begin an exploration of the connection between the similarly emergent processes of writing together and cooking together.

***

Interestingly, Elbow, in *Writing without Teachers* (1973), draws on the metaphor of "cooking" to discuss writing processes, describing cooking as generative interaction: "Cooking consists of the process of one piece of material (or one process) being transformed by interacting with another: one piece of material being seen through the lens of another, being dragged through the guts of another, being reoriented or reorganized in terms of the other, being mapped onto the other" (49). Yet here, and echoed in the 1999 *Composition Studies* article on collage and collaboration, we find the deeply humanist perspective that guides so much of Elbow's understanding of collaboration as an interaction between individual human subjects, whether a form of weak collaboration, where writers' individual responses to and from one another "*influence* each others' thinking and writing," or strong collaboration, which "requires agreement or consensus" among individual collaborators (10, emphasis in original). As we have reflected on how the material practices of cooking and making translate to our writing together, we have come away with a richer understanding of the ways in which material, multisensory, and multi-agentive forces and practices shape writing together—a perspective that can enrich and complicate our field's understanding of collaborative authorship.

***

"The collaborative collage is a gathering of pieces each written from an 'I' point of view–for the sake of a 'we' enterprise" (Elbow "Using the Collage," 11).

"[C]ollaborative composition, like all discourse production, is materially situated in ecologies we can only ever partially distinguish by observing the various relations between and among the many objects populating these environments, including the collaborators themselves" (Duffy 4-5).

***

In *Beyond Conversation: Collaboration and the Production of Writing*, Duffy notes that in the current context of new materialist and post-human theories of writing, "now is the opportune time" for an inquiry into collaborative writing and for rethinking our prevailing theories of collaborative authorship (21). Such an exploration would include not just the shared conversations between collaborators but also a consideration of "the material-discursive ecologies that provide the complex of objects with which they interact as *collaborators* to write together" (48, emphasis in original).

***

Thinking about the collaborative practice of writing together in relation to/alongside cooking draws our attention to the deep relationality at work in both, a relationality that is epistemological as well as ontological, involving "knowing with" (Broudy 12) not just each other as collaborators, but also knowing with objects such as recipes, cookbooks, ingredients, the physical space of the kitchen, utensils, bowls, pans and pots, timers, and the stove. This relationality also involves knowing with sensory experiences such as taste, smell, and sound, as well as factors such as temperature, and knowing with temporal relations such as cooking time, serving time, and the coordination of various dishes. This deep relationality disrupts and expands our understanding of agency, as the boundaries between actors (human and other than human, animate and inanimate) are blurred and intentionality is distributed in more dynamic, intra-active ways (Barad). Cooking helps us reveal and cultivate this relationality in ways that have informed, consciously and unconsciously, our collaboration, which also includes working and distributing agency across media, modalities, and objects as we take notes by hand; look up sources online; make lists of topics/sources we want to include; discover new sources; and interact with physical texts, writing pads, laptops, and online resources. This process is continuous and recursive. We are constantly moving across media, modalities, and objects.

But how does the concept of "assemblage" authorship (and agency as emergent, distributed) and of the dynamic interaction of objects, texts, people, technologies across material-discursive ecologies inform methods and practices of collaboration? Does collage still hold up as an adequate method and form for such assemblages?

***

On Collaborative Collage:

"Each person writes for ten or fifteen minutes—however he or she wants to start. Then people switch papers for the next piece of writing so that what is written is some kind of response to what the first person wrote. And so on" (Elbow "Using the Collage," 9).

On "Turnaround Writing":

"The basic conceit of turnaround is to treat collaborative composition like a dialogue or informal correspondence. I write a bit, then give my text to my writing partner, who then writes a bit, they give the text back to me, and so forth" (Duffy 129).

***

Duffy redefines collaborative authorship as co-writing agency, "as a kind of power or dynamic coauthors cultivate in rhetorical ecologies—or assemblages—of their collaboration" (76). Yet his application of "turnaround writing" is similar to Elbow's collaborative collage, which has the goal of "help[ing] students 'place' their own thoughts and voices–in authoritative dialogue with the voices of others, especially of published writers" (12) and "to give voice to the multiple views and consciousnesses that inhabit us" (13).

But what does it mean to "place" one's thoughts and voices in authoritative dialogue? And what are these consciousnesses that inhabit us? The process of cooking and writing together can inform our understanding of collaboration as relational, mediated, and codependent with things, places, people, and others.

Our cooking process starts from a common "place"—the couch at one of our houses—as we engage and interact with objects like cookbooks and recipes, pens and notepads, sticky notes to mark pages in the cookbooks, iPhones and laptops to search online recipes or to look up unfamiliar ingredients. These multiple consciousnesses inhabit us as we decide what we want to make, plan the courses, and consider our audience as we decide on a menu. In cooking and writing together, we engage in shared inventions and purposes as well as a sense of synchronicity and being relationally present in time and space with one another. This is what Elbow seems to describe as an interactive process of collaboration, whereas Duffy and other scholars might define it as an intra-active process. How can collage make space for these complex, entangled inter- and intra-actions?

Recently, writing studies scholars (Shivers-McNair; Cardinal; Gries; Micciche; West-Puckett) have turned to the work of feminist philosopher and physicist Karen Barad, whose notion of intra-action challenges the idea that things interact with one another, as if they precede and pre-exist one another and remain separate even as they participate in interaction. As Whitney Stark describes it, intra-action instead understands agency not as "an inherent property of an individual or human to be exercised, but as a 'dynamism of forces' (Barad 141) in which all designated 'things' are constantly exchanging and diffracting, influencing and working inseparably" (Stark). Offered as an alternative to reflection (in which light or soundwaves bounce off of objects that remain the same), diffraction for Barad is an unfolding process of coming into being as things intra-act and intra-fere with one another in dynamic encounters.

***

Once again, we turn to how the material process of cooking together can illuminate the materiality of writing together. When we cook, the ingredients and the pan do not dialogue with or reflect on each other; they diffract and absorb. The heat from the stovetop is conducted through the pan and, in creating a chemical reaction in the ingredients, transforms them. Flavors diffract and absorb one another; the ingredients are not distinct; they are altered through their intra-action. In the same way that in cooking, ingredients diffract one another, our long history of cooking together has taught us how to understand our writing together as similarly diffractive and intra-active.

***

"Writing needs the drama of thinking and the performance of voices" (Elbow 13).

"[C]ollaborators cowrite the agency of their collaboration as it develops" (Duffy 75).

***

What would it mean to think of collaboration NOT as dialogue but as diffraction? And what would happen to the idea of collage as a result? Elbow seems to anticipate this question to some degree as he describes the performance of conflicting voices and perspectives in collaborative collage: "My goal in this activity is not just to make collaborative writing easier and more inviting, but also more complex and conflicted" (13-14).

But while collaborative collage combines multiple voices and points of view, the individual writer stays "in charge of their own writing," a process that moves from individual to co-writer (Elbow 10). Duffy theorizes "co-writing agency" as a state of "emergent potential" (75). In this sense, agency in collaboration is not so much a pre-condition for interaction to occur but an ongoing accomplishment—an emergent process and product of negotiations between individuals, conditions, and objects in constant relation with one another.

We need to imagine a post-humanist collaborative collage that resembles the material, multisensory, multi-agentive processes of cooking together!

***

Our reflection on our twenty-five-year collaboration, through the lens of our cooking together, reinforces the similarly emergent processes of writing/cooking: invention/planning a menu; the tools and timing of preparing to write/ preparing to cook; negotiating the shared labor of cooking/ writing; presenting/publishing/serving the meal; getting audience feedback; and participating in revision/cleaning up, along with reflection on what worked successfully and what to change next time. Our own experiences as long-time collaborators have enabled us to examine how our collaborative cooking experiences cultivate practices of creativity and connection that translate into and enrich collaborative writing processes. It is interesting to reimagine collaborative collage as assemblages and the collaborative process as emergent, intra-active, affective, and relational.

***

"One powerful impetus, and subsequent reinforcement, for our collaboration is our friendship. We enjoy being together, and even though we spend much of the brief periods we're together—a weekend during the term, four to six days over Christmas, a luxurious two weeks in summer—working, we always find time for jokes, shopping sprees for exotic foods, and laughter-filled late-night dinners" (Lunsford and Ede 37).

Works Cited

Barad, Karen. "Posthumanist Performativity: Toward an Understanding of How Matter Comes to Matter." *Signs: Journal of Women in Culture and Society*, vol. 28, no. 3, 2003, pp. 801-831.

Bennett, Jane. *Vibrant Matter*. Duke UP, 2009.

Boyle, Casey. *Rhetoric as Posthuman Practice*. Ohio State UP, 2018.

—. "Writing and Rhetoric and/as Posthuman Practice." *College English*, vol. 78, no. 6, 2016, pp. 532-554.

Broudy, H. S. "Types of knowledge and purposes of education." *Schooling and the Acquisition of Knowledge, edited by* R. C. Anderson, R. J. Spiro, and W.E. Montague, Erlbaum, 1977, pp. 1-17.

Cardinal, Alison. *How Literacy Flows and Comes to Matter: A Participatory Video Study*. 2019. University of Washington, PhD dissertation.

Clary-Lemon, J. "Gifts, ancestors, and relations: Notes toward an indigenous new materialism." *Enculturation*, 12 Nov. 2019. enculturation.net/gifts_ancestors_and_relations

Cooper, Marilyn M. *The Animal Who Writes: A Posthumanist Composition*. U of Pittsburgh P, 2019.

Duffy, William. *Beyond Conversation: Collaboration and the Production of Writing*. Utah State UP, 2020.

Elbow, Peter. "Using the Collage for Collaborative Writing." *Composition Studies*, vol. 27, no. 1, 1999, pp. 7-14.

—. *Writing Without Teachers*. Oxford UP, 1973.

Gries, Laurie E. *Still Life with Rhetoric: A New Materialist Approach to Visual Rhetorics*. Utah State UP, 2015.

Hawk, Byron. *Resounding the Rhetorical: Composition as a Quasi-Object*. U of Pittsburgh P, 2018.

Lunsford, Andrea, and Lisa Ede. *Writing Together: Collaboration in Theory and Practice*. Bedford St. Martin's, 2012.

Micciche, Laura R. "Writing Material." *College English*, vol. 76, no. 6, 2014, pp. 488-505.

Shivers-McNair, Ann. *Beyond the Makerspace: Making and Relational Rhetorics*. U of Michigan P, 2021.

Stark, Whitney. "Inra-action." New Materialism: How Matters Comes to Matter. 15 Aug. 2016. https://newmaterialism.eu/almanac/i/intra-action.html

West-Puckett, Stephanie J. *Materializing Makerspaces: Queerly Composing Space, Time, and (what) Matters*. 2017. East Carolina University, PhD Dissertation.

Differences within Difference: Everyday Praxis from Latinx Lived Experiences

Yvette Chairez, Victoria Ramirez Gentry, and Sue Hum

Latinx bodies challenge conventional historical, ideological, and institutional narratives that seek to fix, define, and render legible racial identities. These traditional accounts of race, racialization processes, and narratives imposed on Latinx student populations present a monolithic approach to difference. However, Latinx bodies confound simple narratives about race, community, and belonging: "Latinx reflects the shifting terrain of identification and the ongoing commitment to building unity through embracing the diversity of Latinidad by not erasing difference and specificity" (Blackwell et al. 129). By foregrounding this difference and specificity—what we call "differences within difference"—we seek to illuminate the degree to which focusing on a single narrative erases and silences diversity. By so doing, we underscore contextual complications to undermine the racial logics and static narratives about Latinx educational experiences. We engage with a recent article on Latinx responses to mentorship and belonging, where authors Christine Garcia, Les Hutchinson Campos, Genevieve Garcia de Müeller, and Christina V. Cedillo bear witness to their painful experiences of racial narratives and systemic racism. In particular, Garcia et al. describe the ways in which Latinx experiences are co-opted, exploited, and controlled by white mentors, who explicitly announce and embrace "anti-racist" predispositions. In response to this problem, the authors focus on deploying rhetorical practices that "more closely reflect our everyday praxes" an approach in which anti-racist theory and practice interact to produce a cycle of action and reflection that both supports and stays true to an antiracist agenda (56). We reflect on and augment this agenda with our own voices, sharing narratives of three sites of praxis: heritage language acquisition, journeys to educational attainment, and supporting differences in the classroom. Our narratives contribute to the "everyday praxes," by foregrounding lived experiences of individuals who are complex assemblages of difference.

Heritage Language Acquisition

A rise in English-only speakers in Latinx communities can be attributed not only to the privileging of standard-edited English in schools but also Mexican American parents and communities who want success, power, and social mobility for their children (Beckstead and Toribio). Structural inequalities, racialized ideologies, and personal histories combine to compel the inevitable heritage language loss for Latinx students, including Yvette and Victoria. This loss, along with the psychic toll of consistent microaggressions, results from their (in)ability to speak Spanish at home and in academe. Regardless of the variety of Spanish, being able to speak one's heritage language becomes proof of authentic performances of racial identity. Heritage language acquisition provides a rich context for highlighting the value of everyday praxes and the dynamics of differences within difference.

Victoria: As a multiracial Latina, my experience with racial identity was tied to my experience with speaking Spanish. My father is Latino (Mexican), and my mother is Caucasian. My father was taught in public school that English was the language for success. He was even sent to summer school with other Mexican children to learn to speak English "properly," even though he already knew English. His experiences with this colonialist oppression moved generationally to me, as he spoke English at home with me and my siblings to protect us from experiencing the shame inflicted upon him through public education (see Vasquez-Tokos). While my inability to speak Spanish did not bother me at first, I experienced shame and sorrow over my inability to speak to my abuela, was made fun of for mispronouncing Spanish words, and I eventually shut my mouth to protect myself. To me, my lack of Spanish exacerbated my own perceived illegitimacy of Latinx identity. These feelings of shame are countered by my parents' unquestioning support and fervent encouragement. When my mom read my master's thesis, she expressed pride and love over the work I had done, reminding me, "You were never a quitter." As I started my Ph.D., my dad began calling me "Dr. Mija," an affectionate moniker he has continued to use. The love, pride, and support from my parents keep me tied to my Latina identity.

Yvette: Like Victoria, I am also Mexican-American and white. I grew up solely around the Mexican side of my family on a predominantly Mexican/Mexican-American side of San Antonio, Texas. My family ostracized and teased me for looking and being white (see Castillo Planas), and my abuela frequently lied to her friends that my father was half-Mexican to avoid being shamed. Although my mother and her siblings were fluent in Spanish, they risked being "paddled" at school if caught speaking it; therefore, in order to avoid what was believed to be the dangers of bilingualism, they did not pass the language on to my sibling, my cousins, and me. Paddling was still administered at our elementary school so, and while we dared to behave in other ways that might get us paddled, we dared not speak Spanish at school. Although we were not really encouraged to speak it inside the home, either. I still managed to understand much of what our family said in Spanish, and much of what was written in my mom's Spanish-language *Cosmopolitan* magazines. And I spoke the taboo words and other choice phrases in secret with my cousins and friends, which prompted relentless teasing about how stupid I looked by speaking Spanish in my white skin. Eventually I stopped trying, and effectively stopped learning to speak Spanish.

Journeys to Educational Attainment

Societal views about Latinxs and other populations of color are based on widely held assumptions and master narratives about the value of education (Rendón et al.). Mentors, susceptible to these firmly entrenched narratives, may be influenced by a deficit model that frames *all* Latinx students as culturally deprived, at-risk marginal learners whose families do not value education. To counter this deficit model, Tara Yosso proposes a "community cultural wealth" model that reframes racialized master narratives to focus on the range of knowledge, skills, and abilities that communities of color bring to education (Yosso 77). Our narratives underscore the complexity and challenges of entering academe. For example, Yvette's experience echoes the deficit model while Victoria's familial and societal support underscores cultural wealth. Narratives of educational attainment provide a crucial site of everyday praxis that spotlight the specificity of differences within difference.

Yvette: In second grade, I declared I would be a writer when I grew up. The criticisms were swift and abundant. While my mom thought it was cute, my friends made fun of me for wanting to do something "white," and my cousins laughed at me so much that I had to hide my notebooks every time they came over. By fifth grade, all of my writing was done in secret. When college application time came around, I was too embarrassed to major in English. My mom who was terminally ill with brain cancer begged me not to go away. She asked me to settle down with my high school boyfriend so she would know I was safe when she died. My mom passed away in 2001 right before spring break of my senior year. A few weeks later, my college acceptance (and rejection) letters began coming in. My stepfather approved of me going to college because he was tired of dealing with me. But my abuela reminded me my mom did not want me to. She said it was selfish and asked what my boyfriend would think of it since he would be attending college in town. My uncle, who obtained a college degree while in the United States Army, wondered what would become of my younger sibling, who would be left without a mother figure. Meanwhile, my cousins acted like I was trying to be better than them. The internalized *machismo* in my family's responses—shaming me for wanting to leave the domestic sphere for college while the men were encouraged to further their education—prompted my adoption of Chicana feminist pedagogical practices that encourage me to, as Torrez expresses, "merge… knowledge from the home with the community" (103). I draw on my Anzaldúan mestiza consciousness – the awareness of straddling two or more opposing cultures – against systemic structures, including machismo, that aim to block (primarily female) students from realizing their potential.

Victoria: My experience with education is different than scholarship tends to imagine for Latinx students. My mom homeschooled all five of us. She made the decision to homeschool us when she noticed my oldest sister learning to read quickly. My mom dedicated her life to our learning to ensure we had the best education she could provide. I took homeschooling for granted as a child, not realizing the social and cultural judgment my parents faced for doing so. Homeschooling the five siblings resulted in a strong familial connection so that not a day goes by that we do not speak to one another. Further, she and my dad provided a foundation that emphasized education was not marginalizing or oppressive. Thus, by the time I was sixteen, I had started taking dual-credit courses at the community college where my father taught, and I soon began tutoring other students in math and English. My early education at home with my mother inspired me to become a teacher; homeschooling enabled my academic success. In hindsight, I realized how much stigma my parents endured (from multiple communities) to educate me.

Supporting Differences in Our Classrooms

Current and future mentors engaging in antiracist pedagogy must avoid "white-washing," or "a deliberate erasure of the ontologies and epistemologies" of their students (Garcia et al. 8). Contributions to antiracist pedagogy might attend to the specificity of differences in classrooms. Informed by our experiences with struggling to acquire our heritage language and our journeys into academe, we seek to support and foreground the racialized, gendered, and classed experiences of Latinx students specifically, and our minoritized and underserved populations more broadly. Narratives of lived experiences are the first step to enabling social engagement and challenging the racial logics that silence some facets of Latinxs' complex, contextual, ever-changing identity performances.

Victoria: To broaden awareness about the complexity of acquiring one's heritage language, I encourage my students to write Language Literacy Narratives that spotlight their experiences with their heritage languages. In particular, I focus on how multiracial/ethnic Latinx students bring diverse experiences that are a result of their communities, upbringing, and educational journeys. Additionally, through a qualitative study of students' multilingual literacy narratives, I have noticed students who are neither multiracial/ethnic nor Latinx also provide insight into the hybrid linguistic experiences of students at Hispanic Serving Institutions. Building on scholarship on translingualism which prioritizes "cross-language interactions and contact relationships," I encourage monolingual and multilingual students to embrace their cultural and linguistic hybridity in ways that I felt I lacked as a Latina who struggled to speak Spanish (Canagarajah 2). My praxis foregrounds the ways in which hybrid, Latinx identities enable students to embrace translingualism in their narratives so that their unique voices and experiences may be heard by others.

Yvette: Majoring in English as I see it, and have experienced it, is an act of resistance, and I treat it as such in my classroom. To drive this concept home, I assign work by writers like Gloria Anzaldua, Ariana Brown, and Ilan Stavans, who embrace Spanglish in their works, alongside linguists who spell out the legitimacy of AAVE and women in history who have created their own languages to survive. In my upper-division composition class, I ask my students, "When/How did you decide you wanted to major in English?" Interestingly, but not surprisingly, about half of my Latinx students express similar cognitive and emotional dissonance in their own responses. The other half tend not to mention anything about conflicting messages at all. Many, like me, cultivated a love for writing through creative pieces composed in hiding. To justify their choice of major, many choose "practical" pathways such as professional writing or teaching. As an instructor, I mentor my students on the effects that colonization, segregation, the patriarchy, and public school district zonings have had on literacy in the United States and how restricting access to reading and writing has often been a fairly successful method of oppression for immigrants, people of color, those living in poverty, and women. These topics, as part of my approach to antiracist pedagogy, help my students conceptualize possible reasons for their families' opposition to their majoring in English. It is likely they are under the impression that having, or aspiring to have, a high command over reading and writing makes one an oppressor. I explain that this reaction is by design, and that as students of writing, rhetoric, and language, they are in a prime position to begin dismantling this racist practice.

Conclusion

Our voices, stories, and journeys testify to the urgency to pay attention to the differences within difference, countering erasure, silence, and marginalization imposed institutionally and communally. Totalizing categories that limit us to specific racial identities and roles as students, teachers, and mentors, can be countered with intentional acknowledgement of the specificity of difference. We encourage students to identify their own sites of lived experiences, thereby redefining themselves through their own narratives and with their own voices and in so doing enacting an everyday praxis. The foundation of antiracist pedagogy, this praxis provides opportunities for students to push against limiting definitions, define themselves, and find belonging even as they undermine those totalizing categories.

Works Cited

Beckstead, Karen, and Almeida Jacqueline Toribio. "Minority Perspectives on Language: Mexican and Mexican-American Adolescents' Attitudes toward Spanish and English." *Mi Lengua: Spanish as a Heritage Language in the United States*, edited by Ana Roca and M. Cecilia Colombi, Georgetown UP, 2003, pp. 154-70.

Blackwell, Maylei, et al. "Special Issue: Critical Latinx Indigeneities." *Latino Studies*, vol. 15, no. 2, 2017, pp. 126-137.

Canagarajah, Suresh. *Literacy as Translingual Practice: Between Communities and Classrooms*. Routledge, 2013.

Garcia, Christine, Les Hutchinson Campos, Genevieve Garcia de Müeller, and Christina V. Cedillo. "'It's not you. You belong here.' A Latinx Conversation on Mentorship and Belonging in the Academy." *Composition Studies*, vol. 49, no. 2, 2021, pp. 53-69.

Planas, Melissa Castillo. "Latinx Enough?: Whiteness, Latinidad and Identity in Memoirs of Finding 'Home.'" *Prose Studies*, vol 41, no. 2, 2020, pp. 179-92.

Rendón, Laura, Vijay Kanagala, and Ripsime Bledsoe. "Shattering the Deficit Grand Narrative: Toward a Culturally-Validating Latino Student Success Framework." *New Directions: Assessment and Preparation of Hispanic College Students*, edited by Alfredo de los Santos, Laura Rendón, Gary Francisco Keller, Alberto Arereda, Estela Mara Bensimón, and Richard J. Tannenbaum, Bilingual P, 2017.

Torrez, J. Estrella. "Translating Chicana Testimonios Into Pedagogy for a White Midwestern Classroom." *Chicana/Latina Studies*, vol. 14, no. 2, 2015, pp. 101-130.

Vasquez-Tokos, Jessica M. *Mexican Americans Across Generations: Immigrant Families, Racial Realities*. New York University Press, 2011.

Yosso, T.J. "Whose Culture has Capital?: A Critical Race Theory Discussion of Community Cultural Wealth." *Race Ethnicity and Education*, vol. 8, no. 1, 2005, pp. 69-91.

Rhetoric 2050: In Honor of Richard M. Coe's "Rhetoric 2001"

Sidney I. Dobrin

> But these are extraordinary times. The world is changing, and human consciousness with it.
>
> —Richard M. Coe, "Rhetoric 2001"

I began my academic publishing career thirty years ago while in graduate school. That year, I published three pieces, two of which appeared in *Composition Studies*: a review of Wendy Bishop and James Strickland's *The Subject is Writing: Essays by Teachers and Students* and an interview called "Turning the Tables: An (Inter)view with Gary A. Olson." At the time, Olson was editor of *Journal of Advanced Composition* (which would later be known simply as *JAC*), and his in-depth scholarly interviews in *JAC* redefined how the interview format could be used as scholarship. Olson was also my mentor and dissertation director. The third piece I published that year was a review of M. Jimmie Killingsworth and Jacqueline S. Palmer's landmark book *Ecospeak: Rhetoric and Environmental Politics in America* which Olson and, at the time *JAC* Book Review Editor, John Frederick Reynolds agreed to publish. (There's nothing like a little scholarly nepotism to jump start a new grad student's career.) After the review was published, Olson advised me not to waste my time writing about ecological or environmental subjects anymore. Environmental subjects, he told me, were, at best, trendy fads in which everyone would lose interest quickly. Ecology and environment, he explained, were not substantive concepts for writing studies and that *real* composition scholars would see work that addresses those subjects as substandard, as irrelevant to the field, and counter to humanistic resistance to the sciences. There would be no way, he said, I'd get a job if my dissertation took up ecology or environment or if I published any more reviews, essays, or articles about the subjects. For the next six years, I honored his advice. It wasn't until I had been out of graduate school for three years that I returned to subjects of ecology and environment when I published "Advanced Exposition: Rhetoric and Environment" in *Composition Studies*. It would take another ten years before Olson (now President of Daemen College) would say to me, "Wow was I wrong about what I said about working in environmental areas."

Nineteen years before I wrote that review of Killingsworth and Palmer's book, *Freshman English News* (*FEN*), the precursor to *Composition Studies*, published Richard M. Coe's "Rhetoric 2001." Coe's article had been selected as the winner of *FEN*'s annual essay contest (as judged by Edward P.J. Corbett, Mina Shaughnessy, and Peter Elbow) and was featured in the Spring 1974 issue. Coe's title, "Rhetoric 2001" alluded to a speculative—or perhaps anticipated—future of rhetoric and composition instruction (think of Orwell using the title *1984* for his 1948 book). Coe begins his essay by noting that "the assertion that we live in a century of major technological and social transformation is already cliché" (1). In "Rhetoric 2001," he establishes, well ahead of his time, a context in which ecological methodologies and concern for environmental crises, as well as the interactions between writers and computer technologies, would become dominant aspects of both composition instruction and the very understanding of writing itself. Coe anticipates ecological methodologies in rhetorical studies and writing studies as emerging as a fundamental school of thought as he links ecological crises to "three determining factors: (a) technological progress, (b) population increase, and (c) certain outmoded attitudes and thought patterns" (1). He shows us the need to take up systems theories and complexity theories, the very theories that would become critical to the development of ecocomposition, place-based composition, and ecological rhetoric thirty years following the publication of "Rhetoric 2001"—as accurately predicted in his title. Coe connects ecological and environmental disaster to technological advancement and to the role of communicative practices, which he demonstrates as fundamental to composition and rhetoric's pedagogical imperative. He also foresees posthumanist thinking in showing that the parts of what we have assumed to be "natural" aspects of the human are called into question by both the way of technological transformation and the very ideas of what we understand to be "natural" or "human consciousness." Perhaps most telling, though, is Coe's anticipation of a new era of interdisciplinary work that demands the collaboration between science/technology research and humanities research. Interdisciplinarity, he contends, has "implications for the future of the humanities in particular and human consciousness in general" (1). "The task of the humanities," Coe explains, "is to teach human-ness" (1). But Coe does not adhere to an essentialist understanding of what "human-ness" might be or how we might define and understand the humanities as a discipline. Instead, Coe alerts us that "within academia, the coming of a new mode is foreshadowed by the increasing necessity to violate the old classifications and compartmentalizations of knowledge" (2).

Coe's insight regarding shifts in the classifications of knowledge-making seems like an evident response to the academic climate of the time. Fifteen years prior to the publication of "Rhetoric 2001," C.P. Snow delivered the now famous Rede Lecture, "The Two Cultures and The Scientific Revolution," in which he argues that "the intellectual life of the whole of western society is increasingly being split into two polar groups" (4). Snow defines these groups as the Sciences and the Humanities (he defines the Humanities as literary intellectuals). These academic cultural divisions have remained central to the disciplinary demarcations employed in Western education, divisions which tend to promote academic silos, disciplinary territorialism, and intellectual hierarchies, many of which affect larger cultural, political, and economic valuing of and within education. In the past quarter century, that value has manifested culturally as an embrace of Science, Technology, Engineering, and Math (STEM) education. In response to this cultural tide, the Humanities, as Coe anticipated, have begun to pay particular attention to STEM-related approaches to humanities research, as seen in the emergence of environmental humanities and digital humanities, among others.

Since the early 2000s, ecological methodologies and questions regarding environmental concerns have been central not only to rhetoric and composition, but to the humanities more generally. And, as Coe correctly anticipates, the ecological turn in composition paralleled a similar influx of methodologies and inquiries regarding the role of advanced technologies. The emergence of environmental humanities and digital humanities (as well as other subsets like energy humanities, medical humanities, blue humanities, and so on) demonstrate the prevalence and relevance of Coe's claims. Perhaps the ecological/environmental turn in composition is a result of the extensive desire—amidst ongoing environmental crises—for those in the Humanities to consider the question "what can we do?" Such a question asks in what ways the humanities might contribute to the larger environmental problem-solving initiative in response to environmental crises—problems that had been traditionally understood as scientific in nature and requiring scientific solutions. However, what Coe so rightly projects is the inseparability of environmental crises and the role of communication, both as the cause of such crises and as necessary in finding any solution. That is, Coe anticipates the role of cultural communication in perpetuating, circulating, and reinscribing those "certain outmoded attitudes and thought patterns" (1) he sees as at the heart of all environmental crises.

Though it would take until 1985 and the publication of Coe's *College Composition and Communication* article "Eco-Logic for the Composition Classroom" and Marilyn M. Cooper's 1986 *College English* article "The Ecology of Writing" before ecological methodologies would begin to take root in composition and rhetoric—and then only slowly propagating throughout the field for the next decade until the ecological turn emerged in full in the late 1990s—ecological methodologies have become central to work in writing studies. Perhaps this is the case because, as Coe implies, such thinking requires understanding writing as a cardinal component of the complex systems and networks through which cultures "comprehend, order, evaluate, and control their experience" (1). For Coe, then, writing—and specifically teaching writing in the composition classroom—offers the "power to make a contribution which may be crucial to the future of our species" (1). Certainly, Coe's 1985 article and Cooper's 1986 article solidified ecological methodologies as an important advent in composition studies, but "Rhetoric 2001" initiated the conversation, and there is remarkable value in being the initiator of a conversation, particularly one which has had such a significant impact on writing studies. (Cixin Liu, in *The Dark Forest*—the sequel to his Hugo and Nebula Award winning book *The Three Body Problem*—best describes this phenomenon in this way: "Judas became who he was because he was the first to kiss Jesus, and that made him fundamentally different from the second one to kiss him" (451)).[1]

Coe explains that "within academia, the coming of a new mode is foreshadowed by the increasing necessity to violate the old classifications and compartmentalizations of knowledge" (2). This violation, he explains, is inevitable as "every major scientific advance has implied a shift of human consciousness" (2). For Coe, the awareness of and ability to communicate information that both inform and critique such shifts are elemental to the future of composition studies and composition pedagogy's influence on the world. This means reorienting the very idea of what composition classes can be because "to create the composition course of the future, we will have to make explicit and reevaluate the values implicit in the traditional composition course" (2).

Of course, ecology—as a methodology and as a general concept—has become central to many academic approaches as well as ways of thinking generally. As Erich Hörl explains, "There are thousands of ecologies today: ecologies of sensation, perception, cognition, desire, attention, power, values, information, participation, media, the mind, relations, practices, behavior, belonging, the social, the political" (1)—to which I would add rhetoric and writing. Hörl contends that ecology has been denaturalized and removed from its original connections with nature and environment and semantically redefined to occupy any field where it might find utility—or, at least, convenience. While Hörl's position regarding new iterations or reformations of the idea of ecology are important to how we might conceive of ecology and writing studies moving forward, Coe had already anticipated the need for ecology to mutate as a methodology that might inform our understanding of writing and writing instruction. Crucially, too, Coe saw the inevitability of the link between these new formations of ecology and emerging technologies. If, as Jean-Luc Nancy puts it, that "an ecology properly understood can be nothing other than a technology" (47), then the intersection between ecology, technology, and communication, particularly written communication, have become, as Coe alerted us nearly fifty years ago, central to the very nature of what we do as scholars of rhetoric and writing and, perhaps most importantly, as teachers of composition.

Given the range of and influence of the scholarship published in the last fifty years of *Composition Studies* and *Freshman English News*, it would be an oversimplification to point to a single moment in the journal's history as having the most profound influence on the field. Yet, Coe's "Rhetoric 2001" may have anticipated better than most how the field of rhetoric and composition would unfold and why ecological approaches to thinking about composition instruction would become so crucial. If, as I have quoted from "Rhetoric 2001" in the epigraph to this short piece, the time when Coe made his claims were indeed "extraordinary times" during which the world was "changing, and human consciousness with it" (1), then we might identify that these times, our times—like all times—are extraordinary as well. And, with the foresight of Coe, writing studies has been better prepared to engage them.

Notes

1. By no means, though, do I use this analogy to imply that Coe betrayed the field in any way, only to indicate the uniqueness of a first.

Works Cited

Coe, Richard M. "Rhetoric 2001." *Freshman English News*, vol. 3, no. 1, 1974, pp. 1-13.

———. "Eco-Logic for the Composition Classroom." *College Composition and Communication.* Vol. 26, No. 3 (Oct., 1975), pp. 232-237.

Cooper, Marilyn M. "The Ecology of Writing." *College English*, vol. 48, no. 4, 1986, pp. 364-375.

Dobrin, Sidney I. "Turning the Tables: An (Inter)view with Gary A. Olson." *Composition Studies*, vol. 21, 1993, pp. 32-45.

Dobrin, Sidney I. "Review of Ecospeak: Rhetoric and Environmental Politics in America." *Journal of Advanced Composition,* vol. 13. 1993, pp. 272-73.

Dobrin. Sidney I. "Review of The Subject is Writing: Essays by Teachers and Students." *Composition Studies*, vol. 21, 1993, pp.102-03.

Hörl, Erich. "Introduction to General Ecology: The Ecologization of Thinking." *General Ecology: The New Ecological Paradigm*, Bloomsbury, 2017, pp.1-73.

Liu, Cixin. *The Dark Forrest*. Tor Books, 2016.

Nancy, Jean-Luc. *The Sense of the World*. Translated by Jeffrey S. Librett, U of Minnesota P, 1997.

Snow, C. P. "The Two Cultures." *The Rede Lecture*. Cambridge UP, 1959.

The Democratization of Writing and the Role of Cheating

Peter Elbow

This is an exciting 50 year anniversary for our field's oldest independent peer-reviewed journal. I'm grateful that I have been able to write for its pages previously, and I give deep thanks to the editors, Matt Davis and Kara Taczak, for inviting me to write as part of this birthday party.

The occasion prompts rumination about names. (Ruminate. Ruminants. I've always wished I could chew my cud like a couple of graceful Nubian goats we had during some childhood summers—beautiful and playful with long ears hanging down. When you watch ruminants like goats and cows, you can't help wondering what they are thinking.) This journal's first name was *Freshman English News,* but it was later rechristened *Composition Studies.* Does that matter? The change went along with a deeper change: under its new name, the journal was notable for being more inclusive and multiracial in a field that had been white-centered, white-focused, and white-oriented.

And, much as we like to think we've outgrown magical thinking, we can still detect a trace of it in everyday language. Skinner may have been discredited by Saussure and Chomsky, but his behavioral model of language helps us understand why names often seem to function magically. That is, Skinner insists that our response to a word carries a tiny trace of our response to the thing it names. Mostly we don't notice this behavioral dimension of language, but think of when you are in a formal meeting or living room and someone says "shit." Notice carefully and you'll see how some people will betray a tiny marginal trace of their response to the thing itself.

We've been fighting magical thinking for a long time. Socrates led the attack, but even he, with his theory of forms, remarked that tall people possess more tallness or participate in "Tallness" *(Phaedo* 102). In the twentieth century, Saussure seemed to have finished off the idea that names carry real traces of things. Yet still, when we read descriptions of torture—mere words—most of us cringe. In short, neither Socrates nor Saussure were capable of wielding words that could free us completely from the primitive tendency to feel a marginal link between words and the things they name. A name change–from *Freshman English News* to *Composition Studies,* say–reflects an actual change in the field itself.

I'm old enough to remember when the name of our field was up for grabs. "Freshman English" felt too local and ad hoc. I argued for "writing" as the most natural and obvious choice, but those with more scholarly clout carried the day with a fancier name: composition. I remember a walk in the woods with a doctor friend. I smelled dog poop, but he sniffed and said, "fecal matter." He was a professional and used a professional term. In those fecund years, the 1960s, there was just a small group of us interested in the process of writing and who were—it later turned out—starting a new academic field: composition. As for the name, I guess there was a hunger for some professionalism and legitimacy. I liked plain "writing" for our name, but composition seemed to carry more prestige with the big kids in the other disciplines. Still, I saw it as a bad omen to run away from the common everyday name for our field: writing. Why avoid the vernacular?

Democratization as Cheating

If we had used the everyday word "writing" for our field, we would have been highlighting a goal I had in mind with the titles of my two early books: *Writing Without Teachers* (1973) and *Everyone Can Write* (1981). I wanted to show that the activity of writing could be easy. But professionals and literate people seemed to resist. It's understandable that if they suffered in learning to write, they didn't want to make it too easy for others. I can claim that I suffered, too (see "Illiteracy and Oxford and Harvard"). But my goal was to make things easy.

There's something deeply human about the impulse to exclude or preserve privilege—whether you were born to it or had to struggle to earn it. Literacy has tended to function as a way to exclude. Christians don't highlight Jesus as an excluder, but he sometimes was, and he didn't mince words when he was asked why he used parables:

> It has been given to you to know the mysteries of the kingdom of heaven, but to them it has not been given. For whoever has, to him more will be given, and he will have abundance; but whoever does not have, even what he has will be taken away from him. Therefore speak I to them in parables: because they seeing see not; and hearing they hear not, neither do they understand. (*New King James Bible,* Matthew 13:11-12)

The poor will stay poor while the rich get richer.

From the earliest times, people who could write had palpable power and prestige. And as late as the Renaissance, you needed Latin if you wanted to write. Women and children and folks in the street had only the vernacular (meaning "close to the earth"). Yet Dante in writing the *Divine Comedy* insisted on using this language of the street—this language of the people that had never been used for serious noble purposes. By using it, he gave birth to the language we now call Italian.

In an earlier small book, *De Vulgari Eloquentia*, Dante argued that eloquence could just as well be found in "the vulgar," that is, the language of the street, of women and nursemaids. But he felt he needed to use Latin to make this argument that Latin wasn't necessary. I paid homage to Dante in the title of my last book, *Vernacular Eloquence: What Speech Can Bring to Writing* (vernacular being the exact translation of his word "vulgar.")

My whole career has been a battle against literacy as an exclusionary force. (When I see "No Trespassing" and a fence, I find I want to go there. Perhaps there are good blueberries in that field. I don't want to be kept out, and writing was trying to keep me out.) If something is difficult, I always look for an easier way. I had to quit graduate school in my second semester when I first set out for a PhD at Harvard. I couldn't write any more—or rather I couldn't write clear organized prose anymore because of the psychological tangle the effort put me into. In truth, I wrote reams and reams—but it was all personal private freewriting about my fear and frustration at being unable to write. Luckily, I've been able to build a career exploring the implications of my inability to write (see "Illiteracy at Oxford and Harvard").

To conclude this introduction, I'd like to explore three difficulties in writing—and how I used cheating to get around them.

Writing is hard but we can cheat by speaking onto the page.

Because I was a good student and always tried to write properly, I ground to a halt when I could no longer manage this feat. It took me a long time to learn to shift into a completely different mental and linguistic gear and use speech for writing—or as I like to phrase it, "to speak onto the page." That is, I learned to freewrite—and that's what I needed in order to learn to write garbage. That is, to write whatever words came to my mouth when I was tangled in a knot or trying to find words for what I mean. I published this idea in the appendix to *Writing Without Teachers*, before there was dictation software, indeed before anyone had ever imagined such a thing as software. (I didn't invent freewriting; Ken Macrorie did. He is massively underappreciated.)

When I followed my lazy shortcut, I found that freewriting is not just easier; it leads to linguistic and cognitive improvements that are hard to get any other way. That is, when we use our mouths and write by speaking onto the page, those words on the page are experienced by readers as alive, and voiced; they resonate with more of the writer's self.

We can understand how this mysterious improvement happens by peering under the hood. What we find are not carburetors or distributors but rather intonation units. That is, if we speak normally or unselfconsciously, our words come out in spurts that linguists call intonation units. (For example, look at the naturally conversational phrases or spurts that I just used: "when we speak," "in normal unselfconscious speech," "the words come out." In normal speech, there are places where we pause and places where we don't pause. If you want to be technical, you can find that intonation units correlate with aspects of grammar [see Part Three in my *Vernacular Eloquence*].) When we cheat by speaking onto the page and produce these intonation units, readers tend to hear the sound of these words—audibly but in their heads. And when this happens, readers often hear a person on the page, and the words are often more easily understood and more resonant and memorable.

There's something almost magical about intonation units—those unpausing words that spurt from our mouths. They embody a process I call easy-out, easy-in. Because the words come out of the mind so easily (thanks to the mouth), they go into the mind easily. The mouth has the ability to shape words characteristic of natural speech; and probably because we evolved as speaking animals, the mind comprehends those intonation units easily. This explains why so much writing, especially by academics, is ungratifying to read. When we write slowly, haltingly, and deliberately—stopping every third word to make conscious choices—we tend to create much less fluent prose. Often enough it is downright stiff, stilted, or even tangled. We fail to create intonation units.

Let me note two false conclusions you might draw from what I've said. I am not saying that our goal should necessarily be simple conversational language, a la Hemingway. No. Look at the prose of Henry James: it is also very much built out of intonation units. Even from that sometimes stilted writer, we also tend to hear those spurted intonation units—but James' units are longer and more intricate and sometimes more fragilely connected.

A brief note about spelling. I like to imply that speaking onto the page is the answer to all your questions. (My wife, after hearing me too often speak about these matters, once remarked, "Peter, whatever the question is, the answer is always freewriting.") And, of course, I benefited from a standard education, so I am lucky enough: I don't worry so much about spelling. But to write a word, we have to spell it. I remember interviewing a guy who lived mostly on the street, and he was more eloquent than most highly educated people. But he couldn't write and once, tragically said, "I have no words." Our culture had tricked him into thinking that if he couldn't spell a word, he didn't have that word.

I'm sure all my readers know about the amazing breakthroughs in teaching writing to children that come from ignoring spelling. There's been a big movement in teaching toddlers to "speak onto the page"—with whatever spelling results. With this approach, children learn to write before they learn to read: they can write any word or sentence they can say—whereas they have trouble reading words they're unacquainted with. And, of course, people in our culture didn't used to care so much about spelling. For instance, Meriwether

Lewis wrote eloquently in the *Lewis and Clark Journal*, and he was typical in not worrying about idiosyncratic and inconsistent spelling. He was appointed Secretary to the President by Thomas Jefferson. Interestingly, in both Finland and in Korea, taking different routes, they grasped the nettle and radically transformed their national spelling to make it conform better to pronunciation. In the case of Korea, this was a decision from the top—by the king in the seventeenth century!

Organizing is hard, but we can cheat by using the form of collage.

When we are working on a draft or revising, it's sometimes hard to know what order to put things in. Indeed, sometimes we are still struggling to decide what the main point is. But we can cheat our way around this difficulty by using the structure of collage. That is, we can write as much as possible about the topic; then choose the best bits and clean them up; then decide on an order that is random but somehow pleasing.

Collaborating is hard, but the solution is so easy that it doesn't feel like cheating.

When people have to agree, there are always tiresome arguments about everything–words, ideas, organization. By invoking the collage principle, we can divvy up the ideas or sections according to preference or temperament then settle for a random order. But it's probably worth agreeing about which bits to start and end with.

When Pat Belanoff and I wrote a textbook together, *A Community of Writers* (short edition, *Being a Writer*), we divvied up the sections according to preference, and then each wrote very, very rough drafts—drafts that sometimes just fell into rough notes and phrases; then we traded and each took over the other person's almost-draft and gave it a first rough revision; then we traded again and revised again. We did that at least two more times till we finally couldn't remember whose fingerprints were on the first version.

***

Language may be the realm of life more democratic than any other. People are in charge. What comes out of peoples' mouths is what ends up in dictionaries—as long as there are enough mouths. Dictionaries can do nothing but record decisions made by speakers—who like to take shortcuts and cheat.

Previous publications in this journal:

Elbow, Peter. "Using Collage for Collaborative Writing." *Composition Studies* vol. 27 no. 1, 1999, pp.7-14.

Trimbur, John, Keil, Charles, and Peter Elbow. "Making Choices about Voices." *Composition Studies* vol. 30, no. 1, 2002, pp. 61-65. (My bit was just a tiny, almost mystical reflection.)

Bean, Janet, Eddy, Robert, Grego, Rhonda, Irvine, Patricia, Kutz, Ellie, Matsuda, Paul Kei, Cucchiara, Maryann, Elbow, Peter, Haswell, Richard, Kennedy, Eileen, and Al Lehner. "Should We Ask Students to Write in Home Language? Complicating a Yes/No Debate." *Composition Studies,* vol. 31, no. 1, 2003, pp. 25-42.

Works Cited

Dante, Alighieri. Translated by Steven Botterill. *De Vulgari Eloquentia*. Cambridge UP, 1996.

Elbow, Peter. "Illiteracy and Oxford and Harvard: Reflections on the Inability to Write." In Richard Larson and Tom McCrackin, eds. *Reflective Stories: Becoming Teachers of English and English Education*. NCTE, 1997. (Reprinted in *Everyone Can Write: Essays Toward a Hopeful Theory of Writing and Teaching Writing*. Oxford UP, 2000.)

—. *Vernacular Eloquence: What Speech Can Bring to Writing*. Oxford UP, 2012.

—. *Writing With Power*. Oxford UP, 1980.

—. *Writing Without Teachers*. Oxford UP, 1973.

—. *Everyone Can Write*. Oxford UP, 2000.

Elbow, Peter, and Patricia Belanoff. *A Community of Writers*. McGraw-Hill, (short edition, *Being a Writer*), New York, 2002.

Plato. *Phaedo*. Translated by F.J. Church, Liberal Arts Press, 1951.

The Holy Bible, New King James. Thomas Nelson, 1975.

Creating Space for Emotion in the *Composition Studies* Archive

Alexis Sabryn Walston and Jessica Enoch

Fear, anger, frustration, anxiety, worry, compassion, empathy, exhaustion–these emotions and more have marked and shaped our administrative and pedagogical work over the past two years, and, of course, we're not alone. Writing teachers and administrators across the country have attempted to create a community of support for our students and ourselves as we've faced a terrifying global pandemic, a hotly contested presidential election, as well as injustices, violence, and protests related to race, gender, sexuality, and gender expression. Now too we watch a world at war. The emotional toll the past two years have had on us and our students is evidenced by articles in the *Chronicle of Higher Education* and *Inside Higher Ed* such as "Covid-19 Has Worsened the Student Mental-Health Crisis" (Brown and Kafka), "Faculty Members are Suffering Burnout" (Pettit), "How to Manage through Emotional Exhaustion" (O'Grady), "Academe, Hear Me. I Am Crying Uncle" (Anonymous), and "Honoring Ourselves and Each Other Through Burnout" (Godbee). We're exhausted and burnt out; our emotions are at frayed edges, as we've seen and experienced the need to create space for those in our communities to mourn, to breathe, to rest, to recover, and even to hope for a better future.

As writing program administrators, we've (Lexi and Jess) paid especially close attention to how we can support writing teachers and students. The program we direct at the University of Maryland is a large one: 60+ instructors teaching over 2,000 students per semester in 120 sections of English 101: Academic Writing. As we've worked to support this large community of students and teachers over the past two years, our administrative focus has been guided by principles of antiracist pedagogy, empathy, resilience, and community building, and we've prioritized instructional support based in social and linguistic justice, critical thinking and reading, reflection, and communicating across difference. Learning more about trauma-informed pedagogy has become a key concern for us.

The invitation from Kara Taczak and Matt Davis to take stock of the *Composition Studies* archive gave us the opportunity to explore how its trove of articles from 1972 to the present speak to our current circumstances. As we perused the archive and contemplated the journal's impact on the field, articles that meditated on the emotive dimension of teaching and administration resonated powerfully with us. Thus, here, we spotlight just a few articles from the *Composition Studies* archive that make space for us to engage with emotion, and we track lines of conversation within the journal that fortify our conviction that attention to emotion must be a critical part of writing, teaching, and administration, especially now. Our goal is to consider how *Composition Studies* has laid the groundwork for centering emotion in our pedagogy in a way that supports our administrative and pedagogical exigencies over the past two years.

Not surprisingly, *Composition Studies* is at the cutting edge of this conversation with recent scholarship that engages the pandemic and its emotional effects on us, our students, and our classrooms. In her 2021 article, "Pandemic Pedagogy: What We Learned from the Sudden Transition to Online Teaching and How It Can Help Us Prepare to Teach Writing in an Uncertain Future," Jennifer Sheppard conducts a survey of writing instructors in which instructors articulate "a plea for attention to personal/professional well-being," indicating a desire for an ethic of care and empathy in the teaching and administration of writing courses (61). Carrie Hall also investigates how emotions–specifically, duress–impact the writing classroom in her 2021 essay, "'How am I Supposed to Watch a Little Piece of Paper?': Literacy and Learning Under Duress." Here, Hall interrogates the complex relationship between literacy and duress, exploring the strains duress places on focused attention. Critically, Hall speaks to and broadens our pandemic experience, explaining "Even without a pandemic, experiences that tax attention–like poverty and trauma–disproportionately affect students of color, disabled students, LGBTQIA+ students, and women, due to societal influences like homophobia, poverty, misogyny, transphobia, sexual violence, police brutality, and institutional racism" (16). Referencing Asao Inoue, Hall cites paying attention as one way to better comprehend how students can be affected by duress: "in order for students to pay attention, they must be paid attention to. We should assume our students are making meaning, though that meaning may not always be immediately clear" (16). Hall argues that we can pay attention to our students by employing empathy to better understand how duress affects students' attention and that we should use this understanding to inform how we craft flexible assignments, schedules, and syllabi (22). Ultimately, Hall posits that instructors should incorporate pedagogical tenets that accommodate students under duress–a practice that will serve students well both during and beyond the pandemic.

Our current exigencies have not been the only catalysts to consider attention to emotion, of course. Arguments in favor of valuing students' well-being and emotions can be tracked to early issues of *Composition Studies*, formerly known as *Freshman English News*. As early as the 1970s, editors and writers were developing an ethic of care for instructors and their students. Clearly, there were elements of stress and frustration in these early years of our discipline when teachers felt isolated and diminished by the lack of support they received from their universities and the need for greater community and conversation across institutions. Such feelings are indicated in titles like Merle Thompson's "Let's

Be Human about Behavior" (1972), Andrea Lunsford's "How to Combat the Freshman English Blues" (1976), and Maurice Hunt's "Preventing Burnout in Teaching Assistants" (1986).

Donald Murray's 1981 essay, "The Politics of Respect," stands out to us because he meditates on respect as an emotion necessary for effective teaching, learning, and writing program administration. Murray guides readers not to dismiss students, their ideas, or their writing, but instead to deeply engage and value students' intellectual growth and to extend respect for what instructors may dispel or trivialize. Murray explains that a major problem composition instructors face is students not having self-respect for their own ideas. We must, Murray claims, "respect our students' potential so they can begin to believe they have potential, and through the work with us earn self-respect" (1). Importantly, Murray goes on to turn this message on its head to consider the fact that faculty may not feel respected given composition instruction's low status in many universities. Murray calls for respect for these instructors and the important courses they teach, asserting, "If faculty who actually teach Freshman English are going to be able to respect their students they must be respected themselves and respect themselves" (1). Murray establishes that student, instructor, and administrative respect is vital for a successful first-year composition course.

Twenty years later, Kia Jane Richmond builds on Murray's call for respect in her 2002 essay, "Repositioning Emotions in Composition Studies." Here Richmond considers how scholars, teachers, and administrators should respect, rather than minimize or ignore, the place of emotion in composition pedagogy and makes it her work to invite more conversation around the role of emotion in our field. Richmond explains that "composition, historically, has challenged the validity of emotions" in an attempt to "legitimize itself in the academic community" (69). She recalls her own training:

> I was taught, during my training as a secondary educator and in my courses on pedagogy in composition, that a student's emotional well-being is not as important to my teaching (or his/her learning) as his or her intellectual development. I believe, however, that this attitude toward students suggests an educational philosophy that emphasizes humanistic education without wanting to view its participants as (fully) human" (Richmond 78-79).

Her goal in this essay is to center emotions and the attendant relationships they enable in the writing classroom. Richmond calls instructors to invite students to interrogate the ways emotions shape the work of the classroom, recognizing and reflecting especially on how emotions impact their writing processes (75).

Richmond also underscores the need for teachers to interrogate our own emotional impact on the classroom by contemplating how the emotions we circulate affect both learning and teaching (76). Instructors should reflect on how shifting attitudes toward students can potentially encourage or discourage their writing process and product as well as their writerly identity. Richmond spurs scholars to deepen our thinking on this score and continue pursuing the connections between writing and emotion, explaining "Further opportunities for research exist in the areas of intuition, spirituality, fear, and health," as well as mental health (Richmond 77). Scholars have indeed responded to her call, with *Composition Studies* articles by Sally Chandler, A. Abby Knoblauch, and Amy Williams contributing to the conversation Richmond helped to sustain and invigorate.

As we, too, take up Richmond's call, realizing now how important these investigations should be for us in 2022, one emotion we want to turn to and cultivate is hope. And, once again, the *Composition Studies* archive helps us to consider how. In her 1986 essay, "Ground of Hope: The Freshman English Class," Mary Savage inspires readers to see opportunities for hope in the work we do. Savage reminds us of the "transformational potential" (25) that lies in our classrooms, for it is here that we teach students "to enact change and challenge power" (24). Through Savage's lens we are emboldened by the feelings of hope we need to face our contemporary contexts; we must have hope to do the work we want to do: to create pedagogies invested social and linguistic social justice, embedded in careful and critical reading, invested in communicating across difference. For, as Savage makes clear, the first-year course provides the "ground for hope . . . [b]ecause it is through language that we learn how to mean and be in the world, it is also through *learning how we learn to mean* that we may come to have choices about how we will be in the world" (27, emphasis original). In this time of strife and emotional turmoil, we take a moment to dwell on Savage's reminder of first-year composition's "transformational potential" and echo her emphasis on seeing hope as a key element of first-year composition (25).

Since its inception, *Composition Studies* has pushed the field to consider the role of emotions in the writing classroom. Murray, Savage, and Richmond, along with all the scholars in conversation with them, helped lay the groundwork for writing instructors to center the range of emotions students and teachers experience in the classroom. We see respect and hope as especially important emotions to call on and cultivate as we try to facilitate more empathetic teaching during the difficult times we face. A focus on respect and hope for students, instructors, and administrators has helped us through these past two years of sickness, stress, and burn out, and–as Hall demonstrates–will continue to aid us in supporting students under duress. As we persevere, we especially hope the significance of emotions remains a foundational element of our composition pedagogy and administration and that *Composition Studies* will help to make it so.

Works Cited

Anonymous. "Academe, Hear Me. I Am Crying Uncle." *Inside Higher Ed*, 22 Apr. 2022, https://www.insidehighered.com/advice/2022/04/22/burned-out-professor-declares-academic-chapter-11-opinion.

Brown, Sarah and Alexander C. Kafka. "Covid-19 Has Worsened the Student Mental-Health Crisis. Can Resilience Training Fix It?" *The Chronicle of Higher Education*, 11 May 2020, https://www.chronicle.com/article/covid-19-has-worsened-the-student-mental-health-crisis-can-resilience-training-fix-it/.

Chandler, Sally. "Fear, Teaching Composition, and Students' Discursive Choices: Re-Thinking Connections between Emotions and College Student Writing." *Composition Studies*, vol. 35, no. 2, Fall 2007, pp. 53–70.

Godbee, Beth. "Honoring Ourselves and Each Other Through Burnout." *Inside Higher Ed*, 6 May 2022, https://www.insidehighered.com/advice/2022/05/06/problems-burnout-are-collective-not-just-individual-opinion?fbclid=IwAR02cI9Ry2urO7T04bDe6oe0-foc5HzOP2ebu7YTiA2GuC3oLt6n2WmInIM.

Hall, Carrie. "'How am I Supposed to Watch a Little Piece of Paper?' Literacy and Learning Under Duress." *Composition Studies*, vol. 49, no. 3, 2021, pp. 13–30.

Hunt, Maurice. "Preventing Burn-Out in Teaching Assistants." *Freshman English News*, vol. 15, no. 1, 1986, pp. 12–15.

Knoblauch, A. Abby. "Bodies of Knowledge: Definitions, Delineations, and Implications of Embodied Writing in the Academy." *Composition Studies*, vol. 40, no. 2, 2012, pp. 50–65.

Lunsford, Andrea A. "Those Freshman English Blues." *Freshman English News*, vol. 5, no. 1, 1976, pp. 16–17.

Murray, Donald M. "The Politics of Respect." *Freshman English News*, vol. 9, no. 3, 1981, pp. 1–3.

O'Grady, Kerry L. "How to Manage Through Emotional Exhaustion." *The Chronicle of Higher Education*, 22 Feb. 2021, https://www.chronicle.com/article/how-to-manage-through-emotional-exhaustion.

Pettit, Emma. "Faculty Members Are Suffering Burnout. These Strategies Could Help." *The Chronicle of Higher Education*, 25 Feb. 2021, https://www.chronicle.com/article/faculty-members-are-suffering-burnout-so-some-colleges-have-used-these-strategies-to-help.

Richmond, Kia Jane. "Repositioning Emotions in Composition Studies." *Composition Studies*, vol. 30, no. 1, Spring 2002, pp. 67–82.

Savage, Mary C. "Ground of Hope: The Freshman English Class." *Freshman English News*, vol. 14, no. 3, 1986, pp. 24–27.

Sheppard, Jennifer. "Pandemic Pedagogy: What We Learned from the Sudden Transition to Online Teaching and How It Can Help Us Prepare to Teach Writing in an Uncertain Future." *Composition Studies*, vol. 49, no. 1, 2021, pp. 60–83

Thompson, Merle. "Let's Be Human About Behavior." *Freshman English News*, vol. 1, no. 2, 1972, pp. 11.

Williams, Amy. "'I Can't Do Cartwheels, So I Write': Students' Writing Affect." *Composition Studies*, vol. 47, no. 2, 2019, pp. 68–87.

Embodying Mentorship and Friendship: A Love Letter to Villanueva's "Tradition and Change"

Alexandra Hidalgo

Some people who change your life are consistently by your side, holding your hand as you stumble through your story's most gnarled passages. Some, like spectral mentors in fairy tales, appear only when you need them most. Your time together is brief but suffused by a mythical air that causes the encounter to reverberate for years. Victor Villanueva is the latter kind of mentor to me, and in this essay, I describe three pivotal interactions we shared, connecting them to ideas he proposes in his 2021 "Tradition and Change" *Composition Studies* piece. From one Latinx memoirist to another, I aim to show he not only espouses his scholarly ideas, but also enacts them through interactions with others. If this special issue is as much a looking forward as it is a looking back, my hope is that in the next 50 years we follow Victor's example of living like the teachers, researchers, and leaders we conceptualize in our scholarship.

The Laughing Apparition

I attended my first Conference on College Composition and Communication (CCCC) in 2009, during the first year of my PhD. Like countless graduate students before me, I shared a diminutive room blocks away from the conference hotel with three of my Purdue classmates. I flexed my body in a corner during my daily yoga practice while they tried not to trip over me, performing their own morning rituals of ironing dresses and poring over the conference program.

On the conference's opening day, I left the last panel feeling like the kid who moves to a new school halfway through the year. I called my husband and cried into the phone in some semi-secluded hallway. My sleeping quarters were too crowded, but I preferred them to the conference experience, which was teeming with people conversing animatedly and walking with purpose. Where were they going with such certainty? How come everyone knew each other? And what was this thing called the Latino Caucus? Being Venezuelan, it seemed like a place for me to investigate.

I showed up to the Caucus meeting early and, wanting to curtail my isolation, sat next to one of the few people already there. He acknowledged me with a smile, and I did a double take. He looked like the author of *Bootstraps: From an American Academic of Color*, the book I'd signed up to present about in my Minority Rhetorics class. The room filled quickly, and those coming to pay their respects confirmed I was, indeed, sitting next to Victor Villanueva. He knew everyone's names and the projects they were working on. He asked about their recent predicaments and triumphs. He found a way to laugh—honestly and with gusto—with everyone.

As the meeting ended, I steeled myself and mentioned my impending presentation and how I'd love to ask him a few questions about *Bootstraps*. I wanted to tell him his book had made me feel like I could find my path in rhetoric and composition, in spite of being a filmmaker and fiction writer who cried in hotel hallways. Yet others were waiting for their moment with him. He glanced at the gathering crowd and said if I emailed him, he'd answer any questions I had. I did, and he did. On my presentation day, I beamed as I shared my PowerPoint filled with Victor's reflections on having written one of the most impactful books in our field.

Our student bodies have become more diverse since Victor published *Bootstraps* in 1993. In "Tradition and Change," he writes, "Over the most recent decade or two, I have met more students like I was: of color, first generation, from poverty, new to the culture of the university" (156). His observation is palpably true at meetings of what—honoring developments in gender—we now call the Latinx Caucus. While in 2009 we gathered in an intimate circle of chairs, we now fill copious tables at hotel ballrooms. As Victor points out, universities have tried to adapt to these changes. From "students' right to their own rhetorics" to "translingualism [and] counterstory" (156), administrative and pedagogical policies aim to accommodate the diversification of student bodies. As he adds, however, "despite a rising consciousness about diversity among students and professionals, the deficit presumption far too often remains in assessing students" (156). As academia attempts to make room for these new voices and perspectives, it has a tendency to treat them as being unprepared and in need of help. That perspective can blind us to how these students and the experiences they bring into the Ivory Tower can help transform academia into a place that reflects the needs and demographics of today's society.

As Victor reminds us, seeing diverse students as deficient springs from long and entrenched educational traditions. Still, he argues, there are faculty who "try to look at traditions differently, and in so doing, change the traditions, perhaps" (156). For me, he is saying that even if some aspects of the educational system are intrinsically flawed, those of us with some level of power inside it—particularly tenured faculty—can work individually to support diverse students. That work involves revising admissions criteria, curricula, and by-laws, but it also unfolds in less quantifiable ways. Keeping track of a graduate student's dissertation progress even though they study at a university across the country, helping a faculty member you only see at conferences articulate the value of their community engagement work for tenure. And yes, taking time from your unspeakably busy schedule to deliver insightful answers to questions from a first-time CCCC attendee—even if those answers will never be published anywhere, just shared with a few students you've never met. Making room for diversity in higher education requires a blend of the administrative and the personal, the tangible and the ephemeral. Victor has done both during his career, inspiring countless others to follow suit.

The Gracious Host

After graduating from Purdue in 2013, I became an assistant professor at Michigan State University. I completed *Vanishing Borders*, my first feature documentary, a year later. Like he does with so many of us, Victor followed my career. In 2015 he invited me and author and scholar (and dear friend) Cecilia Rodríguez Milanés to come to Washington State University. I screened my film, Ceci read her work, and we met with students and faculty. It was the first time anyone took my work seriously enough to bring me to campus. Not only did Victor take a chance on me, he didn't flinch when I said I'd need to bring my youngest son, Santiago, who was still breastfeeding. Victor arranged for a hotel room that was sizable and equipped with a kitchen. He found (and covered the cost of) a student to babysit Santiago while Ceci and I were presenting. During every other moment we spent together, he also seemed genuinely pleased by the presence of my dark-eyed baby with the mischievous smile.

He gave Ceci and me tours of campus and the town and shared scrumptious meals with us, asking questions, telling stories, laughing as we sipped red wine. I felt like my work and the person who made that work mattered to him, and by extension to others in the field. By bringing me to Washington State, he was sanctioning my documentary as valuable to rhetoric and composition, even though it isn't a theoretical piece. It tells the story of four immigrant women living in New York City, whose professional accomplishments and personal interactions leave a positive mark on the city. When Victor invited me, I was theorizing the process of making the film into what would become my 2017 video book, *Cámara Retórica: A Feminist Filmmaking Methodology for Rhetoric and Composition*. The conversations I had with Ceci and him allowed me to deepen my ideas about what the filmmaking process could offer our field.

Victor argues that "it is important to know something of one's philosophical framework in order to act—in scholarship, research, teaching, in all one does—within the consistence of a conceptual framework" (159). He invites us to identify and weave together the intellectual, ethical, and affective threads that make up our backbone as human beings. Once we identify those threads, we can return to them over and over as we decide how to act and what we want to say through our intellectual, pedagogical, and creative work. I couldn't have articulated it back in 2015, but I now know that my framework involves fostering and nurturing relationships in my personal and professional lives. Through the exchange of ideas, feedback, and affection with those I collaborate with in work and in life, I produce artistic and scholarly pieces centered around storytelling and intersectional feminism. The making of *Vanishing Borders* and the film itself abide by that framework, as does *Cámara Retórica*. Victor's invitation to find our guiding framework allows us to explore a variety of intellectual and creative outlets while maintaining a cohesive thematic trajectory in our professional and personal experiences. Of course, that doesn't mean our framework can't evolve. Mine certainly has, and it will continue to be revamped by projects and collaborators. However, articulating that framework allows us to create a larger narrative around our work and our lives, synthesizing what they accomplish for others and ourselves.

Victor warns that while developing our framework, we should avoid getting lost in the mounds of scholarship that surround us. He explains that as a student, "I went out of my way to review the lit for whatever I was writing. I was thorough, every source till the sources started looping back" (157). Mentioning that he sees a similar approach from early-career scholars, he warns that "thoroughness in and of itself can be a problem. It can lead to contradictory sources" (157). It can also make us reticent. We wonder what we can add to existing conversations by others who seem more erudite and eloquent than we are. Yet at some point we must take the plunge and trust we have something significant to say. Having metaphorical stamps of approval from mentors like Victor—ranging from words of encouragement to campus visits—can give us confidence to develop our own framework and explain how it fits with what came before us and with the intellectual future we want to inhabit.

The Breakfast Companion

Until the pandemic shut everything down, I would email Victor before each CCCC and ask if he had time to get together. He always made room for a meal, usually before the Thursday morning Opening General Session. We'd become friends and now told each other stories about navigating parenthood and romantic relationships, about our parents and the knotty richness of being Latinx in the US. I looked forward to this deep personal connection during a conference that was now crowded with professional interactions. For years now, I've been one of those attendees who seems to know everyone and who is always rushing from panel to meeting to interview to lunch. Having a moment to be a full-fledged human (not simply an academic) friend to someone I care for and admire was one of the conference's joys for me.

As he wrestles with the fact that his intellectual fascination with Marxists like Gramsci and Freire makes others assume he has no room for spirituality in his framework, Victor writes, "I cannot accept materialism to the exclusion of the spiritual. No spiritual equals no faith (even faith in humanity is spiritual). At bottom, I'm a teacher. A teacher has to have faith, faith in the possibility of something better" (158). Victor's expansive brilliance comes through in everything I've ever read by him, but what I miss in his writing is his delicious wit and his ability to navigate personal, theoretical, and societal conundrums through humor. His laughter comes from a deep-seated faith that no matter what calamities we're slapped with, our work as scholars, teachers, and friends can make our tiny fraction of the world a little better. He certainly did that for me and for many who have the fortune to count him as a mentor. As we embark on the next fifty years of this journal and of the scholarship and pedagogies it documents and theorizes, I hope we can do so through our own version of Victor's geniality, generosity, and hope for a better future. He embodies the approach to composition I hope to share with others, whether we spend years or a few formative hours together.

Works Cited

Hidalgo, Alexandra. *Cámara Retórica: A Feminist Filmmaking Methodology for Rhetoric and Composition*. Computers and Composition Digital P/Utah State UP, 2017.

Vanishing Borders. Directed by Alexandra Hidalgo, featuring Teboho Moja, Melainie Rogers, Daphnie Sicre, and Yatna Vakharia, Sabana Grande Productions, 2014.

Villanueva, Victor. "Tradition and Change." *Composition Studies*, vol. 49, no. 1, 2021, pp. 156-159.

Critical Distance in *Composition Studies*

Rebecca Lorimer Leonard

I have had criticality on the mind of late. My recent teaching in a community-engaged writing project follows Tania Mitchell's tradition of critical service learning, so my students and I have spent much time staring at the word critical on the board, asking each other, what do we mean by critical? What does it look like when we do it? We have especially wondered how criticality happens in terms of writing. In this short essay, I use the notion of critical distance as one lens to explore how criticality has been taken up in fifty years of *Composition Studies*. I review authors' use of "critical awareness" as related to "critical distance," consider what notions of "distance" have to do with writing, and speculate about how certain spaces allow writers to create and traverse critical distance, together.

In *Composition Studies* in the last fifty years, "critical" has meant everything from important to analytic to liberatory—and this range has stayed consistent, with a few shifts. In the eighties, there was increasing use of critical in terms of references to "critical theory"; the period after *Freshman English News* saw an increase of engagement with critical pedagogy. Articles from the last ten years show more explicit attention to power relations and use of theoretical frames that explicitly include "critical," as in Aja Martinez' enactment of critical race theory through counterstory and Alex Hanson's application of Gesa Kirsch and Jacqueline Jones Royster's critical imagination. Martinez and Hanson's specificity of criticality—in which stock stories of racial and gendered privilege are carefully and methodically de-naturalized (Hanson 37; Martinez 51)—supplies authors and readers a much-needed "mechanism for seeing the noticed and the unnoticed, rethinking what is there and not there, and speculating what could be there instead" (Kirsch and Royster 20). Thus, "critical" can signal writing approaches that seek to go "beyond cognitive awareness and move toward social and political consciousness-raising and action" (Alim 215).

In *Composition Studies*, the phrase "critical awareness" has been used primarily to indicate a potential student (e.g., Comer; Lockett and RudeWalker; McCarty) or teacher (e.g., Alexander; Shamoon and Schwegler) learning outcome. For example, in 1986, Mary Savage presents critical awareness as a feature of a "Freshman English" course grounded in a "realistic hope based on the fundamental character of the Freshman English enterprise itself," which Savage describes as "the moment" when "students can come to consciousness about the power—as well as the problematic—of language in and through which they live" (24). Her essay illustrates why critical awareness needs the space of writing to manifest. She says,

> Writing, just because it can go beyond the immediate present, is a powerful capacity. Writing can separate me from my experience to allow me to objectify it so I can analyze it and explain it to someone else who wasn't even there when I had the experience in the first place. Writing decontextualizes experience and re-contextualizes it again as writing. (26-27)

Savage suggests that it is critical distance—separation from experience—that makes room for critical awareness to be realized. To return, then, to the question above—How does writing mediate awareness and what happens along the way?—it seems that awareness needs some kind of discursive space to occur.

Critical Awareness Needs Distance?

In keyword searches, critical distance often appears in the company of critical awareness. The phrase appears in one article in *Freshman English News* from 1972-1991 and in six articles from 1992-2017. In the last five years "distance" shows up but not described as "critical." I briefly consider that fact in the conclusion below.

In the nineties, the addition of "distance" to critical seems related to authors' uptake of dialogic and dialectic pedagogy. For example, in a 1990 article on the dialogic classroom, Frank Farmer evokes what he says is Paulo Freire's belief that "critical distance [is] necessary for authentic literacy" (21). Farmer describes dialogic pedagogy as driven by students' own text selections and text-based questions, explicitly leading students and teacher together toward understanding not just what to ask but "why particular questions are asked" (21). This pedagogical "social dialogue" is meant to raise students' awareness of the rhetorical effect of style. Following Richard Lanham, though, Farmer also claims that such dialogic pedagogy "makes possible dialogue with ourselves, and thereby enables us to foster a keen self-consciousness about human perception and knowledge" (Lanham qtd. in Farmer 22). Farmer forwards a pedagogy that creates the distance-making conditions for "such encounters"—with others, with the self—in order to "help our students develop an awareness of how the plurality of language communities betokens a multiplicity of approaches to knowledge" (17).

Like Farmer, Dale Jacobs' "re-vision" of critical pedagogy says it is "through such dialogue" that "students and teachers can attempt to gain a critical distance from their own circumstances so that they can locate themselves . . . and engage with other possible identities or roles" (43). He hopes for his students "to think about their locations in cultures and discourses in which they reside" and be thus "better able to recognize and negotiate their own uses of language and the uses of language around them within specific contexts" (43). This recognition-for-negotiation found in both Farmer and Jacobs resonates with other understandings of criticality in terms of dialectic as well. For example, in his examination of the "critical" in critical language awareness (CLA), Terry Males argues that when an individual encounters a new discursive subject they experience a distance between their current and former self that allows criticality to "dialectically unfold" (159). For Males, the "critical instance" resides in the dialectic space of an individual reasoning through their experiences, a space in which "new understanding dialectically unfolds" and "new discourse practices can arise" (159).

In *Composition Studies* articles from 2005-2015, "critical distance" is more specific: something student writers "gained" through a pedagogy (Goggin and Waggoner), a "position" they could assume to carry out critical analysis (Jackson 21), a "tool" to use to "see how they are products of culture" (Rohan 62), or an outcome generated by the multimodality of certain genres like comics (Sealey-Morris), many of which are described as a process of making the familiar strange. For example, in Peter Goggin and Zach Waggoner's course description of a sustainability-focused writing course, students "defamiliarize the familiar as a means of gaining critical distance from the reading and writing activities they are engaged in as well as the social and cultural contexts in which their meaning making occurs" (55). In Gabriel Sealey-Morris' article on comics, defamiliarization takes on a specific form in that visuals in comics contain a "visual distortion of reality," a "collision of words and images," and a "static rendering of temporal experience" that helps "dictate a critical distance" in their multimodality (38). Following Hatfield, Sealey-Morris explains that because authors portray themselves through caricature, they can "recognize and externalize" their subjectivity at a remove that makes critical distance possible (Hatfield qtd. in Sealey-Morris 36).

Writing at a Distance

In terms of what distance does for critical awareness, then, *Composition Studies* authors suggest that distance makes space for criticality to develop. The role of writing in that process seems to be what is well-established in writing studies: writing can slow down meaning-making, leave a record to be reviewed later by the writer, and create visual representations to be reviewed by a reader at remove. Writing provides an occasion for dialogue, whether during invention or revision, among writers, or with oneself. In other words, if criticality is initiated in the distance between former and new understandings, as Males suggests, then writing leads people to traverse that space.

I'll demonstrate what I mean briefly. In the beginning of his ethnography *Illegal Alphabets and Adult Biliteracy: Latino Migrants Crossing the Linguistic*

Border, Tomás Mario Kalmar describes a scene in a grocery store basement, where a small group of migrant fieldworkers gathered to strategize how to protect themselves with language. The meeting was motivated by the likely murder of a fellow migrant and the mutual agreement that the law, in rural Illinois where they worked, did not protect them. Using an easel to record their written deliberations, they reasoned through phonetic approaches to language learning, eventually agreeing to write "doló dasn't protect as" (the law doesn't protect us) (Kalmar 23). The group gave and took suggestions, collaboratively "fudged" the rules of English-language literacy, and voted on written versions of the phrase until they were satisfied with this first entry of several Spanish/English *diccionarios* they eventually composed (88).

Kalmar emphasizes that the scene was extracurricular: there was no teacher, no students, no funding, no tests, no start or end time. It was not a class; it was a community gathering built out of communicative necessity. He points out the migrants' collaborative impulse, their tendency to play with rules, their scholarly approach to language. But a few additional elements from the basement scene have long stayed with me. When I think of this literacy event, I see people sitting and standing around, looking together toward the easel. They deliberate what is written there, from a distance. What I remember is that they stop and look at the text, with the steady determination that what they wrote down would help them *dominar* the language.

Returning to the classroom image I began with, my students and I, too, position ourselves back from the board, sitting or standing together as we regard the writing over there, nodding at our perplexities. But the small difference in the way "critical distance" is used in the articles reviewed above and evoked in these two images of learning is the presence of many people. That is, while writing studies has tended to frame distance within a student and teacher's dialogue or between a writer's former and present understandings, my and Kalmar's scenes show multiple people creating distance together. Can we locate criticality in distance—stepping back and seeing an idea anew—as a dialectic not within the self, but among the self and others? Early on, Norman Fairclough grounded the criticality of CLA in a social science orientation that explains structural relations in terms of social practices, which include "material activities, institutional rituals, social relations, beliefs and values" articulated together with "the dialectical tension between structure and event" (79). Such a dialectic treats criticality as forged in long cultural histories and experiences beyond the self. In other words, criticality here comes from the distance of experience—re-imagining writing from a new vantage—but specifically in the dialectic tension between the social structures and events that shape collective literacies.

Therefore, to move beyond critical distance as individually gained awareness, we need to understand critical distance, and thus awareness, as formed among others, in community. This enactment of distance lets writers attend to inward-facing awareness, of their sense of self, family or community writing practices, as well as to outward-facing awareness of the sociocultural components and effects of writing in the world around them. This approach might purposefully shift which writing questions or problems matter and are accounted for, to individual writers, to classrooms, and to communities.

In one last speculative turn, I'd like to return to *Composition Studies* authors' most recent uses of "distance," which I noted early on in this piece are not described as "critical." There are only two uses of "distance" in the last five years. The first, published in 2020, is Pennie Gray's use of linguistic politeness theory to understand how writers enact "social distance" during peer review. The second, published in 2021, is Zhaozhe Wang's first-line evocation of pandemic "division, disconnection, and distance" that sets the stage for his exploration of professionalization in the field. Neither use of distance is described as "critical," but as a pair, the articulations of distance call for attention. Given the pandemic's discursive saturation of the term social distancing, our notions of distance have drastically changed. Certainly, the last three years of journal publishing (and maybe our minds?) simply have not had a chance to consider the nature or consequence of newer concepts of distance. How does distance happen now, in writing or otherwise? What does it mean now for writers to be more critically distant, from each other and from themselves?

Works Cited

Alexander, Kara Poe. "From Story to Analysis: Reflection and Uptake in the Literacy Narrative Assignment." *Composition Studies*, vol. 43, no. 2, 2015, pp. 43–71.

Alim, H. Samy. "Critical Language Awareness." *Sociolinguistics and Language Education*, edited by N. H. Hornberger and S. L. McKay. Multilingual Matters, 2010, pp. 205–31.

Comer, Kathryn. "Illustrating Praxis: Comic Composition, Narrative Rhetoric, and Critical Multiliteracies." *Composition Studies*, vol. 43, no. 1, 2015, pp. 75–104.

Fairclough, Norman. "Global Capitalism and Critical Awareness of Language" *Language Awareness*, vol. 8, no. 2, 1999, pp. 71–83.

Farmer, Frank. "A Language of One's Own: A Stylistic Pedagogy for the Dialogic Classroom." *Freshman English News*, vol. 19, no. 1, 1990, pp. 16–17, 20–22.

Goggin, Peter, and Zach Waggoner. "Sustainable Development: Thinking Globally and Acting Locally in the Writing Classroom." *Composition Studies*, vol. 33, no. 2, 2005, pp. 45–67.

Gray, Pennie L. "Politeness Profiles in the First-Year Composition Classroom." *Composition Studies,* vol. 48, no. 1, 2020, pp. 71–87.

Hanson, Alex. "Career Killer Survival Kit: Centering Single Mom Perspectives in Composition and Rhetoric." *Composition Studies,* vol. 48, no. 1, 2020, pp. 34–52.

Jackson, Brian. "Teaching the Analytical Life." *Composition Studies*, vol. 38, no. 2, 2010, pp. 9–27.

Jacobs, Dale. "Beginning Where They Are: A Re-vision of Critical Pedagogy." *Composition Studies*, vol. 25, no. 2, 1997, pp. 39–62.

Kalmar, Tomás Mario. *Illegal Alphabets and Adult Biliteracy: Latino Migrants Crossing the Linguistic Border.* 2nd ed. Routledge, 2015.

Kirsch, Gesa E., and Jacqueline Jones Royster. *Feminist Rhetorical Practices: New Horizons for Rhetoric, Composition, and Literacy Studies.* Southern Illinois UP, 2012.

Lockett, Alexandria, and Sarah RudeWalker. "Creative Disruption and the Potential of Writing at HBCUs." *Composition Studies*, vol. 44, no. 2, 2016, pp. 172–178.

Males, Terry. "What Is Critical in Critical Language Awareness?" *Language Awareness*, vol. 9, no. 3, 2000, pp. 147–59.

Martinez, Aja Y. "A Plea for Critical Race Theory Counterstory: Stock Story versus Counterstory Dialogues Concerning Alejandra's 'Fit' in the Academy." *Composition Studies*, vol. 42, no. 2, 2014, pp. 33–55.

McCarty, Ryan. "Translational Learning: Surfacing Multilingual Repertoires." *Composition Studie*s, vol. 46, no. 2, 2018, pp. 52–78.

Mitchell, Tania D. "Traditional vs. Critical Service-Learning: Engaging the Literature to Differentiate Two Models." *Journal of Community Service Learning*, vol. 14, 2008, pp. 50–65.

Rohan, Liz. "Everyday Curators: Collecting as Literate Activity." *Composition Studies,* vol. 38, no. 1, 2010, pp. 53–68.

Savage, Mary. "Ground of Hope: The Freshman English Class." *Freshman English News*, vol. 14, no. 3, 1986, pp. 24–27.

Sealey-Morris, Gabriel. "The Rhetoric of the Paneled Page: Comics and Composition Pedagogy." *Composition Studies*, vol. 43, no. 1, 2015, pp. 31–50.

Shamoon, Linda, and Robert A. Schwegler. "Teaching the Research Paper: A New Approach to an Old Problem." *Freshman English News*, vol. 11, no. 1, 1982, pp. 14–17.

Wang, Zhaozhe. "Too Green to Talk Disciplinarity." *Composition Studies*, vol. 49, no. 1, 2021, pp. 160–163.

The Catharsis for Poison: A Counterstory Retrospective on *Composition Studies'* 50th Anniversary

Aja Y. Martinez

It was Memorial Day weekend 2010 in Central Texas. Temperature highs hovered around 95°F, which shouldn't be a big deal for a girl from southern Arizona where summer temperatures soar easily into the 100s. However, in southern Arizona it's "a dry heat" and in the hill country of central Texas—well, there's visible water, palpable humidity. In both locales, central air is a necessity. My daughter Olivia (eight years old at the time) and I had just arrived in Kyle, Texas, to stay in the home of my hosts/mentors, Drs. Octavio and Charise Pimentel. I had secured a summer pre-doctoral fellowship through Octavio and Charise's institution, Texas State University, and I was looking forward to making good headway that summer on my dissertation. However, during the first weekend in Texas, the air conditioning in the Pimentel home stopped working, and the sweltering humidity and heat quickly overwhelmed the entire house. Because it was a holiday weekend, our prospects of getting the air conditioning repaired were slim to none, and we were informed that the soonest an HVAC technician could come out to repair the unit was the Tuesday following the holiday. Ugh. So there we were, facing three whole sleepless sweaty nights, tossing and turning, unable to comfortably drift off to sleep, and it was within this extreme discomfort that my first counterstory was birthed.

3AM. Two nights into this heat filled misery, I gave up on the hope of any sort of restful slumber and decided to instead do what I was in fact there in Texas to do: write. By this point in my career as a graduate student at University of Arizona's Rhetoric, Composition, and the Teaching of English (RCTE) program, I had experienced the insult of being evaluated in my first year of study and being asked to "take the masters and go" (Martinez "A Plea" 43). By this point, I had experienced the various erasures and assaults on my humanity that people of color endure in predominantly and historically white graduate programs. But I had also experienced the hope and joy of witnessing the hiring processes that brought in the first faculty of color in the program's history. By this point I was being mentored by Adela C. Licona, who introduced me to the race critical work of a variety of scholars including critical race theorists like Derrick Bell, Richard Delgado, and Patricia Williams (Martinez *Counterstory* xvi). By this point I had declared my intent to pursue a dissertation project that centralized the framework of Critical Race Theory (CRT) and zeroed in on its espoused methodology: counterstory. However, by this point I had only studied the counterstories of others; I had yet to compose my own.

So, there I was, at 3AM in humid and hot central Texas, unable to sleep, but perfectly able to think and think and think about my looming doctoral project. And within this thought cycling (undoubtedly informed by my context-specific physical miseries) all the various indignities I had endured within my graduate program experience wove and swirled through my mind and body, feeling evermore like poison that required an immediate outlet. Thus, the only seemingly available catharsis in that moment was to compose, and the outburst of counterstory that poured from my discontented carcass onto the cued-up MS Word document was the first draft, the verifiable word vomit version, of what would eventually be honed and shaped into: "A Plea for Critical Race Theory Counterstory: Dialogues Concerning Alejandra's 'Fit' in the Academy."

Looking back, twelve years beyond this initial attempt at a counterstory of my own composition, but also ten years beyond its defense as part of my dissertation, and eight years beyond its eventual publication in a field-specific academic journal, I find myself nostalgically reflective (even a bit misty-eyed) on my counterstory journey. When presently asked by audiences to comment on my decision to go the counterstory route, I am adamant in my assertion that for much of my career as a CRT scholar and counterstoryteller, I have mostly dwelled within the identity category of counterstory "student." The first counterstories I told as part of my dissertation, inclusive of "A Plea for Critical Race Theory Counterstory," were hunches I was pursuing in a greater quest to fully investigate and understand why the counterstories of exemplars such as Bell, Delgado, and Williams are rhetorically effective as a race critical methodology. However, another line of inquiry I was also pursuing was an interrogation of how this methodology could serve as a contribution to the field of rhetoric and writing studies in a quest to deal as productively as they can with race and racism (Gilyard qtd. on *Counterstory* back cover). I was attempting a contribution. But I knew in those initial years of honing my craft as a counterstoryteller that the only way I could fully wrap my mind around the effectiveness and potential contribution of counterstory as methodology would require I compose counterstories of my own.

As I embarked on this composing process and inquiry, I was met with critique and stubborn resistance (Martinez *Counterstory* 20-21). While dissertating, I experienced nothing short of dismissal of my counterstory project. While engaged in discussion with a professor of Education, they were quick to inform me "the field of Education has moved beyond counterstory."

"Counterstory," they declared, "was just formless ranting by disgruntled people of color."

"Counterstory," they concluded, "was over."

The encounter described above was only one among many instances in which my work was met with skepticism, opposition, and in some cases outright disdain. However, this particular encounter was a turning point for me and my project. I knew this Education scholar was wrong, but in the moment, I hadn't developed the vocabulary or knowledgebase in CRT to refute their claims. I had to do more research, I had to stay the path as a student of CRT and counterstory. And as my project took shape through the process of my dissertation, I began to realize that what was missing from the interdisciplinary CRT discussion concerning the methodology of counterstory was a direct and targeted intervention from the humanities, particularly from scholars who are experts in rhetoric and writing studies. What counterstory needed was for the field of rhetoric and writing studies to make a case for counterstory in ways we can uniquely accomplish, due to our field-specific focus on rhetorical effectiveness, pedagogical viability, and writing genre as method. And while field and field-adjacent scholars before me (e.g. Banks; Gutiérrez-Jones; Kynard; Prendergast) have engaged an analysis of and in some cases demonstration of counterstory, I eventually realized there was a gap to fill in terms of establishing counterstory as a research methodology and method through an examination of the counterstory work of CRT exemplars Bell, Delgado, and Williams. But how did I arrive at this conclusion? I wrote counterstories.

I continued to write and defend, write and publish, write and teach, write and share with my family and the public: counterstories. During my 2012 dissertation defense at the conclusion of my doctoral studies, a committee member proclaimed one of my Derrick Bell-esque counterstories read as bad fiction. I was subsequently awarded a doctorate for this project. I subsequently managed to land a tenure-track position at Binghamton University with this project. However, at that moment I was unsure about what was next for me and counterstory. Were the counterstories written for the dissertation viable for publication? Did I dare venture to send these counterstories to academic journals? Would I be taken seriously? I have Dr. Adam J. Banks and the inaugural Smitherman/Villanueva Writing Group to thank for the push to publish.

During summer 2013, Dr. Adam Banks organized a summer writing retreat in Lexington, KY, for early career scholars. Over the course of several days, I was in writerly community with Dr. Steven Alvarez, Dr. Tamika Carey, Dr. Rhea Lathan, Dr. Gabi Ríos, Dr. David Green, Dr. Nazera Wright, and Dr. Bill Endres. Most of us were only a year out of graduate school, working on prospective monographs and other publications, and it was to this group I posed the question of my project's viability beyond the dissertation. I tentatively shared the chapter I was most proud of, but not without reservation and doubt. This chapter engaged the Chicanx Educational Pipeline and offered a Delgado-esque counterstory in the form of "stock story vs. counterstory" (Martinez "A Plea"

34–39). The stock story involves a committee of white professors gathered to discuss a Chicana student, Alejandra Prieto, who they view as a failure in their graduate program. In this counterstory Alejandra is in conversation with her mother concerning her own experiences of racism and discrimination within the same graduate program. Originally composed during that sweltering air conditioning-less 2010 Memorial Weekend sleepless night, this counterstory was informed by my own personal experiences in the RCTE graduate program, and it represents the poison of that program that I poured out of my bodily lived experience and onto the page. This counterstory mattered to me, very much. And beyond the eyes of my four dissertation committee members, at least one of whom thought my project was "bad fiction," no other academics had yet read my counterstories—I hadn't yet worked up the nerve. So, I was beyond relieved when my cohort of fellow scholars responded positively and encouragingly to this great leap of vulnerability I felt I had taken.

Although my Smitherman/Villanueva cohorts heartily agreed my project in counterstory was viable beyond the dissertation and encouraged me to send a revised version to journals, the feedback I received from Dr. Gabriela Raquel Ríos proved vital. Dr. Ríos and I share a similar racial-ethnic background as indigenous Mexican Americans. Upon reading the counterstory involving Alejandra and her mother, Dr. Ríos pointed out that although the stock story amongst the white professors rang true in tone and voice, the voices of Alejandra and her mother rang false—too stifled, too academic, not authentic to Dr. Ríos' experience of the ways a Mexican American mother and daughter would engage. And Dr. Ríos was 100% correct. In my attempt to act and sound the part of a highly-educated scholar within my dissertation, I missed an element of what has become central to my own counterstory methodology: the tenet of accessibility (Martinez *Counterstory* 18). Where was the voice of these minoritized women, represented on their own terms, relating their own experiences? Dr. Ríos' astute critique prompted me to engage a writing and revising process that had not ever been taught or modeled for me during my formal education: to write with rather than for or over my community (Martinez *Counterstory* 18). As the acknowledgements of "A Plea" indicates (53), the voices of Mami and Alejandra involved a writing process that quite literally required I sit next to my mom on the living room couch and read through the counterstory dialogue with her, asking for her responses to Alejandra's prompts. As is also indicated in the acknowledgements of "A Plea," the voices of the mother-daughter exchange would not/could not be genuine without my mother's touch (53).

Now that the chapter had been revised into publishable form, there remained the question of where to send it. At CCCC 2013, I attended a panel on publishing and was inspired to hear *Composition Studies*' then-editor Dr.

Laura Micciche declare her commitment to publishing diverse voices and perspectives. For me, nervous as I was about publishing this risky and deeply personal counterstory, I took Dr. Micciche's words at face value and only ever considered *Composition Studies* as a venue for my first attempt at publishing counterstory. True to her commitments, Dr. Micciche deserves credit for taking my work as a counterstoryteller seriously as she pulled out all the stops to publish "A Plea."

Looking back, eight years beyond the 2014 publication of "A Plea," I offer my sincere gratitude to *Composition Studies* as a platform that made space for the publication of my first counterstory. Had Dr. Micciche and *CS* not supported me at this crucial juncture of my career, I am not sure I would have continued to write and publish the body of work I have amassed ever since—a body of work that amounts to sixteen published counterstories as journal articles and edited collection chapters, and my 2020 book, *Counterstory: The Rhetoric and Writing of Critical Race Theory*. My heartfelt thanks to Kara and Matt for this opportunity to reflect on this journey and to give credit where credit is due to the people who have helped me along the way. Huge congratulations to *Composition Studies* on its 50th anniversary.

Works Cited

Banks, Adam J. *Race, Rhetoric, and Technology: Searching for Higher Ground*. Lawrence Erlbaum and NCTE, 2006.

Bell, Derrick. *And We Are Not Saved: The Elusive Quest for Racial Justice*. Basic Books, 1987.

—. *Faces at the Bottom of the Well: The Permanence of Racism*. Basic Books, 1992.

Delgado, Richard. *The Rodrigo Chronicles: Conversations about America and Race*. New York UP, 1995.

Gutiérrez-Jones, Carl. *Critical Race Narratives: A Study of Race, Rhetoric, and Injury*. New York UP, 2001.

Kynard, Carmen. "Teaching while Black: Witnessing and Countering Disciplinary Whiteness, Racial Violence, and University Race-Management." *Literacy in Composition Studies*, no. 3, vol. 1, 2015, pp. 1–20.

—. *Vernacular Insurrections: Race, Black Protest, and the New Century in Composition-Literacies Studies*. State U of New York P, 2013.

Martinez, Aja Y. *Counterstory: The Rhetoric and Writing of Critical Race Theory*. NCTE, 2020.

—. "A Plea for Critical Race Theory Counterstory: Stock Story versus Counterstory Dialogues concerning Alejandra's 'Fit' in the Academy." *Composition Studies*, vol. 42, no. 2, 2014, pp. 33–55.

Prendergast, Catherine. *Literacy and Racial Justice: The Politics of Learning after* Brown v. Board of Education. Southern Illinois UP, 2003.

Williams, Patricia J. *The Alchemy of Race and Rights: Diary of a Law Professor*. Harvard UP, 1991.

Composing in the Discomfort of Institutional Violence

Cruz Medina

It's been a dozen years since my first publication in *Composition Studies,* Volume 39, Number 2. I wrote a book review for an edited collection on writing program administration after a WPA course with Ed White. Future CCCC chair Asao Inoue was the book editor at the time, so thinking back on that experience has me feeling a bit like Forrest Gump in his montage with notable historical figures. The archive of the last 50 years suggests that the journal has followed, and in some cases led, in the shifts of the field; from early pedagogically-oriented writing to more postmodern theory taken from the influence of literature, the journal has focused on composition as a field and what concerns the field. I deeply appreciate the innovations in topics in *Composition Studies,* such as the special issue on comics (43.1) that I used for teaching; the course designs, such as "Decolonial Theory and Methodology" (46.1), that I have conversely used for research; and the articles that helped to push the field in directions that many researchers have wanted or never even knew to ask for. For this celebratory moment, I have chosen to discuss Aja Martinez's 2014 article, "A Plea for Critical Race Theory Counterstory: Stock Story versus Counterstory Dialogues Concerning Alejandra's 'Fit' in the Academy." This article might fall into the category of research, a kind research with which the field has had an uncomfortable relationship because it disrupts and complicates narratives of institutional white supremacy. In Martinez's article, she advocates for critical race theory (CRT) counterstory and shares the vulnerable experience of being a graduate student of color (with a research interest centered on race) in a graduate program that is in its resistance to this interest, emblematic of the field. But her research that would continue and become her 2020 book, *Counterstory: The Rhetoric and Writing of Critical Race Theory.* Martinez and I were in the same graduate program, so re-reading her article took me back to my own experiences, and I found myself needing to stop and take breaks. The counterstory dialogue triggered relatable feelings of uncertainty from graduate school, where the future seems to hinge on every CV line and networking opportunity. The uncertainty Martinez captures was, of course, exacerbated by cultural and ethnic differences with the composite characters of the professors in a program that identified itself as central to the field of rhetoric and composition. Martinez's definitions of "stock" and "majoritarian" stories help to explain how her narrative functions: "These [majoritarian] stories privilege whites, men, the middle and/or upper class, and heterosexuals by naming these social locations as natural or normative points of reference" (Martinez "A Plea" 51). As her stock story illustrates, these differences leave many graduate students of color feeling as though they fall short of their professors' ideal expectations by default. In Martinez's counterstory, the use of "fit"–a term that has since come under fire and is advised against using in job searches–represents the homogeneous replication of whiteness that Martinez points out (Flaherty).

Martinez's article contributes to the groundwork for what others and I have been able to do with critical race theory (CRT) and anti-racist scholarship. On a personal note, I also feel indebted to Aja Martinez for successfully negotiating what had been a predominantly white program, thereby making my own experience much less traumatic.[1] In "A Plea," one of Martinez's composite tenured professor characters, Tanner, grapples with how the race-conscious research of Alejandra (our protagonist) "fits" within the program. The sympathetic but untenured character, Hayden, helps to articulate: "I think her work is difficult for us to wrap our minds around because it's unconventional, probably by and large due to the fact that she approaches it from a perspective we're not trained in or accustomed to" (43). The untenured professor, Hayden, provides a perspective that presages the growing acceptance of anti-racism in the field (e.g. in special issues, like *Composition Studies* (49.2), in 2021, guest edited by Ersula Ore, Christina Cedillo, and Kim Wieser, where the theme and contributors push for a move beyond diversity to transformation for the purpose of justice). These conversations–in print and in dialogue–are strengthened, in part, by CRT scholarship that acknowledges the permanence of racism and values the experiential knowledge of Black, Inidgenous and people of color (BIPOC) and their scholarship.

Martinez's "Plea" also highlights the dedication of *Composition Studies* to continue the discussion of pedagogy and curricular content that began in the early stages of the journal, while also addressing what is not often taught. The unsympathetic tenured professor character, Tanner, tacitly acknowledges the topic of the hidden curriculum that many graduate students contend with: "Are you seriously suggesting we all, as faculty, shoulder the responsibility of teaching her how to be a student, a scholar, and a professional in our field?" (44). When Tanner questions whether faculty should teach graduate students to be scholars and professionals, I find myself wanting to ask the composite character: If we are not teaching the next generation of graduate students to be students and professionals, then what are we doing?

The resistance that Tanner embodies is institutional, though it is not the objective logic that it purports to be. A defensive logic of white supremacy is communicated by the tenured professor who says: "Alejandra is just not a good fit for this program ... her comments always drew the material back to her comfort zone of social oppression, particular to race....there's no focus and no connection or contribution to the field" (42). The student's research and, by default, the student are "not a good fit," so much so that Tanner, tenured, threatens the untenured Hayden: "You, Hayden, of all people should be wary of this situation, what with your teaching load and the fact you still have quite a publishing quota to meet before you go up for tenure in a couple years" (44). These serve as not-so-subtle reminders: this tenured colleague will no doubt serve on a departmental personnel or promotion committee that will evaluate the untenured faculty member's case for promotion. In the scenes that Martinez constructs, the reader can see the emotional violence and career-altering consequences that racism inflicts on the graduate student. Similarly, the reader can see how those consequences play out against allies who might challenge the status quo.

Although Martinez's article on counterstory appeared in 2014, the article raised issues that she further builds upon in her book, *Counterstory: The Rhetoric and Writing of Critical Race Theory* (2020). In Louis M. Maraj's review of *Counterstory* in *Composition Studies* (49.1), Maraj attests to how the book resonated for him in the summer of 2020. In expressing how much the field still needs scholarship like Martinez's, Maraj explains that:

> [T]he first of eight, then nine, core tenets of critical race theory (CRT) highlighted in *Counterstory*'s introduction—still needs reiterating in the fields of rhetoric and writing studies. One might think that by 2021 these disciplines might have gotten it together well enough that our scholars, teachers, and students would not need a monograph like Martinez's. But here we are. And, yet again, a woman of color is doing the work. (196)

In thinking about the last 50 years of *Composition Studies* the journal, we can see how much the field has changed…and not changed as much as we might have hoped. Maraj captures this sentiment in describing the epigraphs in Martinez's book: scholarship like this still fights the "widespread ignorance of scholars in our field who ask for justification for CRT methods that have been around for decades" (197). (To further support Maraj's point, I would add that the Gary Olson chapter about critical race and teaching composition that Martinez mentions in her 2014 article was published in 2003, nearly two decades prior to Maraj's review.)

As someone who has contributed to *Composition Studies* over the last dozen years, I am appreciative of the kinds of editorial practices that have created space for work like Martinez's article and the experiential knowledge of BIPOC. Martinez's "A Plea" helps communicate the important message about trusting voices of color and building knowledge from those experiences. Referencing

CRT's emphasis on experiential knowledge, Martinez explains that "voices from the margins become the voices of authority in the researching and relating of our own experiences" (33). When I submitted the manuscript for what would become my 2019 *Composition Studies* article "Decolonial Potential in a Multilingual FYC" (47.1), then-editor Laura Micciche and former editor Bob Mayberry reminded me of my focus: the students' words and experiences. They helped me to re-see how my predominantly Latinx students had motivated me to write. They facilitated my revisions so that the multilingual students' writing came much earlier, instead of their experiences simply being relegated to the data section. I also felt empowered to voice my own experience in my course design (49.2), where I described teaching a diverse curriculum as professor of color at a predominantly white institution.

Recently, CRT became the rhetorical strawman for then-President Donald Trump to attack: first by misrepresenting CRT in order to stoke his ideological base; then as scapegoat for an executive order banning federal funding from agencies teaching CRT (Samuels). Martinez's description of "stock stories" reveals how power circulates through the repeated lies of white supremacist narratives until they are normalized:

> Stock stories feign neutrality and at all costs avoid any blame or responsibility for societal inequality. Powerful because they are often repeated until canonized or normalized, those who tell stock stories insist that their version of events is indeed reality, and any stories that counter these standardized tellings are deemed biased, self-interested, and ultimately not credible. (38)

According to the *Washington Post*, Trump's lies (normalized as "false or misleading claims") totaled 30,573 during his four years in the White House (Kessler, Rizzo, and Kelly). Trump's executive order and lies about CRT point the finger at scholarship that makes racial dynamics clear. One common response–to dismiss Trump's thirty thousand lies by saying that all politicians lie–ignores his appeals to a white nationalist ideology and how his stock stories about the "good people on both sides" contributes to the normalization of racism in courts, schools, and police interactions.

It's important that scholars in rhetoric and composition sit in the discomfort of the violence of institutional white supremacy. Martinez's counterstory about Alejandra reminds us of the material consequences for many in the field who also did not "fit." I am thankful for the many in our field who resemble the composite character Hayden: more prepared to come to terms with how racism operates on all levels of teaching, assessment, and administration. I appreciate this reflective moment to be reflexive about where we still have potential for growth. Without Martinez's article and the vision of the *Composition Studies* editors, my own scholarship and the scholarship of many whom I respect and cite might not be published, much less considered a part of our field. And this is no small feat. The editors of *Composition Studies* have done this work while maintaining a focus on student writing, pedagogy, and theories that provoke us to rethink how composing and the teaching of writing respond to and influence the world around us.

Notes:

1. It should also be noted that the department's hiring of Adela Licona and Damián Baca (before I started) helped with the cultural shift within the program that I greatly benefited from.

Works Cited

Composition Studies (Special Issue: Comics, Multimodality, and Composition), vol. 43, no. 1, Spring 2015.

Flaherty, Colleen. "A Bad Fit? Study finds the Concept of Faculty fit in Hiring is Vague and Potentially Detrimental to Diversity Efforts." *Inside Higher Ed*. 14 Jul 2020. Accessed 8 Feb 2022. https://www.insidehighered.com/news/2020/07/14/study-concept-faculty-fit-hiring-vague-and-potentially-detrimental-diversity-efforts

Kessler, Glenn, Salvador Rizzo and Meg Kelly. "Trump's False or Misleading Claims Total 30,573 Over 4 Years." *Washington Post*. 24 Jan 2021. washingtonpost.com/politics/2021/01/24/trumps-false-or-misleading-claims-total-30573-over-four-years/ Accessed 11 Feb. 2022.

Maraj, Louis M. "*Counterstory: The Rhetoric and Writing of Critical Race Theory* (review)." *Composition Studies*, vol. 49 no. 1, pp. 196-199.

Martinez, Aja Y. "A Plea for Critical Race Theory Counterstory: Stock Story versus Counterstory Dialogues Concerning Alejandra's 'Fit' in the Academy." *Composition Studies*, vol. 42, no. 2, University of Cincinnati on behalf of Composition Studies, 2014, pp. 33–55, http://www.jstor.org/stable/43501855.

---. *Counterstory: The Rhetoric and Writing of Critical Race Theory*. National Council of Teachers of English (Studies in Writing and Rhetoric Series), 2020.

Medina, Cruz. "Decolonial Potential in a Multilingual FYC." *Composition Studies*, vol. 47, no. 1, 2019, pp. 74-95.

—."Rhetoric of Storytelling (Course Design)." *Composition Studies*, vol. 49, no. 2, 2021, pp. 96–104.

Mukavetz, Andrea Riley. "Decolonial Theory and Methodology." *Composition Studies*, vol. 46, no. 1, 2018, pp. 124-140.

Olson, Gary A. "Working with Difference: Critical Race Studies and the Teaching of Composition." *Composition Studies in the New Millennium: Rereading the Past, Rewriting the Future*. Eds. Lynn Z. Bloom, Donald A. Daiker, Edward M. White. Carbondale: SIUP, 2003. 208-21.

Samuels, Brett. "Trump extends Ban on Racial Discrimination Training to Federal Contractors." *The Hill*. 22 Sept 2020. thehill.com/homenews/administration/517707-trump-extends-ban-on-racial-discrimination-training-to-federal. Accessed 25 Feb 2022.

Composition Studies at 50: The New Work of Writing Instruction as a Way Forward

Staci Perryman-Clark

This journal, originally, *Freshman English News*, is our field's oldest independent journal. It evolved from publishing news-based items related to first year writing courses to "reflecting the changes going on in the developing fields of rhetoric and composition" ("History"). It is this theme of evolution that I want to take up in my reflections of the 50th anniversary of what is now *Composition Studies*, occurring during the same year as the CCCC 2022 convention, where I served as chair. From evolution, I then will chart a path forward as we consider the next 50 years of scholarship in *Composition Studies*.

As articulated in the call for proposals for the 2022 CCCC convention, higher education has evolved from a gate-keeping, admission-based enterprise toward a student-based decision-to-attend enterprise, one with declines in enrollment ("College Enrollments"). In the call, I wrote:

> Let's consider the following facts: (1) There are fewer high school graduates, and the rate of high school graduation continues to decline (Nadworny 2019); (2) postsecondary enrollment has continued to decline since 2011 (Nadworny 2019; Nietzel 2019); (3) in 2017–2018, whites comprised the minority of college enrollment for the first time; and (4) despite the fact that the pool of Black and Latinx 18-year-olds in the US is not shrinking at the same rate as the pool of white 18-year-olds, especially in regions like the Midwest and Northeast, Black enrollment has fallen sharply since 2017 (Miller 2020). Given these sobering statistics, students are now making choices about whether or not they want to enroll in a postsecondary institution, making competition among postsecondary institutions keen with more pressure being put on chief marketing and recruitment/enrollment officers to sell the optimal college experience to prospective students. ("2022 Call")

This changing landscape invites us to reflect historically, to when we as a field were required to consider open-access and open admissions (especially within two-year colleges) as part of writing pedagogy in higher education. In 1971, *Guidelines for Junior College English Teacher Training Program* was published in response to the open admissions movement and the "community college boom" (567). As Jensen and Toth also note, "The 1971 *Guidelines* anticipate the 1974 *Students' Right to Their Own Language* statement, which was authored by a committee that included several of the same two-year college faculty (most notably Elisabeth McPherson, who became the first community college faculty member to chair CCCC in 1972–see Smitherman; Parks" (567). That year, 1972, is the year in which *Freshman English News/Composition Studies* was established. The *Guidelines* anticipated increased instruction for diverse learners including "minority literature" and critical language awareness, as applied to student demographics and populations deemed to be remedial (567).

We can learn many lessons from the shifting demographics associated with the open admissions movement 50 years ago and the declining enrollments we see happening today. Here are three.

It is no accident that many institutions, including those with some of the lowest acceptance rates, are now considering test-optional admissions–with the whole California state system now going test optional (Neitzel). In fact, two-thirds of all U.S. higher education institutions are now test-optional (College Post "Two-Thirds"). Institutions of higher education understand that they are no longer in a position to keep students out of higher education, especially when based on culturally-biased metrics. Given that the shifting demographics of U.S. higher education institutions reflect a more culturally diverse student body, test-optional admissions policies are seen as a way to create fewer barriers in access in order to increase enrollment.

Test-optional practices have a great impact on how we do writing placement into first year writing. If this wasn't already "Freshman English News" to readers, it certainly requires greater agency than we once imagined. Considering writing placement "democracy's open door," Christie Toth analyzes the impact of directed self-placement practices at two-year colleges, a population ripe for making connections between historical open admissions movements and current test optional admissions practices (7). All of the 12 institutions from which Toth collected interviews previously used standardized and multiple-choice tests to make decisions about placement into writing courses (8). Seven institutions changed to directed self-placement to accelerate progress toward degree completion, while participants from five colleges

> reported that these changes were fueled by institutional involvement with non-profit organizations like Achieving the Dream, funding from large foundations, and/or the influence of reform-oriented higher education research emerging from academic centers like the CCRC. In five cases, developmental education reforms affecting placement were also a response to state-level policies either encouraging or mandating change. (8)

Similar to test optional admissions practices, another lesson we can learn from the current enrollment landscape of higher education also has a great deal to do with access: cost. While revisions to admissions decisions do open up new opportunities for access, admission in and of itself does not address the lack of affordability with earning a college degree. To improve timely progress toward the degree, as Toth suggests, institutions consider directed self placement to enable students to move directly into first year writing courses that fulfill general education requirements without taking basic or remedial writing courses that only count for elective credit. But timely progress toward the degree isn't the only consideration at work here: While basic writing courses typically count for elective credit only, students are in fact still stuck with the tuition costs associated with enrolling in these courses. Thinking back to the enrollment picture I outlined in the Call for Proposals for the CCCC 2022 convention, I noted how students are flipping the script. They are making decisions about whether or not they want to enroll in college in the first place, in part because college is expensive ("2022 Call").

In a recent *Forbes* article, "A New Study Investigates Why College is so Expensive," Preston Cooper identifies the following reasons for this reconsideration of college's affordability: "students overestimate the return to a degree; colleges are not transparent about their true prices; too few institutions operate in each regional market; and there are significant barriers to entry for new educational providers" (par. 4). In terms of solutions to these problems, Cooper identifies a two-pronged approach: 1) transparency in terms of providing better financial aid data and net pricing, and 2) "opening the higher-education marketplace to competition by removing accreditors from their role as gatekeepers of federal financial aid, and instead allocating funds based on student outcomes" (par. 14). Again, the solution is eliminating gatekeeping mechanisms that deny access by making college less accessible and affordable.

The final lesson we can learn from the shifting demographics of higher education enrollment requires us to have candid conversations about what these shifting demographics mean. While there are fewer high school graduates due to lower birth rates, the most recent projections reveal the following:

> the racial/ethnic distribution of U.S. high school graduates will reflect the strong increases in high school graduation that have occurred in recent years. What used to be the coming diversity of U.S. graduates is now reality. Among the 90 percent of Class of 2019 high school graduates who were from public schools and for whom race/ethnicity data are provided: 51 percent of U.S. public high school graduates were White non-Hispanic, 25 percent were Hispanic of any race, 14 percent were single race Black non-Hispanic, 6 percent

were single-race non-Hispanic Asian or Native Hawaiian/Other Pacific Islander (of these, 6 percent were Native Hawaiian/Other Pacific Islander graduates), 3 percent were non-Hispanic multiracial, and 1 percent were single-race non-Hispanic American Indian/Alaska Native. ("Appendix")

Put simply, the population from which colleges and universities must find students appear to be more brown and diverse, and higher education depends on these populations of students in order to survive. While test-optional admissions and affordability may provide access to a more brown demographic, those practices are front-ended and do not address ways to retain students, especially as related to academic excellence and culturally responsive curricula. It is, perhaps, for this reason that I connected the 2022 Call to diversity, equity, and inclusion work. This is, perhaps, where composition studies (as a field) can make its greatest contribution: in considering higher education's enrollment challenges in relationship to access. An approach that addresses both admission and retention is necessary to make sure that students graduate from our institutions.

Connecting retention and first year writing is, again, not "Freshmen English News." Pegeen Reichert Powell's scholarship has explored at length connections between retention and first year writing. Building on this scholarship, Lockett et al. also provide data as evidence that first year writing initiatives can significantly shift institutions' first-to-second year retention rates. Based on their retention initiatives in first year writing, the retention rate "increased from 36 percent to 64 percent with the population of students with the highest likelihood of leaving the university, students who would have failed first year writing" (132). What is also significant about these efforts is the fact that two-thirds of the students participating in a retention-based first year writing course, designed to provide intervention for those in danger of failing, were nonwhite. Initiatives such as these provide one of many potential roadmaps for how we make our work as a field relevant with regard to diversity and inclusion and higher education enrollment.

In summary, we have a number of challenges as teachers and scholars navigating the new higher education landscape; however, our previous and existing scholarship equipped us to address higher education's challenges. As I move from the 2022 Program Convention Chair's role into the CCCC Chair's role, I'd like to conclude by highlighting three key foci that and themes that consider our future in higher education:

1. *Higher Education enrollment and our responsibilities as a discipline.* Questions we need to be equipped to address include how we re-

think our approaches to dual enrollment, directed self-placement, and recruitment and retention in ways that enable the institutions from which we come to survive. If the institutions where we work cannot survive or thrive, how can we support members of the field in doing the work of the field and our organizations?

2. *Diversity, equity, and inclusion across the discipline.* Every new initiative, working group, or policy we adopt or take a stance on must align with the organization's commitment to DEI principles. Not only does the survival of institutions and higher education depend on it, but as a field, our expertise and influence within the broader higher education landscape also depends on it.

3. *Public facing outreach and dissemination of knowledge.* As a discipline, we need to be the leading voice on how writing pedagogy and institutional practices influence the landscape of higher education. We need to explore more deeply how we demonstrate our ethos as experts and leading scholars to the broader public, and begin to influence public policy and decision-making, especially within this new higher education landscape.

As we remember the past 50 years of *Composition Studies*' influence on the field, it is my sincerest hope that you will join me in charting a new path for our work and higher education over the course of the next 50 years.

Works Cited

"2022 Call for Proposals." Conference on College Composition and Communication, 13 Apr. 2021, https://cccc.ncte.org/cccc/call-2022.

"Appendix Table A-2. Coefficients of Variation for ... - Wiche." Accessed April 6, 2022.https://knocking.wiche.edu/wp-content/uploads/sites/10/2020/12/Appendix-Table-2.pdf.

Bransberger, Peace, Falkenstern, Colleen, and Patrick Lane. Wiche. "*Knocking at the College Door: Projections on High School Graduates.*" Western Interstate Commission for Higher Education (WICHE) with support from College Board, 2020. https://www.wiche.edu/wp-content/uploads/2020/12/Knocking-pdf-for-website.pdf

College Enrollments Continue to Drop This Fall, Inside Higher Ed, 26 Oct. 2021, https://www.insidehighered.com/news/2021/10/26/college-enrollments-continue-drop-fall

Cooper, Preston. "A New Study Investigates Why College Tuition Is so Expensive." Forbes. *Forbes Magazine*, December 10, 2021. https://www.forbes.com/sites/prestoncooper2/2020/08/31/a-new-study-investigates-why-college-tuition-is-so-expensive/?sh=d814dde17a05.

Jensen, Darin and Christie Toth. "Unknown Knowns: The Past, Present, and Future of Graduate Preparation for Two-Year College English Faculty." *College English*, vol. 79, no. 6, 2017, pp. 561-592.

Lockett, Alexandria et al. "Reflective Moments: Showcasing University Writing Program Models for Black Student Success." In Staci M. Perryman-Clark and Collin Lamont Craig, eds. *Black Perspectives in Writing Program Administration: From the Margins to the Center*. NCTE, 2019, pp. 114-140.

Nietzel, Michael T. "University of California Reaches Final Decision: No More Standardized Admission Testing." *Forbes*, Forbes Magazine, 19 Nov. 2021, https://www.forbes.com/sites/michaeltnietzel/2021/11/19/university-of-california-reaches-final-decision-no-more-standardized-admission-testing/?sh=79d881292ec5.

Powell, Pegeen Reichert. *Retention and Resistance: Writing Instruction and Students Who Leave*. Utah State UP, 2014.

Toth, Christie. "Directed Self-Placement at Two-Year Colleges: A Kairotic Moment." *Journal of Writing Assessment*, vol. 12, no. 1, 2019, pp. 1-18.

"Two-Thirds of US Colleges Going Test-Optional in 2022: Report." *The College Post*, 9 Sept. 2021, https://thecollegepost.com/colleges-test-optional-2022/.

Generation(al) Matters: Story, Lens, and Tone

Louise Wetherbee Phelps

This essay tells a story of how "generation" came to matter in rhetoric and composition/writing studies; analyzes and advocates for "generation" as a lens through which to examine disciplinary studies and activities; and considers how we can productively engage in generational relations between individuals and groups. It adopts a framework of "hospitality" (adapted from Richard and Janis Haswell) to develop a concept of "cross-generational relations" as an aspirational category. An ethic of hospitality is proposed to facilitate respectful, productive relations among generational groups, which recognize and enact interdependence but allow for a wide range of stances and strategies of interaction in action and scholarly discourse.

Introduction

When pondering how to contribute to this special issue, I was startled to realize that my career, the journal's history, and the development of the discipline—rhetoric and composition/writing studies (RCWS)—had run in parallel for 50 years. I noticed uncanny correspondences and intersections among these timelines at key moments (Table 1):

Table 1

Self (LWP)	Journal (*FEN*→*CS*)	Field (RCWS)
1971-72: entered field (graduate studies)	Spring 1972: first issue of *FEN* published	"around 1971": beginning of discipline formation, first generation scholars (process; rhetoric revival)
1979: finished PhD; first article published (in *FEN*); attended Ottawa conference	1982: *FEN* broadened focus from Freshman English to the study and teaching of writing	"around 1979": discipline emerged (Ottawa conference; founding of doctoral programs, journals; first cohort of tenure-track hires)
	1992: new title *CS/FEN*	1990s: expansion, division, conflicts, disciplinary instability

1995: published article in *CS/FEN* on reproducing field in graduate programs	Fall 1995: special issue on doctoral education 1999: FEN dropped from title	1990s-2000s: Conversations around doctoral education as center of disciplinary definition and development
2009: "retired" and started post-retirement position; 2010: co-founded SIG for seniors and retirees		"around 2009": wave of retirements accelerated and began to impact the field, higher education
2013-14: organized 1st cross-generational conversation (CCCC) and initiated cross-generational project		2014: CCCC cross-generational task force (2014-2018) began work, including survey of retirees
2018/2020: published work on age/literacy and seniority	Spring 2021 issue: Intergenerational Exchanges; Pinkert and Bowen on results of retiree survey	"around 2018": seniority studies; lifespan writing studies; age/literacy studies; nextGEN group formed 2020: SIG for Senior, Late Career, & Retired Professionals became CCCC standing group (SGSLR) 2022: Writing and English Studies Co-organizational Collaborative (WESSC) survey of graduate students and early-career professionals
2021-22: 50 years in field	2021-2022: 50 years of publication	2021-2022: 50 years of disciplinary development

In 1971 I went back to graduate school to study rhetoric and language, coinciding with the founding of *Freshman English News* (*FEN*) that year. Scholars like Martin Nystrand and David Fleming identify that year as the moment that a teaching practice acquired the potential to become a discipline.

In 1979—the year I finished my PhD and published my first article (in *FEN*)—I attended the Ottawa conference, a coming-of-age event for the discipline. It capped off a decade of disciplinary growth—a Cambrian explosion of doctoral programs and journals. My microhistory of the conference depicts 1979 as the watershed year the conference (and field) crossed into a new era (Phelps, "Ottawa"). In 1982 the journal recognized this by expanding its scope to encompass the discipline's scholarly and teaching mission.

My second article (Fall 1995) in the renamed *Composition Studies/FEN* proposed that efforts to define the discipline had passed into a heterogeneous body of doctoral programs (Phelps, "Reproducing"). Contributors to this special issue joined an array of conversations about doctoral education amid divisions and conflicts associated with the growth and maturation of the burgeoning field, many of which showed up in the journal.

With the passage of personal and disciplinary time, generational themes gradually emerged in the field, intensifying with the "Age Wave" of baby-boomer retirements. Beginning around "2009," the aging of the professoriate defined a new generational identity of "seniors," many retiring from their positions but not necessarily from the field. I co-founded a special interest group (SIG) (now a Conference on College Composition and Communication (CCCC) Standing Group) to recognize this group and attend to its interests, but my larger concern was the consequences for all generations of this worldwide demographic shift, which could only be addressed together. Working with the SIG and younger colleagues, I initiated a multi-faceted project to foster cross-generational ("X-Gen") conversations and activities (CCCC Task Force). At the other end of the age spectrum, the nextGEN movement asserted a generational identity for graduate students. Concurrently, new areas of study emerged to connect age, literacy, lifespan writing, and disciplinary lifecycles—now a focus of my own scholarship.

These developments had come together by 2021 to define a new salience for generational relationships and their complexities in all three timelines. In the Spring 2021 issue of *Composition Studies*, thirteen scholars participated in "Intergenerational Exchanges." Two other articles feature generational themes: Zachary Beare's on the WPA-listserv and a study of disciplinary lifecycles by Laurie A. Pinkert and Lauren Marshall Bowen (whose retiree survey originated in the X-Gen project). Together these inspired my response for this 50th anniversary issue.

My essay unfolds in three parts. I'll tell a story of how "generation" came to matter in the field; analyze and advocate for "generation" as a lens through which to examine disciplinary studies and activities; and consider how we can productively engage in generational relations between individuals and groups (tone). I use the term *generation/al* here generically, to refer to groups or social identities based on age/time, in relation to the field's becoming over time. Later I'll introduce more precise terms to talk about such groups and their relationships.

Story

The mutual and intertwined aging of rhetoric and composition/writing studies (RCWS) and its scholars underlies a rising generational consciousness over the last two decades. I want to trace its trajectory in a series of overlapping moments in which members of the field came to 1) experience "generation" (implicitly, age) as a social identity; and 2) frame the history of the field as a succession or progression of generations. This consciousness brings the potential for convergence or divergence between generational identity groups—terms I'm borrowing from other contexts to refer to directions that interactions among generations can take, based on their perception of intergroup differences.[1]

This story deserves to be documented fully in a proper history, but here I can only tell it as my own: in Kierkegaard's phrase, how—"living forward"—I witnessed and perceived it and now, "understanding backward," I make sense of it. Like the stories of my colleagues in the Intergenerational Exchanges or in collections like *Talking Back* (Elliot and Horning), the intersections in my chart aren't arbitrary but reflect the kinds of relationships among individuals, generations, and sociohistorical location that connect age and time in a life-course perspective. Its first principle is that "the life course of individuals is embedded in and shaped by the historical times and places they experience over their life-time" (Elder).

Here's a roughly chronological overview:

- new interest in researching the twentieth-century development of RCWS as a discipline;
- attention to lived experiences of scholars, teachers, professionals as a dimension of that history;
- conversations *about* "generational" groups, their interests and relations, and disciplinary lifecycles;
- organizations, activities, and controversies that make generational identities explicit.

Not coincidentally, the field is now expanding the scope of its subject matter and approaches to account for age and time in literacy lives and its own work (Bazerman et al.; Dippre and Phillips; Bowen).

Why do both older and younger generations seek history? For one, disciplines need to establish and sustain continuity over time. That means, for older generations, recruiting and mentoring new members who will advance the field while preserving and honoring their legacy. Younger scholars, regardless of how much they bring new agendas, need to claim forebears. If the dominant ideas and people don't fit, they look for others to justify their visions of the future. Thus in the 1990s new cohorts of scholars (trained rigorously in historical methods) turned away from taxonomies to develop a more complex, multifaceted understanding of disciplinary development in the twentieth century. These "alternate histories" (in Kristopher Lotier's account, revisionist and "local")— replaced any single master narrative.[2]

Although they might argue against limitations of earlier historical scholarship, younger scholars recognized older generations as resources for their research—"the living memory of the field's development" (Miller et al.). They sought out older scholars for interviews and oral histories (Detweiler; Detweiler and McGhee Williams); claiming their legacies, they helped gather older scholars' work in collections and honored them with festschrifts and awards. Generational consciousness became increasingly explicit in genealogies (Miller and Miller et al. on the Writing Studies Tree), citation studies (Mueller) and studies of scholarly networks (Mueller et al.)

Fortuitously, these purposes complemented older scholars' own impulses to capture their lived experience of the field's development (Roen et al.; Flynn and Bourelle). Hoping to preserve their legacies, enrich historical accounts, and correct oversimplifications and gaps in the historical record, they've not only written about their memories but interacted with younger scholars in interviews, dialogues, oral histories, and collaborations. This synergy was dramatized in the 1996 Watson Conference, which brought scholars of different generations together to engage dialogically in—aptly named—"history, reflection, and narrative" (Rosner et al.). It perfectly represents the convergence of generational interests in historizing the discipline.

During the same period, the centripetal forces that joined disparate interests and traditions to claim a place in the academy gave way to centrifugal forces that fractured its original "founding" unity around all sorts of differences (Phelps, "Reproducing"). While these conflicts at first presented as scholarly (theoretical, methodological, pedagogical) and then increasingly as political and ideological, generational change played a tacit role as young scholars sought to make their mark by challenging prior scholarship and overturning dominant paradigms. However, even as identity became a dominant theme in the field's scholarship, these differences seldom became explicitly generational. One notable early exception was the exchange between Janice Lauer and Robin Varnum (Varnum; Lauer, "Response") over a 1992 CCCC panel in which Lauer and other scholars referred to themselves as "first generation." Varnum challenged this claim as neglecting scholars of the 1950s and 1960s for their roles in disciplinary history. Lauer responded that the panelists were offering oral histories, hers on the work of developing graduate programs. You see here early signs of generational divergence: older scholars trying to enrich histories with their reminiscences (and affectively, to be appreciated for their work); newer ones eager to complicate accounts of the field's origin. Each makes legitimate points, but they're talking past one another. Ironically, each accuses the other of discounting the work of previous generations. Lauer also makes explicit a tacit generational dynamic she criticizes: "scholarship that launches itself by denigrating or misrepresenting previous work" ("Response" 253).

The wave of retirements that gathered steam around 2009, coupled with crises and pressures on younger cohorts in higher education, set the stage for the emergence of self-identified generational identity groups. These have tended to polarize at opposite ends of the age spectrum, obscuring the rest of the generational span. Seniors and graduate student groups have sought ways to assert their identity and support their interests in organizations, collectives, advocacy spaces, research, and narratives. These include, for seniors, the Standing Group for Senior, Late Career, and Retired Professionals in RCWS (see Pinkert and Bowen; Bowen and Pinkert); for graduate students, nextGEN, Digital Black Lit and Composition (often DBLAC), Writing Program Administrators–Graduate Organization (often WPA-GO) and Writing Across the Curriculum–Graduate Organization (often WAC-GO), and GenAdmin (Charlton et al.). Younger generations have foregrounded horizontal and peer mentoring over traditional mentoring (Browdy et al).[3]

When "generation" becomes a social identity for groups, many forces of divergence operate to separate them, as illustrated by the recent controversy around the WPA listserv and the nextGen response (Kumari et al; Beare; WPA-L Reimagining Working Group and nextGen Start Up Team; Glotfelter and Tham). However, in RCWS forces for convergence also seek to balance those of divergence among generations.

Lens

Generational Identification/Identities

Generation matters, beyond its role in disciplinary history and professional identity: it's a lens we can turn on almost any phenomena we study, tools we use, and activities we engage in (see Yancey's "Notes on Intergenerational Exchanges"). If our sense of generation develops from the nexus of age and time with individual, cohort, and historical context, its scope of application is potentially enormous. For example, writing instruction is a classic site of intergenerational relations, but these can't be isolated from the complex web of generational identities and relations that every teacher and learner participates in across and outside schooling. I'm proposing we open that whole span to disciplinary inquiry.[4]

It's impossible to ignore a lens once it becomes salient, but we need to deploy it with caution. While "generation/al" is useful as a generic term, it's ambiguous (among many kinds of "generations") and, when referring to disciplinary generations in our field, difficult to apply precisely.

"Generation" is laminated (see Prior); individuals participate in multiple generational systems that are foregrounded or backgrounded in particular situations and are reconstructed and renegotiated continually over the lifespan. Individuals entering a discipline are already generationally identified in their families and in popular culture ("social generations" like "Generation X") and potentially in other life activities (like chess or sports) that are organized by an age and time-based nexus. These identities, intermingling and influencing one another, acquire reality from both external (systemic/sociocultural) and (inter)subjective (phenomenological) perspectives. To add to the complexity, generational and other social identities are intersectional, as evidenced by Martin J. Finkelstein et al.'s research on a "new generation" of faculty defined by demographic change (more diverse in race/ethnicity, nativity, and gender).

Keeping in mind that generational analysis has to account for these laminations and complex interminglings, how can we identify our field's disciplinary generations? In popular culture, "generation" typically refers to individuals born within a span of dates, who share experience of transformational events (World War II, the digital revolution) and/or a cultural milieu during formative years: i.e., it places an individual by an intersection of age (birth cohort), time, and historical worlds. Generational talk in our field ("I'm a fourth-generation scholar") has tacitly assumed an analogous nexus for disciplinary identity. In a traditional career arc, elements in the nexus align predictably: individuals enter through PhDs in the discipline, which frame a generation defined by age (youth), era in the field, and a cohort moving forward collectively up the academic ladder. Alternately, "generation" is sometimes rendered as descent: a mentor lineage or successive cohorts in a doctoral program.

But do these ways of identifying disciplinary generations work for RCWS careers? Consider the field's membership. As Pinkert and Bowen demonstrate, RCWS scholars are atypical in their status and relationship to the academy and their heterogeneous career patterns. RCWS careers deviate from the presumed norm by scholars' routes *into* the discipline and *through* their careers: crucially for generational identity, in terms of credentialing and timing.[5] The reasons include such historical disciplinary features as the labor situation with respect to First Year Writing; the gender imbalance (feminized); the role of community colleges; the recency of the discipline's doctoral programs; the role of administrative work; and relations (of training or experience) with other disciplines or external workplaces. Despite growing more like other disciplines in many respects, RCWS careers still display these anomalies, some even exacerbated by recent trends in higher education, in patterns of labor inside the academy and work in disciplinary spaces outside it.

It's clear that no single model can be used to identify generations of RCWS professionals (not just faculty) without falsifying this complexity. The nexus-based or genealogical models apply best to the elite who participate directly in vertical networks at research universities: they acquire their generational identity from doctoral programs and mentors and then educate the next cohort of scholars. (With social media and digital communication among graduate students, their nextGen cohort identity now transcends local programs.) But many RCWS careers, in their temporal messiness and unpredictable trajectories, don't fit traditional models, and even those that do may not look so conventional when closely examined.

Without consistent ways to distinguish disciplinary RCWS generations, generational research will need to adopt perspectives and choose criteria to fit methods to a particular purpose, situation, historical moment, or research question (see Urick). Examples might include point of entry/time working in the discipline; major shifts in scholarship, as in feminism's generational "waves"; or a transformative event.[6]

Such definitions may or may not correlate with RCWS scholars' *experiences* of generational identity. But it is phenomenological and intersubjective perspectives that matter in addressing intergenerational relations. We know generational consciousness has risen in our field, but it remains an empirical question exactly how and when RCWS scholars ascribe generational identities to themselves and others, and which identities are salient enough to articulate and act on as a group. Unsurprisingly, the voices heard most clearly about generational identity come from those who, by following privileged routes into or through the profession, have greater access to its public written and oral venues. Otherwise, generational consciousness seems to be largely binary—oldest vs. newest. The many individuals who fall in-between or outside these groups may have a very fuzzy sense of generational boundaries or disciplinary location. That means we need more nuanced understandings of generational experience to develop multigenerational models for justice and care that apply to all members of the field.

Generational Relations

Despite all this, scholars do have some sense of generational identification that informs their thinking: for example, in a 2022 CCCC panel on intergenerational exchange, scholars identified themselves as "early career," "mid-career," "late career," or "retired" ("Mutuality"). I find it helpful to distinguish generational relations as follows, building on generation's generic sense.

- Intergenerational: refers to exchanges and relations among distinct groups or individuals experiencing their generational identity as salient in relationships. An *inter*group perspective on generational relations highlights processes like "(group-based) categorization, social comparison, self- and other-stereotyping, prejudice, and discrimination" (Williams and Nussbaum 10), but generational groups (and interpersonal relations interpreted generationally) have the potential for convergence (emphasizing commonalities, reciprocal benefits, complementarity) as well as divergence (emphasizing difference, antagonism, conflict).

- Transgenerational: understands a discipline as analogous to a polity (Thompson) in which members' sense of belonging to a community transcends their own experience/lives in it, so that they accept duties—"relations of obligation and entitlement"—to those who precede and follow them: "they are heirs to a legacy that is the work of many generations and they will in turn provide an inheritance for their successors" (2).
- Cross-generational: an aspirational category for productive, respectful relationships among co-temporal generational groups belonging to a transgenerational scholarly community, which recognize and enact interdependence but allow for a wide range of relations and strategies of interaction, along a spectrum from convergence to divergence. In scholarly communication, individuals engage in transgenerational exchanges that can extend these relationships (and mutual duties) beyond the bounds of contemporaneous lives.

Tone

In her famous 1984 article on composition as a dappled discipline ("Composition"), and reaffirmed 30 years later (Vealey and Rivers 175-77), Lauer described the field's "tone" as a distinctive feature: a mutually respectful, collegial ethos that has survived counterforces of discord as the field developed and diversified. Her examples of tone cast it in generational terms, for example, contrasting "new work that builds on previous work" with the adversarial tone of new scholars "carv[ing] out niches for themselves by enlarging loopholes in previous work" ("Composition" 27-28). And her claim for this tone in composition (RCWS) roots it in a transgenerational sense of community, one in which successive generations are invested in the past and future of a continuing, shared project of disciplinary inquiry and learning.

Lauer's discussion offers a discipline-specific precedent—and "tone" as a useful shorthand—for exploring qualities of cross-generational relations in the field. I defined a category of "cross-generational" relations earlier as aspirational: imagining an authentic attempt by generationally identified individuals and groups to engage in relations across the spectrum from divergence to convergence in mutually productive ways. This formulation acknowledges the necessary role of both divergence and convergence in scholarly interactions and discourse, treating these forms of relationship as ethically neutral (i.e., I don't equate Lauer's "tone" with convergence).[7]

I asked myself, what resources does the discipline have to develop concepts and strategies for cross-generational relations? I'll answer this question differently for two means and contexts for enacting cross-generational relations: embodied, material action and scholarly discourse (meaning here exchanges among scholars over primarily textual, but also oral public inquiry).[8] However, as an overall framework for analyzing both contexts I'm adopting the concept of "hospitality" as developed by Richard and Janis Haswell, originally for pedagogical relations (teacher/learner, writer/reader). Its foundation is a traditional notion of hospitality as a reciprocal relation of friendly welcome, mutual respect, dialogue, and exchange of gifts between stranger-host and stranger-guest, who treat each other as equal in dignity, potential, and human worth, despite inequalities (asymmetry) between them.[9] The "[r]ules governing the traditional relations between guest and host included swapping of information, unspoken assumption of social equality, unspoken assumption of the equal validity of differing customs, and a respect for privacy" (*Authoring* 261). The Haswells specify three postures of hospitality: intellectual, which welcomes reciprocal learning through exchange of ideas, experiences, and perspectives; transformative, whereby host and guest both willingly risk being destabilized and transformed by their exchanges; and *ubuntu*, through which host and guest recognize in each other a common humanity that transcends differences of identity, experience, and culture (*Hospitality* 8, 53-55). From their rich, complex elaboration of this idea I've selected a list of features I will draw on to characterize a "hospitable tone" in cross-generational relations:

- the roles of host and guest: upon first encounter, they meet as strangers; relation is asymmetrical; roles are reversible (in an encounter or over time), can evolve beyond hospitality into long-term relationships
- mutual respect: despite asymmetry, host and guest meet as equals (valuing one another's "singularity" and "potentiality": see *Authoring* for more on these concepts)
- disidentification: valuing difference but "looking through social identities to the singular Other" (*Hospitality* 14)
- exchange of gifts, including information/ideas/knowledge/learning
- hospitable spirit (attitude, disposition, ambience): generous, open, compassionate; creates a sense of "ease" to enable risk-taking.[10]

Action

To examine how hospitality operates in action—embodied, material modes of cross-generational interaction and exchange–my resource is disciplinary practice: specifically, evidence of practices in RCWS that exemplify *beneficence* in generational relations, meaning actions that advance the interests and well-being of the other (generational group or individual).[11] Broadly, such actions may be regarded as gift-giving, but they also include affective components of hospitality in action like empathetic listening. I'm borrowing this definition from medical ethics, where, usefully, beneficence is paired with a concept of nonmaleficence (do no harm) as well as two other principles relevant to hospitality: autonomy (respect for persons) and justice (Varkey; Bester). Unlike the doctor-patient model, though, in the hospitality framework beneficence is expected of both host and guest— reciprocal between generations.

RCWS has a historical claim to a habitus of beneficent or hospitable action directed toward others (cross-generationally) in two modes: group to group and individual to individual (although the line between them blurs: "the interindividual-intergroup split. . . [is] a dialectic that is continuously in play across all our interactions [Williams and Nussbaum 288]).

The group to group examples I'm thinking of are the plenitude of means by which the (host) field welcomes and supports emergent scholars (as strangers) to the field through a variety of material and symbolic means, sponsored by professional organizations and their sub-groups or affiliates. The "gifts" offered to younger generations by groups like the Conference on College Composition and Communication (CCCC), Rhetoric Society of America (RSA), the Council of Writing Program Administrators (CWPA), and the Association of Teachers of Technical Writing (ATTW) have been steadily increasing over the years. They include grants for research, career advancement, and travel; recognition through awards; workshops, institutes, and meetings (orientation, welcome, group mentoring) targeted toward newcomers; opportunities for in-person and virtual dialogue; and access to positions in professional organizations. Most of these efforts (presupposing a traditional career arc) focus on early career stages; very little generational help has been offered for later career stages or alternate forms of advancement (one exception is the RSA Career Retreat for Associate Professors).

Although these forms of beneficent action may appear to be one-way gifts (from elders to younger generations), they exemplify hospitality because there is an exchange of benefits within the common project of building a transgenerational community. Broadly, older generations (as noted earlier) are invested in sustaining the field through recruiting and supporting new members, especially in their own lines of work and specialties. Besides continuity, they also have a futurist interest in encouraging innovation and change, in part through diversifying people and ideas entering the field.

I must acknowledge, of course, counterexamples of maleficent intergenerational actions in RCWS, although these are hard to distinguish from endemic (and interdisciplinary) academic practices of inhospitable behaviors, ranging from exclusion, exploitation, deception, and incivility to bullying (Elder and Davila). Although multidirectional, such behaviors often exploit age-related inequities in rank, power, and authority. Recently, as senior and very junior groups have begun to identify themselves generationally and pursue divergent strategies, there is a potential for intergenerational conflict or competition to become negative in tone and consequences.

However, divergence is a necessary predicate to forming generational identities, and it has potentially positive benefits. Divergent strategies like separation and competition, used to express a group identity and pursue common goals, can be healthy elements of cross-generational relations as long as they remain nonmaleficent. (Indeed, relations within a generational group can be hospitable, as in peer-to-peer mentoring and horizontal networks.) But overall, in generational group relations, convergent actions tend to outweigh divergent ones, if we look at the historic patterns within our professional sites of interaction. I suggest multiple reasons for this:

1. RCWS members do share a transgenerational intellectual project and community, which is the basis (according to Thompson) of a rational, life-time transcending interest in transgenerational justice.
2. Age, as many observe, is a unique kind of social identity in that it isn't fixed: it is reconstructed (indeed, transformed) constantly as individuals and cohorts pass through the same phases of aging as their predecessors: in effect, becoming the "other[s]." In Ruth Ray Karpen's words, "unlike race, class, gender, ethnicity, sexual orientation, and other cultural categories that divide us, age is the one thing that unites us all . . . For the benefit of both society and the individual, young people need to learn to see old people as a mirror of their future selves" (55).
3. As Karpen affirms, generational groups are intrinsically interdependent, complementary in their changing needs and interests and the gifts they can offer each other.

This interdependence among generations isn't just practical. There is a hospitable disposition toward dialogue, mutual caring (even caregiving), and affective bonds among professional generations, as with familial ones. This disposition is present, but more abstract in group to group beneficence than in direct interpersonal relations, which I will exemplify in our disciplinary practice by mentoring, as depicted in the collection *Stories of Mentoring* (Eble and Gaillet). In documenting the scope and variety of their mentoring experiences, contributors enlarge and transform the traditional apprentice model of this relationship. I see this collection as a capacious representation of the host-guest relationship in all its complexities, risks, potential corruption, and–at best–profound mutual value. It shows how, unlike beneficent group action in RCWS, still largely flowing one-way, the field's interpersonal concept of mentoring has evolved to aspire to the host-guest relation in its mutuality and reciprocity, as well as in many other qualities: asymmetry but equality of worth; reversibility of roles; respect for persons in their singularity and potential; friendly, welcoming spirit; and the capability of developing into deeper relations as colleague, friend, collaborator. Although much mentoring remains one-on-one, the host-guest framework is modified in this reimagined practice to multiply relationships in collaboration and mentoring networks and, generationally, to recognize mentoring as multidirectional: peer-to-peer and vertical; multigenerational rather than binary (see Eble and Gaillet, "Reinscribing").

Krista Ratcliffe and Donna Decker Schuster's chapter lays out a non-utopian case for pragmatic interdependence: in which mentoring "effects are envisioned as flowing in all directions and benefiting everyone involved, albeit in different ways and to different degrees" (248). By recognizing differentials (asymmetries) in experience and power, "commonalities and differences among people become visible and serve as sites of agency" through interdependence: i.e., "everyone may learn how one's own agency arises in conjunction with the agencies of other people and institutional structures" (248-49). But many chapters in *Stories of Mentoring* (as well as responses from younger scholars to seniors in *Talking Back*) demonstrate the bonds of affection that arise cross-generationally when their interchanges are conducted in a hospitable spirit—generous, caring, with humility and ease. Looking at mentoring alongside group to group action tells us that beneficent action in the field needs to become more thoroughly multigenerational, multidirectional, and fully reciprocal in dispensing care and justice. In particular, both middle generations and seniors, who are subject to ageism in the broader culture (and the academy), need attention to their practical and affective needs as well as appreciation and opportunities to offer benefits to other generations.

Much of what I've described here reflects personal experience in watching generational identity groups cycle through divergence and convergence, reflecting emergent understandings of their interdependence and desire for communication and connection. The SIG I co-founded (now SGSLR)—originally for retirees but soon broadened to encompass late career and senior professionals—has benefited (like other identity groups) from the divergent strategy of separation: articulating its distinctive identity and pursuing its own "special interests" and needs. But the SIG quickly realized that seniors couldn't thrive purely as an enclave, so they sought out other generations for interactions and mutual help (compare nextGEN founders' comments in Glotfelter and Tham's interview). From this grew the X-Gen project, whose task force report lays out a menu of ideas for pursuing cross-generational connections and communication (CCCC Task Force). It began strikingly in 2013 with a CCCC "cross-generational conversation," in which Shelley Rodrigo and I asked people sitting at cross-generational tables to compile lists of what they wanted from and could offer to other generations. As participants left the room, they stopped to exclaim how much they enjoyed this rare opportunity to meet (hospitably) and encouraged us to pursue both further conversations and the practical action items they had proposed. Unfortunately, this agenda has so far had too little uptake, given major disruptive events and urgent concerns that have recently taken up all the disciplinary attention space. But there are local projects like the BRAWN network (see Brereton and Gannett), as well as the Spring 2021 issue of *Composition Studies*). The opportunity remains, and the desire: in Zhaozhe Wang's words, "I do not think we as a disciplinary community have done enough to frame our trans-generational exchanges around the notion of 'partnership' and foster trans-generational collegiality.... We wish for more" (161-163).

Scholarly Discourse

The field's resources for examining intergenerational relations and defining hospitality in scholarly discourse are almost limitless: virtually all of rhetorical theory offers relevant concepts. In a kind of strange loop, much rhetorical scholarship has been devoted to debates over convergent vs. divergent models of scholarly exchange, especially as they intersect with feminist controversies over argumentation as violent or agonistic vs. peaceful or dialogic. But these seem to have reached an impasse (see Lloyd). The same is true in a parallel argument within academic feminism regarding models for generational relations; for example, Kathleen Woodward rejects a Freudian, two-generation-model based on "struggle for dominion" for a three-generation maternal "heritage of care for the next generation" (151-52), but ultimately decides to move away from familial models entirely and calls for alternate models. Host-guest relations in hospitality offer such an alternative, which has the advantage of allowing for both convergent and divergent modes of generational relationships (and was originally applied by the Haswells to writer-reader relations). Like Lloyd, I want to account for the fact that vigorous conflict is an essential feature of intellectual networks, which test ideas against one another in a limited attention space (Collins); but so is the dependence of new scholarship on prior scholarship, whether building on its findings and concepts or critiquing them. Convergence can be synergistic, but it also risks stagnation if it doesn't challenge the status quo: "conflict. . . can be fundamental to rendering possible processes of social change and innovation" (Valentim 594). Scholarly discourse, therefore, needs to operate flexibly across the range from convergence to divergence, allowing for (in Lloyd's words) "articulations of possibility, openness, community, as well as expressions of frustration, antagonism, and group identity" (103). In C. Jan Swearingen's wonderful phrasing, "She who would speak must speak (*eiro*) irenically at times, eristically at others, elenchically with some opponents, maieutically with the young and tender hearted, and inescapably with the irony of those who believe in the incompleteness and incommunicability of thought that relentlessly necessitates dialogue" (158).

The question of hospitality in scholarly discourse becomes, then, not how to balance or choose between divergence and convergence, but how scholars engage one another in either mode—in what spirit or tone. That is really the crux of objections to what Lloyd calls "dichoto-negative rhetoric": not the mere fact of conflict but the way it dismisses and disrespects other scholars and their work in service of "winning" the competition for intellectual dominance. (That goal is often tacitly generational, as both Lloyd and Lauer imply.) Lloyd's proposal for applying a fuzzy, multivalent logic to reading other scholars' work is a pragmatic methodological solution to cultivating openness and reducing the potential for inhospitable tone. But principles of hospitality run deeper than critical method.

At heart, the "moral axis" (Haswell and Haswell, "Hospitality," 17) of an ethic of hospitality is treating the Other as an embodied person, with all that implies: understanding each unique human being as on a trajectory of learning and becoming, filled with rich potential for growth and change. Risking themselves in scholarly writing makes persons vulnerable, which is why hospitality asks more of us than respect or even civility; its welcoming spirit offers kindness, openness, concern for the other's well-being. That is what Alexandra Hidalgo is asking for (and trying to practice) in responding to a *College English* article about the work of herself and her colleagues: "I want you . . . to know that real human beings with lives and families are affected by the words we write and that those human beings feel wounded when we express ourselves in ways that unkindly portray them or their work (2-3). In teaching graduate students, she tells them, when citing and discussing another scholar's work, "to imagine that they are sitting across from that person, uttering the very words they wrote about them and holding their gaze, seeing their reactions as their words settle. At some point, they are likely to end up at some committee, panel or dinner with any living person they cite" (6-7).

Written scholarly discourse is inherently inter-generational because, unlike generational actions, which typically occur in the here and now among living scholars, it extends scholars' "meetings" outside the temporal bounds of co-presence. Scholars encountering one another as host and guest, writer and reader, are not co-present in time and, in fact, their texts transcend their own lifetime, as well as other boundaries like discipline and place. So, thinking trans-generationally, we need to revise Hidalgo's advice to mean acting "as if" the textual encounter could become an in-person meeting—and to take into account, even for living scholars, their lives over time. But the conventions of written scholarship make it hard for writers and readers—as hospitality requires—to perceive and address one another as unfinished persons with unrealized potential, that is, as living and changing. The present tense used in citing scholars fixes their work—and the scholar-author—in a timeless space that becomes identified with the current moment in which it is read and cited. This convention leads to a double erasure of cited scholars as living in time: first, from the life course perspective, as human beings whose thought is shaped by their generational location in history and the exigence of a historical moment of writing; second, as authors who continue writing and developing as scholars, unpredictably, after a time-bound piece of their thinking becomes public. Like the light from stars, a scholar's words reach us only over time; by then, they are already speaking for that person's former self.

The gifts that writers and readers of different generations can bring to one another depend, in part, on these very differences in their relation to time and history: as the Haswells put it, the guest "promises news from a different world—the world of a different generation, age, gender, class, or ethnicity, and the world of that singular person's experiences, hopes, mullings, insights, and interpretations" (*Hospitality* 54).

"One way or another, we all live intergenerational exchange; it's how we live it, and what we learn from it, that matters" (Yancey 168). Knowing what hospitality expects of us is one thing; living it consistently in times of great tension and stress is another. When practicing it becomes most difficult, I remind myself of these precepts—passed on to me by a former student from her mentor—posted in my office: "BE FAIR. BE KIND. BE BRAVE."

Notes

1. The terms "convergence" vs. "divergence" are attributed by Angie Williams and Jon F. Nussbaum to communication studies, where they describe how people accommodate others' communication styles, but Joaquim Pires Valentim uses divergence as I do, more broadly, to discuss intergroup relations.

2. For graduate courses in 2014 and 2017, I collected alternate histories. I see many as fractal representations of the field, since even the most local, micro-level, or

specialized claim a relationship to the field as a whole. A growing number of alternate histories seek to historicize the contributions, experiences, and rhetorics of groups defined by their social identities (race and ethnicity, gender, ability, sexuality, and so on). Others view the whole through a particular lens, e.g., technology, instructional programs, labor, research methods.

3. My 1995 FEN article "Reproducing Composition and Rhetoric" anticipated and argued for cross-institutional networking among graduate students to overcome the apparent incommensurability of visions of the discipline expressed in their doctoral programs. I hoped then that the Consortium of Doctoral Programs in Rhetoric and Composition could play a facilitative role in "creating collegiality horizontally among graduate students so that they will not encounter one another as strangers but will reproduce the discipline as a human community linked across programs, institutions, and differences by discourse, common information, intellectual exchanges, collaborative projects, and friendships" (125). Instead, those networks have developed organically as an expression of generational consciousness and identity.

4. This reflection on "generation" as a lens is based on my own observations, but working on this essay introduced me to sources of theory and research on intergroup relations (Ana Figuerido et al.; Valentim), generational identity (Urick), and intergenerational communication (Barker et al.; Williams and Nussbaum) that could prove fruitful for the discipline's future research on generational identity and relations.

5. One of the five principles of life course theory is timing: "The developmental antecedents and consequences of life transitions, events, and behavioral patterns vary according to their timing in a person's life," (Elder, Jr.) such as the timing of motherhood or military service relative to education or professional advancement; the timing of life transitions relative to age-norms or to disruptive social, economic, or technological change. Timing (relations among age, life stages, credentialing, and positions) is often unconventional in RCWS careers, including my own.

6. See Marek Kwiek's study of academic generations in Poland before and after the fall of communism in 1989. One can imagine studying pre- and post-Covid pandemic RCWS generations.

7. My view of the roles played by divergence and convergence in scholarly (specifically, generational) relations is influenced by the complementary views of Randall Collins and Mary Catherine Bateson regarding how intellectual networks function: see Phelps, "Ottawa" 66-68.

8. Scholarly discourse in this sense is only a subset of all the professional discourse we engage in, including the discourse required to accomplish actions. Everyday professional discourse in departments, organizations, and across digital space has major issues with tone (it could benefit from a hospitality ethic), but falls outside my parameters here, generational relations among scholars in the discipline.

9. The Haswells' idea of hospitality as an "asymmetrical" relation is complex. I take this to mean, first, the intrinsic nature of the host's role as insider welcoming outsider; but, more deeply, that human relationships always involve inequalities (i.e., lack perfect symmetry) in multiple respects (age, social status, rank, power, expertise, experience, empathy).

10. "Ease" translates Giorgio Agamben's term *"agio"*: "ease, opportunity, coziness"; hospitality sets people at ease by giving others "elbow-room" to learn, change, realize their potential (Haswell and Haswell, *Hospitality* 178-180).

11. I'm following Johan Christiaan Bester in viewing beneficence as a hybrid concept, incorporating the views of both host and guest as to what constitutes the beneficiary's interests or well-being.

Works Cited

Barker, Valerie, et al. "Inter- and Intragroup Perspectives on Intergenerational Communication." *Handbook of Communication and Aging Research*, edited by Jon F. Nussbaum and Justine Coupland, 2nd ed., Erlbaum, 2004, pp. 139–65.

Bazerman, Charles, et al. *The Lifespan Development of Writing*. NCTE, 2018.

Beare, Zachary. "Cross Postings: Disciplinary Knowledge-Making and the Affective Archive of the WPA Listserv." *Composition Studies*, vol. 49, no. 1, 2021, pp. 42–59.

Bester, Johan Christiaan. "The Two Components of Beneficence and Wellbeing in Medicine: A Restatement and Defense of the Argument." *American Journal of Bioethics*, vol. 20, no. 5, 2020, pp. W4–11.

Bowen, Lauren Marshall, editor. *Composing a Further Life,* special issue of *Literacy in Composition Studies*, vol. 6, no. 2, 2018.

Bowen, Lauren Marshall, and Laurie A. Pinkert. "Identities Developed, Identities Denied: Examining the Disciplinary Activities and Disciplinary Positioning of Retirees in Rhetoric, Composition, and Writing Studies." *College Composition and Communication*, vol. 72, no. 2, 2020, pp. 251–81.

Brereton, John, and Cinthia Gannett. "Intergenerational Exchange in Rhetoric and Composition: Some Views from Here." *Composition Studies*, vol. 49, no. 1, 2021, pp. 119–24.

Browdy, Ronisha, et al. "From Cohort to Family: Coalitional Stories of Love and Survivance." *Composition Studies*, vol. 49, no. 2, 2021, pp. 14–30.

CCCC Task Force on Cross-Generational Connections. *Recommendations from the Task Force on Cross-Generational Connections*. Conference on College Composition and Communication, 2018. cccc.ncte.org/cccc/resources.

Charlton, Colin, et al. *GenAdmin: Theorizing WPA Identities in the Twenty-First Century*. Parlor P, 2011.

Collins, Randall. *The Sociology of Philosophies: A Global Theory of Intellectual Change*. Belknap, 1998.

Detweiler, Eric. "On Podcasting, Program Development, and Intergenerational Thinking." *Composition Studies*, vol. 49, no. 1, 2021, pp. 130–34.

Detweiler, Eric, and Elizabeth McGhee Williams. "A Living Rhetorical Enterprise: The RSA Oral History Initiative." *Rhetoric Society Quarterly*, vol. 49, no. 5, Oct. 2019, pp. 566–82.

Dippre, Ryan J., and Talinn Phillips, editors. *Approaches to Lifespan Writing Research: Generating an Actionable Coherence*. WAC Clearing House/UP of Colorado, 2020.

Eble, Michelle F., and Lynee Lewis Gaillet. "Re-Inscribing Mentoring." *Retellings: Opportunities for Feminist Research in Rhetoric and Composition Studies*, edited by Jessica Enoch and Jordynn Jack, Parlor P, 2019, pp. 283–303.

—, editors. *Stories of Mentoring: Theory and Praxis*. Parlor P, 2008.

Elder, Cristyn L., and Bethany Davila, editors. *Defining, Locating, and Addressing Bullying in the WPA Workplace*. Utah State UP, 2019.

Elder, Glen H., Jr. "Research." *Glen H. Elder, Jr.* University of North Carolina, accessed 25 Mar. 2022. https://elder.web.unc.edu/research-projects/

Elliot, Norbert, and Alice Horning, editors. *Talking Back: Senior Scholars Deliberate the Past, Present, and Future of Writing Studies*. Utah State UP, 2020.

Figuerido, Ana, et al. "Theories on Intergroup Relations and Emotions: A Theoretical Overview." *Psychologica*, vol. 57, no. 2, 2014, pp. 7–33.

Finkelstein, Martin J., et al. *The New Academic Generation: A Profession in Transformation*. Johns Hopkins UP, 1998.

Fleming, David. "Rhetoric Revival or Process Revolution: Revisiting the Emergence of Composition-Rhetoric as a Discipline." *Renewing Rhetoric's Relation to Composition: Essays in Honor of Theresa Jarnagin Enos*, Routledge, 2009, pp. 25–52.

Flynn, Elizabeth A., and Tiffany Bourelle, editors. *Women's Professional Lives in Rhetoric and Composition: Choice, Chance, and Serendipity*. Ohio State UP, 2018.

Glotfelter, Angela, and Jason Tham. "Becoming the Next Generation: An Interview with the Founders of the NextGEN Listserv." Digital Rhetoric Collaborative, 13 Nov. 2018. https://www.digitalrhetoriccollaborative.org/2018/11/13/becoming-the-next-generation-an-interview-with-the-founders-of-the-nextgen-listserv/

Haswell, Janis, and Richard Haswell. *Authoring: An Essay for the English Profession on Potentiality and Singularity*. Utah State UP, 2010.

Haswell, Richard, and Janis Haswell. *Hospitality and Authoring: An Essay for the English Profession*. Utah State UP, 2015.

Hidalgo, Alexandra. "A Response to Cushman, Baca, and Garcia's College English Introduction." *Constellations*, vol. 28, no. 4, Oct. 2021, constell8cr.com/articles/a-response-to-cushman-baca-and-garcias-college-english-introduction/.

Karpen, Ruth Ray. "Toward an Even Longer View." Afterword. *Talking Back: Senior Scholars and Their Colleagues Deliberate the Past, Present, and Future of Writing Studies*, edited by Norbert Elliot and Alice Horning, Utah State UP, 2020, pp. 392–403.

Kumari, Ashanka, et al. "The Necessity of Genre Disruption in Organizing an Advocacy Space for and by Graduate Students." *Xchanges*, vol. 15, no. 1, 2020, pp. 1–8.

Kwiek, Marek. "Academic Generations and Academic Work: Patterns of Attitudes, Behaviors, and Research Productivity of Polish Academics after 1989." *Studies in Higher Education*, vol. 40, no. 8, 2015, pp. 1354–76.

Lauer, Janice. "A Response to 'The History of Composition: Reclaiming Our Lost Generations.'" *Journal of Advanced Composition*, vol. 13, no. 1, 1993, pp. 252–53.

—. "Composition Studies: Dappled Discipline." *Rhetoric Review*, vol. 3, 1984, pp. 20–29.

Lloyd, Keith. "Beyond 'Dichonegative' Rhetoric: Interpreting Field Reactions to Feminist Critiques of Academic Rhetoric through an Alternate Multivalent Rhetoric." *Rhetorica*, vol. 34, no. 1, 2016, pp. 78–105.

Lotier, Kristopher M. *Postprocess Postmortem*. WAC Clearing House/UP of Colorado, 2021, https://doi.org/10.37514/PER-B.2021.1268.

Miller, Benjamin. "When the Family Tree Metaphor Breaks Down, What Grows?" *Composition Studies*, vol. 49, no. 1, 2021, pp. 140–43.

Miller, Benjamin et al. "The Roots of an Academic Genealogy: Composing the Writing Studies Tree." *Kairos: A Journal of Rhetoric, Technology, and Pedagogy*, vol. 20, no. 2, 2016, https://kairos.technorhetoric.net/20.2/topoi/miller-et-al/index.html.

Mueller, Derek. "Grasping Composition by Its Long Tail: What Graphs Can Tell Us about the Field's Changing Shape." *College Composition and Communication*, vol. 64, no. 1, 2012, pp. 195–223.

Mueller, Derek, et al. *Cross-Border Networks in Writing Studies*. Inkshed/Parlor Press, 2017.

"Mutuality in Equity through Intergenerational Exchange." Roundtable sponsored by the Standing Group for Senior, Late Career, and Retired Professionals (SGL-SR). Conference on College Composition and Communication, 12 Mar. 2022.

Nystrand, Martin. "Janet Emig, Frank Smith, and the New Discourse about Writing and Reading; or, How Writing and Reading Came to Be Cognitive Processes in 1971." *Towards a Rhetoric of Everyday Life: New Directions in Research on Writing, Text, and Discourse*, edited by Martin Nystrand and John Duffy, U of Wisconsin P, 2003, pp. 121–44.

Phelps, Louise Wetherbee. "Reproducing Composition and Rhetoric: The Intellectual Challenge of Doctoral Education." *Composition Studies*, vol. 23, no. 2, 1995, pp. 115–32.

—. "The 1979 Ottowa Conference and Its Inscriptions: A Canadian Moment in American Rhetoric and Composition." *Microhistories of Composition*, edited by Bruce McComiskey, Utah State UP, 2016.

Pinkert, Laurie A., and Lauren Marshall Bowen. "Disciplinary Lifecycling: A Generative Framework for Career Trajectories in Rhetoric, Composition, and Writing Studies." *Composition Studies*, vol. 49, no. 1, 2021, pp. 16–41.

Prior, Paul. *Writing/Disciplinarity: A Sociohistoric Account of Literate Activity in the Academy*. Erlbaum, 1998.

Ratcliffe, Krista, and Donna Decker Schuster. "Mentoring Toward Interdependency: 'Keeping It Real.'" *Stories of Mentoring: Theory and Praxis*, edited by Michelle F. Eble and Lynee Lewis Gaillet, Parlor P, 2008.

Roen, Duane H., et al. *Living Rhetoric and Composition: Stories of the Discipline*. Erlbaum, 1999.

Rosner, Mary, et al. *History, Reflection, and Narrative: The Professionalization of Composition 1963-1983*. Ablex, 1999.

Swearingen, C. Jan. "Afterplay: A Fore Letter Word." *Pre/Text: The First Decade*, edited by Victor J. Vitanza, U of Pittsburgh P, 1993, pp. 158–62.

Thompson, Janna. "Identity and Obligation in a Transgenerational Polity." *Intergenerational Justice*, edited by Axel Gosseries and Lukas H. Meyer, Oxford UP, 2009, pp. 25–49.

Urick, Michael J. "Exploring Generational Identity: A Multiparadigm Approach." *Journal of Business Diversity*, vol. 12, no. 3, 2012.

Valentim, Joaquim Pires. "Sherif's Theoretical Concepts and Intergroup Relations Studies: Notes for a Positive Interdependence." *Psychologica*, vol. 52, no. 2, 2010, pp. 585–98.

Varkey, Basil. "Principles of Clinical Ethics and Their Application to Practice." *Medical Principles and Practice*, vol. 30, no. 1, 2021, pp. 17–28.

Varnum, Robin. "The History of Composition: Reclaiming Our Lost Generations." *Journal of Advanced Composition*, vol. 12, no. 1, 1992, pp. 39–55.

Vealey, Kyle P., and Nathaniel A. Rivers. "Dappled Discipline at Thirty: An Interview with Janice Lauer." *Rhetoric Review*, vol. 33, no. 2, 2014, pp. 165–80, http://dx.doi.org/10.1080/07350198.2014.884418.

Wang, Zhaoahe. "Too Green to Talk Disciplinarity." *Composition Studies*, vol. 49, no. 1, 2021, pp. 160–63.

Williams, Angie, and Jon F. Nussbaum. *Intergenerational Communication across the Life Span*. Routledge, 2001.

Woodward, Kathleen. "Inventing Generational Models: Psychoanalysis, Feminism, Literature." *Figuring Age: Women, Bodies, Generations*, edited by Kathleen Woodward, Indiana UP, 1999, pp. 149–68.

WPA-L Reimagining Working Group, and nextGEN Start Up Team. "Dialogue and Disciplinary Space." Where We Are. *Composition Studies*, vol. 47, no. 2, 2019, pp. 203–10.

Yancey, Kathleen Blake. "Notes on Intergenerational Exchange: The View from Here." *Composition Studies*, vol. 49, no. 1, pp. 164–69.

Renewing Commitments to Minoritized Writers

Ray Rosas and Cheryl Glenn

We are in the middle of an extraordinary social experiment: the attempt to provide education for all members of a vast pluralistic democracy. To have any prayer of success, we'll need . . . a philosophy of language and literacy that affirms the diverse sources of linguistic competence and deepens our understanding of the ways class and culture blind us to the richness of those sources.

—Mike Rose, *Lives on the Boundary*, 238

In the fifty-some years that *Composition Studies* [formerly *Freshman English News*] has been mapping our field, much attention has been given to so-called minoritized writers.[1] The initial analysis of minoritized writers in *Freshman English News*, for instance, was almost entirely framed by the construct of remediation—by what we teachers could do for "those" students. In her 1972 "Lessons from Experience: Teaching Minority Students," Susan Koprowski writes,

> The difference in teaching a remedial Freshman English course to educationally deprived white students and teaching the same material to Black and Chicano students may be calculated in terms of a single problem—attitude. Minority students can make the white instructor feel defensive, paralyzed by insecurity in dealing with what may be a fundamentally hostile class. (4)

The following year, William D. Lutz echoed Koprowski, framing the composition course as one of "survival" for minoritized students "because of the additional problems of culture and language differences" (4). Of course, both scholars were writing in response to the nationwide open-enrollment movement of the early 1970s, most famously researched by Mina Shaughnessy, whose 1977 *Errors and Expectations: A Guide for the Teachers of Basic Writing* heralded a new look at the status of so-called Basic Writers, most of whom, according to Shaughnessy, grew up in "one of New York's racial or ethnic enclaves" (3).[2] Since its publication, *Errors and Expectations* has been heavily critiqued, leading to more linguistically aware research that supports students' right to their own language (Baker-Bell; Canagarajah; Clark and Ivanic; Elbow; Gilyard; Horner and Lu; Inoue and Poe; Kynard; Lippi-Green; Milson-Whyte et al.; Paris; Perryman-Clark et al.; Rose; Richardson; Ruiz; Smitherman, and many others). Yet despite our field's awareness of language varieties and prejudice, Black and Latinx students continue to populate our professional imaginary as Basic Writers or as needing to be flagged in first year writing courses on the basis of "the skin that they speak" (Delpit). In short, as Jacqueline Jones Royster and Jean C. Williams so insightfully emphasized, our discipline has conflated students of color with basic writing, to position them as "non-universal outsiders" and "aliens to the traditions which other students lay claim" (569).

Such a perspective reflects the staying power of racism and whiteliness rather than any so-called student need(s). Renewing our field's commitment to minoritized students requires sustained attention—not to any perceived deficits on their part—but to the specific ways minoritized students are challenging this longstanding deficit model (and concomitant racism) to enact their writerly agency and thereby successfully pursue their own writing goals.

The Covid-19 Exigence

> Composition scholars should . . . strive to create pedagogies that . . . take . . . exclusionary practices into consideration.
>
> —Iris Ruiz, *Reclaiming Composition for Chicano/as and Other Ethnic Minorities*, 143

Academe is at the tipping point with regard to an authentic commitment to—and understanding of—minoritized undergraduates, starting during their first year. In addition to being flagged in their writing classes as needing correction and help, these students also regularly face other microaggressions (from peers and instructors alike), experience cultural isolation, and withstand repeated racism—especially at predominantly white institutions (PWIs), which too often lack *authentic*, culturally sensitive programming. Little wonder then that Black and Latinx students attain lower academic credentials than their white counterparts (U.S. Census Bureau, 2019). While 40.1% of white adults over the age of twenty-five have completed a bachelor's or higher degree, only 26.1% of Black and only 18.8% of Hispanic[3] adults have reached the same levels of education (U.S. Census Bureau, 2019). In addition, from Fall 2019 to Fall 2021 during the worst of the Covid-19 pandemic, Black enrollment in higher education declined by 12% while Latinx enrollments declined by 6.9% (National Student Clearing House). Within California's community college system, where more that 40% of students are Latinx, Latinx students account for nearly half of those who have left academe due to the pandemic (Brown).[4]

The preceding statistics paint a grim context for minoritized students, especially given the reverberations of Covid-19 in terms of employment, isolation, socially mediated communication, and educational inequity. The transition to remote learning, for instance, was particularly problematic for Black and Latinx students, who were more likely than their white peers to experience internet connectivity issues that affected academic participation and performance (Means and Neisler).[5] Yet these same students offer us models of engaged pedagogy that not only dispel the myth of the minoritized basic writer but spark a reconceptualization of our teacherly commitment, as we demonstrate in the following section.

Strategic Enactments of Writerly Agency as Excellence and Activism

> I love language. Language, to me, is what sunrise is to the birds.
>
> —Jimmy Santiago Baca, *Stories from the Edge*, 85

Despite the constraints of Covid and the multigenerational persistence of whiteliness in academe, Black and Latinx writers continue to carve space for excellence and activism. For example, Jada, a Black participant in Ray's dissertation research, is majoring in broadcast journalism and serves as the campus ambassador for prospective minority students. Despite the numbing regularity of microaggressions she experiences, Jada repeatedly writes and produces pieces that teach her peers and instructors alike about campus-wide racial hostility—her work is engaged pedagogy that distinguishes her from the white students in their PWI:

> I see my classmates doing fluff pieces . . . like the [football team] won this weekend. . . . But an unarmed Black man just got shot. . . . For me it's important to kind of show the things that people want to like ignore or want to like not pay as much attention to. Because of the white privilege my classmates have, they are able to overlook that and talk about what they want to talk about. I feel like I have an obligation to talk about the things that nobody wants to.[6]

In exerting her writerly agency and controlling some features of the racial narrative, Jada educates her readers about the racial reality of campus and beyond, successfully negotiating what Collin Craig calls the "cultures of insularity" that characterize PWIs and often alienate minoritized students. Yes, Jada sometimes feels alienated, isolated within a PWI, but her writing serves as a vehicle for Black advocacy, a sense of purpose, and a link to the broader Black community. She is a writer with a clear understanding of exigence, audience, context, and purpose. Jada is no basic writer—she is a writer with agency.

One feature of Jada's writerly agency is her deliberate rhetorical strategy at the level of syntax and grammar. In his discourse-based interviews[7] with Jada, Ray identified Jada's strategic shifts to the imperative mood[8] as her way of reminding her white professors that they are implicated in her critiques. For example, in concluding an essay that critiques "culture of poverty" tropes with respect to African American men, Jada writes: "Overall, when passing judgment on these victims, acknowledge the racist and discriminatory factors that have affected them." When asked if she would consider using a grammatical mood more consistent with the rest of the essay, Jada declined, stating she made this shift to help her mostly white readers see themselves in her demand that racism and discrimination be acknowledged as contributing factors to poverty and crime. The tacit knowledge informing her choice demonstrates Jada's keen awareness of the rhetorical situation—as well as some of the affordances—of writing while Black in white spaces.

Such agentive strategies occur across the full range of writing processes. For example, Alexandra, another undergraduate student in Ray's study, demonstrates how she uses a style of culturally informed prewriting (invention) in a way that might not resonate with a writing teacher at a PWI:

> *A lo loco* writing for me is like when I know I have to write something and, like, maybe I have a few ideas or maybe I don't, but that's the first step in my writing . . . kind of like a brainstorming in a sense . . . but I write everything that comes to mind.

In Puerto Rico, *a lo loco* indicates anything done wildly or with crazy abandon, sparking connotations of playful creativity—but such creativity leads to productivity only if the teacher gets out of the way. Decades ago, Peter Elbow admonished us that "freewriting must never be evaluated in any way; in fact, there must be no discussion or comment at all" (*Writing without Teachers* 4). Alexandra informed Ray that grounding herself in the ways of *la isla* allows her to claim her sense of belonging and writerly agency—despite her feelings of cultural isolation at a PWI.

Jada and Alexandra offer writerly experiences of rhetorical action, action rooted in a cultural-ethnic community within a PWI. Their writing processes are purposeful, agential, and didactic. Jada's self-sponsored, activist journalism that speaks "b(l)ack to institutional discourses" (Craig), and Alexandra's *a lo loco* embodies a purposeful writerly negotiation of context that evokes affective traces of the writer's community of belonging (Flower). In short, these two minoritized students know what they're doing—and why. Although the constraints might be considerable, both undergraduate writers are navigating issues of racialized expectations, personal purpose and resilience, and educational inequity within the context of a PWI.

Getting Demands of Whiteliness Out of the Way of Black and Latinx Excellence and Activism

> Caring teachers are . . . enlightened witnesses for our students. Since our task is to nurture their academic growth, we are called to serve them.
>
> —bell hooks, *Teaching Community*, 89

The senseless murders of George Floyd, Breonna Taylor, Philando Castile, Daunte Wright, Andre Hill, and many others—together with the Black Lives Matter movement—catalyzed universities across the nation to become more aware of minoritized students' experience with prejudice/racism, microaggression, and inequity. As communication scholars Karen Ashcraft and Brenda J. Allen observe, these murders created a climate where "readiness to 'take a knee' and declare that Black Lives Matter became a litmus test of organizational credibility, instead of a controversial stance" (598). Large-scale responses at PWIs include establishing social justice initiatives; Offices of Diversity, Equity, and Inclusion (DEI); and other such programs, always with the hope that such programs and centers will level the playing ground.

And on a smaller scale, compositionists are also attending to the inequities that have long been visible and practiced in our writing classrooms. Whether these enterprises culminate in mere image management or authentic implementation, the pivot from a kind of disciplinary obliviousness (success is linked to the acquisition of Edited American English) to one of recognition and respect for multiple ways of languaging is rarely seamless or smooth. Still, these large- and smaller-scale DEI initiatives have become a marker of institutional legitimacy. And such shifts in thinking are encouraging, even if DEI projects risk becoming "feel-good" schemes rather than indicators of a genuine antiracist telos. An open question, then, is whether DEI initiatives will facilitate or frustrate the educational arc of minoritized students. To ensure the former, DEI initiatives must include the voices and perspectives of minoritized students. After all, these students can provide first-hand accounts of which policies actually work for them and which do not, both at the level of individual strategies and institutional structures.

As Beatrice Méndez Newman reminds us, "Student voices are our best source for illuminating the obstacles" of education (20). Therefore, the payoff of listening to students, to asking them how they're navigating the academic terrain of a PWI, is considerable. With more nuanced understandings of how students experience, negotiate, and redefine academe along antiracist and more inclusive lines, university-wide and programmatic equity initiatives can become more focused, more malleable, more successful.

Authentically Renewing Our Commitment

> Commitment to engaged pedagogy carries with it the willingness to be responsible, not to pretend that professors do not have the power to change the direction of our students' lives.
>
> —bell hooks, *Teaching to Transgress: Education as the Practice of Freedom*, 206

The writers in Ray's study evince rhetorical strategies and tacit knowledges that account for the racial dynamics of context. That is, they plan and compose arguments in ways that educate white audiences (peers and instructors alike) about racially motivated violence and everyday racism. These students tap into familiar resources from their communities of belonging, and in ways that promote their self-efficacy, demonstrating day after day their rhetorical qualifications for belonging at a PWI, often going beyond mere requirements to earn the admiration and respect of their instructors and peers. In other words, the participants in Ray's study handily challenge deficit models of "the other" in composition studies via their strategic enactments of writerly agency, all the while negotiating and redefining contexts of academe along antiracist lines.

We can continue to recommit—and learn from—these students when we get our whiteliness out of the way. As the preceding epigraph from the late bell hooks suggests, renewing our academic commitment means taking responsibility for what is humanly possible on our campuses and in our writing classrooms. We can start with getting our whiteliness out of the way, listening to—and learning from our students. We still have much to learn.

Notes

1. This essay represents just a narrow slice of Ray's dissertation project on the writerly strategies and agency of minoritized writers in PWIs.

2. For many compositionists, Shaughnessy's error-awareness scholarship overshadowed the language-awareness scholarship of Geneva Smitherman, whose *Talkin and Testifyin: The Language of Black America* also appeared in 1977.

3. The U.S. Census Bureau uses the term "Hispanic."

4. According to the National Student Clearing House, there was an 8% drop in overall enrollments across the U.S. during the pandemic, with community colleges losing 15% of their students, with Native American students the most negatively affected.

5. According to Barbara Means and Julie Neisler, the rates of internet connectivity issues affecting academic participation were 17%among Black students, 23% among Latinx students, and 12% among white students.

6. This excerpt comes from an IRB-approved study exploring how Black and Latinx undergraduates use writing to pursue goals in the context of a mid-Atlantic PWI. IRB#: 18058. In this study, Ray is working with Black and Latinx undergraduates at a PWI.

7. See Lee Odell, Dixie Goswami, and Anne Herrington.

8. With its second-person subject, "you," either implied or stated.

Works Cited

Ashcraft, Karen Lee, and Brenda J. Allen. "When Words Come to Matter: A Statement on Statements." *Management Communication Quarterly*, vol. 34, no. 4, Nov. 2020, pp. 597–603.

Baca, Jimmy Santiago. *Stories From the Edge*. Heinemann, 2010.

Baker-Bell, April. *Linguistic Justice: Black Language, Literacy, Identity, and Pedagogy*. NCTE-Routledge, 2020.

Brown, Sarah. "The Missing Hispanic Students: Higher Ed's Future, and the Economy, Depends on Their Coming Back to College." *The Chronicle of Higher Education,* 11 Feb. 2022.

Canagarajah, A. Suresh. *A Geopolitics of Academic Writing*. University of Pittsburgh Press, 2002.

—. *Resisting Linguistic Imperialism in English Teaching*. Oxford UP, 1999.

Clark, Romy and Roz Ivanič. *The Politics of Writing*. Routledge, 1997.

Craig, Collin. "Speaking from Different Positions: Framing African American College Male Literacies as Institutional Critique." *Composition Forum*, vol. 30, 2014.

Delpit, Lisa, and Joanne Kilgour Dowdy, editors. *The Skin That We Speak: Thoughts on Language and Culture in the Classroom*. The New Press, 2008.

"Educational Attainment in the United States: 2019." United States Census Bureau, 2019, https://www.census.gov/content/census/en/data/tables/2019/demo/educational-attainment/cps-detailed-tables.html

Elbow, Peter. *Writing Without Teachers*. Oxford UP, 1998.

—. *Vernacular Eloquence: What Speech Can Bring to Writing*. Oxford UP, 2012.

Flower, Linda. *The Construction of Negotiated Meaning: A Social Cognitive Theory of Writing*. Southern Illinois UP, 1994.

Gilyard, Keith. *Voices of the Self: A Study of Language Competence*. Wayne State UP, 1991.

—. *Race, Rhetoric, and Composition*. Boynton/Cook, 1999.

hooks, bell. *Teaching Community: A Pedagogy of Hope*. Routledge, 2003.

—. *Teaching to Transgress: Education as the Practice of Freedom*. Routledge, 1994.

Horner, Bruce and Min-Zhan Lu. *Representing the "Other": Basic Writers and the Teaching of Basic Writing*. NCTE Press, 1999.

Inoue, Asao B., and Mya Poe. *Race and Writing Assessment*. P. Lang, 2012.

Koprowski, Susan. "Lessons From Experience: Teaching Minority Students." *Freshman English News*, vol. 1, no. 2, 1972, p. 4.

Kynard, Carmen. *Vernacular Insurrections: Race, Black Protest, and the New Century in Composition-Literacies Studies.* State University of New York Press, 2013.

Lippi-Green, Rosina. *English with an Accent: Language, Ideology and Discrimination in the United States.* Taylor & Francis Group, 2011.

Lutz, William D. "Teaching Minority Students: Some Additional Comments." *Freshman English News*, vol. 1, no. 3, 1973, pp. 4-9.

Means, Barbara, and Julie Neisler with Langer Research Associates. *Suddenly Online: A National Survey of Undergraduates During the COVID-19 Pandemic.* Digital Promise, 2020.

Méndez Newman, Beatrice. "Teaching Writing at Hispanic-Serving Institutions." *Teaching Writing with Latino/a Students: Lessons Learned at Hispanic-Serving Institutions*, edited by Cristina Kirklighter, Diana Cárdenas, and Susan W. Murphy. State University of New York Press, 2007, pp. 17-36.

Milson-Whyte, Vivette, et al., editors. *Creole Composition: Academic Writing and Rhetoric in the Anglophone Caribbean.* Parlor Press, 2019.

Odell, Lee, et al. "The discourse-based interview: A Procedure for Exploring the Tacit Knowledge of Writers in Nonacademic Settings." *Research on Writing: Principles and Methods*, edited by Peter Mosenthal, Lynne Tamor, and Sean A. Walmsley, Longman, 1983, pp. 220-234.

Paris, Django. *Language across Difference: Ethnicity, Communication, and Youth Identities in Changing Urban Schools.* Cambridge UP, 2011.

Perryman-Clark, Staci, et al, editors. *Students' Right to Their Own Language: A Critical Sourcebook.* Bedford/St. Martin's, 2014.

Richardson, Elaine. *African American Literacies.* Taylor & Francis Group, 2002.

Rose, Mike. *Lives on the Boundary: The Struggles and Achievements of America's Underprepared.* Free Press, 1989.

Royster, Jacqueline J., and Jean C. Williams. "History in the Spaces Left: African American Presence and Narratives of Composition Studies." *College Composition and Communication*, vol. 50, no. 4, 1999, pp. 563-584.

Ruiz, Iris D. *Reclaiming Composition for Chicano/as and Other Ethnic Minorities: A Critical History and Pedagogy.* Palgrave Macmillan, 2016.

Shaughnessy, Mina P. *Errors and Expectations: A Guide for the Teacher of Basic Writing.* Oxford UP, 1977.

Smitherman, Geneva. *Talkin and Testifyin: The Language of Black America.* Houghton Mifflin, 1977.

"Updates on Higher Education Enrolment." National Student Clearing House Research Center, 2021, https://nscresearchcenter.org/stay-informed/

In Search of the Sentence

Hannah J. Rule

In 2017, I published "Sensing the Sentence: An Embodied Simulation Approach to Rhetorical Grammar" in volume 45, issue 1 of *Composition Studies* (*CS*). At its core, the essay calls attention to the dimension and life of languaging—my often preferred, present participle non-word that emphasizes writing as action. In the essay, I explore embodied simulation, a concept that I found game-changing to conceptualizing composing and to teaching at the sentence-level. Embodied simulation, a linguistic-meets-neuroscience theory, suggests in short that we make meaning through language by imagining in our mind's eye and body what it would be like to experience that which the language describes.

Grounded in empirical demonstration, embodied simulation gives name to the material work words do, seeing languaging through 3-D (better 4-D) glasses—as dimensional, spatial, moving, visual, aural, imagistic, connotative, and so on. In other words, embodied simulation sees a sentence as a "dynamic embodied space" (Rule 22). As such and as I argued, this concept and its research has implications for writing instruction, representing the "transformative pedagogical power of emphasizing that words and sentences comprise literal action—language moves us, maps spaces, and makes us see and feel things in myriad and idiosyncratic ways" (Rule 24). Practicing simulation with my writing students—that is, stimulating and sharing with each other the varied sensations language and its structures evokes in us—opens access to sentence style interventions for learners that would otherwise rely on identification of structures and terminology. Writers can begin to sense the varied effects of modulating syntax and style, rather than try to follow a handbook's potentially inscrutable instructions and dictates.

I still wonder today if composition thinks much about the sentence. As I discuss in "Sensing," the sentence remains largely absent or at least uninteresting territory in the discourse of writing instruction (excepting perhaps contexts like the upper-division rhetorical grammar course I describe in the *CS* article or maybe the complex intellectual work of multilingual writing). The sentence is at the very least largely beside the point, a vestige of current-traditional formalism perhaps. Or worst of all, the sentence quickly becomes the domain of racist and classist domination, never not flying the flags of Mainstream White English (Baker-Bell 8), wielded as an invisible and punitive "norm" (reason enough to push the sentence underground). Ultimately, writing is more than sentences, I think we feel: it's expression, identity, language(s); it's thinking, discovery, communication; it's global concerns first (and, maybe in practice, only).

But, at the same time, I can't escape the idea that writing is also only sentences, never not sentences. And by sentences, I don't mean something official or one dialect model enforced as the "Standard." I just mean something like bits of languaging. I mean all fragments, or some other often-deemed violation of sentence "rules." I also mean languaging where words are ☺ or <3 and may or may not use punctuation I mean beautiful and inescapable collisions of multiple dialects and discourses. I mean sentences as fundamentally and only ever deviations on dynamic social forms, never forms themselves. Sentences are just units of languaging. Writing's smallest bites. Making sentences is how one makes their way in writing—by sentencing, by the forming or forging of meaning.

I can muse on, maybe even poeticize, the sentence; but I also must admit that sentences scare me. I'm not comfortable within their geography; I'm not a grammarian (though I admire those who are—not the judgy ones, just those who can see and name the various scaffolding that make sentences work). Sentences are always getting away from me. So, I'm wondering: why sensing the sentence? What was I after? (I know in part what I wanted to disrupt: that a sentence is math that can be "correct" or worse "proper." No.) On the same hand, I wonder: do other compositionists long for the sentence? Can I find the sentence in the archives of *Composition Studies*?

***

I found Winston Weathers before I knew I was looking for the sentence. I didn't find it there, not exactly. Nevertheless, here's how Weathers opens his 1976 article, "Grammar of Style: New Options in Composition" in the two-column, teeny font design of volume 4 of what was then *Freshman English News*:

> Words on paper/ one of the ways I—the human being—communicate. There are all the other ways, of course. Talking. Gesturing. Moving my body. Costuming my flesh. Participating in events 'out there'/ in observable actions. (1)

What are these slashes, I wonder. Are they meant to signal poetry? How very 1976, I presume. Also filed under "very 1976," Weathers' article actually begins with an italicized statement explaining that the lines I quote above (and continue below) are not his own but are rather "found" by Weathers "[a]mong the scattered papers of the late Professor X" (1)—a signal straightaway of the performative and playful powers of composing that Weathers champions throughout this piece. I am struck too by that first phrase: words on paper. How simple but profound. Weathers (or "Professor X" or whomever authored these lines!) goes on:

> But tremendously important always/ words on paper/ the string of words in the code of written language, effecting the composition—the "thing made"/ the verbal artifact—that I transmit to others for them to negotiate into the miracle of understanding what it is/ has been inside the otherwise inaccessible regions of my very human, mysterious brain. (1)

I circle and star "miracle." Weathers is speaking to me. Aren't sentences magic? I note too how I could nudge him, with an embodied simulation perspective, to see those "other ways" of communicating mentioned—gesturing, moving, bodily action "out there"—as not so separate finally from "words on paper."

Weathers never says "sentence." (Not really, though he does embrace the "Sentence Fragment" (12) as a valuable compositional option.) More so he's hoping to convince us of the limits of what he calls "Grammar A": "the well-made box" (1) emphasized in conventional writing instruction, which values "continuity, order, reasonable progression and sequence, consistency, unity, etc." (2). He wants alternatives, a "Grammar B" and its "maneuvers" like crots—short, discrete units of composition not unlike a collection of aphorisms (12); the list (13); or the montage/collage (15). Weathers implores us writing teachers to recognize that conventional college compositions represent just one little part of the things writing can do (17). He begs us to make options available (a tenet of rhetorical grammarians), because "If we'd spend less time trying to 'protect' the language from 'misuse,' and spend more time opening our own minds to all the things that language can do and is doing, we'd be better off" (18). Indeed. A sentiment that bears repeating 46 years later.

***

Irvin Hashimoto (or, as he's identified in the 1993 first issue of volume 21 of *Composition Studies*, "I. Hashimoto") does say sentence. In "Sentence Variety: Where Theory and Practice Meet and Lose," Hashimoto fillets the familiar and still repeated edict that sentence variety is an enduring good for the health of all prose and the sake of all readers. He blasts onto the page as an impassioned and raucous pedagogical persona (a voice that surprised me, one I didn't realize we were sorely missing in our journals today). Poking skeptical, good-natured fun at the surety with which we prize sentence variation, Hashimoto quips about a passage from the "ponderously famous Kenneth Burke" that bogs "his life (and ours) down with abstracted nouns and prepositions and lots of variety" (67). Hashimoto observes too that Henry James' variety makes "graduate students sweat" (68), while compositionists' sentences in our academic journals "bulge with disappointing variety and overweight prose" (68). Enacting their advice literally, Hashimoto also demonstrates how textbooks can rather stupidly insist that variety is noble in itself. How can we be eternally sure of this evaluation, Hashimoto provokes us to ask.

Beware the hubris of the writing teacher: this seems to be Hashimoto's angle on the variety mantra. He doesn't aim to nuance our understanding of this edict as much as question why the writing teacher would pursue edicts at all. Hashimoto demands that we consider the perceptions of students, who he says will likely see through our "stupid boring drills and resent looking at boring, trumped up examples of sentence problems" (77). In the teaching of writing as languaging, we must be willing to admit that "rules are sorta variable" (76).

If I'm trying to find the sentence, in some ways, Hashimoto's rip-roaring takedown of sentence-level lore is what I expected to find (more of). He makes a good case for why we might want to steer clear of sentence instruction altogether. How can we really capture the sentence, or a set of them, long or sufficiently enough to confidently evaluate their architecture? One way to avoid the question in the first place, he implies, is by putting the student (the reader/writer) at the center. Show students that variety isn't a stable good in itself but that gaining access to the infinity of (sentence) options, to bring it back to Weathers, maybe is.

***

My search for the sentence in the 50 years of *Composition Studies* lastly yielded a kind of uncanny mirror in Peter Wayne Moe's 2018 "Inhabiting Ordinary Sentences" (45.2). Naming the sentence "this most fundamental unit of writing" (80), Moe is interested in how student writers "inhabit" (79) everyday "worker" sentences (91) as spaces that position them in discourse and, by extension, in relation to others and to other discourses. That is, the sentence for Moe is "discourse located" (80), "[e]nabl[ing] a writer to speak from a location, to place words and ideas and people in relation to each other" (91). Akin to Hashimoto, Moe turns to the sentence ultimately to vouch for the student writer and their everyday writing. Student sentences are rarely if ever a part of guides or handbooks, Moe observes, crowded out by the exceptional in terms of persona (famous, big name writers), setting (artistic/literary, published), or style (extraordinary, flair!). But there is much to learn from the routine sentence, even the simple use of an adverb (83). Curating student example sentences with moves that Moe refers to as the "And and "But"; "The Pivot"; or "The Parenthetical Aside," Moe uncovers the complex rhetorical action that propels everyday prose (85-87).

It's in the routine, after all, where writers' basic and yet critically essential decisions happen. Moe illustrates this notion elegantly with his discussion of the "Subject and Predicates" move (84). In a set of sentences from a response essay to Anzaldúa's "How to Tame a Wild Tongue," Moe observes how the student writer repetitiously puts themselves (the "I") in the subject position until—eventually—they yield it to Anzaldúa (and in turn push themselves into the object position). One literally staged in the most basic of grammatical options, Moe describes this as a textual "conversation/confrontation" (85) between writer and textual interlocutor. Indeed, who or what takes a sentence's subject position is always a matter of focus—and often a matter of ethics. How powerful for writers, and their teachers, to connect to this most foundational work of ordinary sentence space.

***

If *CS* readers access my essay, or Moe's or Hashimoto's, I wonder what it is they're looking for. I wonder if they're in search of the sentence and if so, what they expect or want to find. For one, I hope they're looking for the creational, not the corrective (Anderson 34). I hope they wish to nurture the spirit of "Professor X": an abiding interest in the "miracle" of sentences, in writing's infinity of options and its uncanny capacities to "transmit the otherwise inaccessible" (Weathers 1).

For fifty years of this journal, the approximate span of our time as a "professional discipline," there isn't much fuss about sentences—as far at least as I could see. I think this makes sense. But it's also maybe a missed opportunity. Part of what I wanted when I wrote "Sensing" was a nonmechanical and sensory way into sentences. I wanted us to privilege, at the core of everything, experiential connections to what words do and do to us. But I now also think I want something bigger and more basic than that. What I want is reverence. Behold the creational power of the littlest bite of languaging. A sentence is a world, one of human invention, a force that makes something where there wasn't before. It's that reverence I want to observe, not for the exceptionally or complexly crafted but the regular old sentence, those we "encounter day after day, week after week, year after year, as both teacher and student" (Moe 83).

Aren't sentences magic?

Works Cited

Anderson, Jeff. "Zooming in and Zooming out: Putting Grammar in Context into Context." *English Journal*, vol. 95, no. 5, 2006, pp. 28-34.

Baker-Bell, April. "We Been Knowin: Toward an Antiracist Language & Literacy Education." *Journal of Language and Literacy Education*, vol. 16, no. 1, 2020, pp. 1-12.

Hashimoto, I. "Sentence Variety: Where Theory and Practice Meet and Lose." *Composition Studies*, vol. 21, no. 1, 1993, pp. 66-77.

Rule, Hannah J. "Sensing the Sentence: An Embodied Simulation Approach to Rhetorical Grammar." *Composition Studies,* vol. 45, no. 1, 2017, pp. 19–38.

Moe, Peter Wayne. "Inhabiting Ordinary Sentences." *Composition Studies,* vol. 46, no. 2, 2018, pp. 79-85.

Weathers, Winston. "Grammars of Style: New Options in Composition." *Freshman English News*, vol. 4, no. 3, 1976, pp. 1-18.

Where We Are: What's Next for (Publishing in) Composition & Rhetoric?

Pushing Through: Moving Beyond Revision to Achieve Substantive Change

Sheila Carter-Tod

What if this darkness is not the darkness of the tomb, but the darkness of the womb?

What if our America is not dead but a country still waiting to be born? What if the story of America is one long labor?

What if all the mothers who came before us, who survived genocide and occupation, slavery and Jim Crow, racism and xenophobia and Islamophobia, political oppression and sexual assault, are standing behind us now, whispering in our ear: You are brave? What if this is our Great Contraction before we birth a new future?

Remember the wisdom of the midwife: "Breathe," she says. Then: "Push."

Now it is time to breathe. But soon it will be time to push; soon it will be time to fight — for those we love — Muslim father, Sikh son, trans daughter, indigenous brother, immigrant sister, white worker, the poor and forgotten, and the ones who cast their vote out of resentment and fear.

—Valarie Kaur, *See No Stranger:
A Memoir and Manifesto of Revolutionary Love*, xiii

As part of the "Where We Are" segment of this anniversary issue, we were asked to contemplate what's next for the discipline and the journal. Before contemplating such a concept disciplinarily or even from the perspective of *Composition Studies*—as an African American female in the United States, in higher education, and in the discipline—I can't help but consider all of the darkness and the labor I and others like me experience nationally, institutionally, and disciplinarily. Any reflection draws my thoughts back to the latest news reports on the ways in which an extremely flawed legal system attempts to hold perpetrators accountable for the racial violence against African American men, women, and children. I also must consider the structures and systems that reinscribe racist practices in higher education institutionally and disciplinarily. Each act of violence, be it overt or covert, is a symptom of darkness that needs to be disrupted, reimagined, and recreated for any real substantive change.

Recent news articles bear witness to the darkness of a racist legal and justice system. News of convictions and acquittals illustrate situational adaptations or accountability. Most recently, a March 2022 article describes how "three white men in Georgia were convicted for committing a hate crime when they murdered Ahmaud Arbery, a 25-year-old Black man jogging in their neighborhood." The article describes how "[d]ays later, three former Minneapolis police officers were convicted of violating George Floyd's civil rights when he died in their custody, a death that previously led to a murder conviction for a fourth officer . . . [and how] in nearby Brooklyn Center, Minnesota, a police officer was convicted of causing the death of Daunte Wright when she mistook her gun for a Taser" (Carrega). But such systemic racist structures, as they exist, can only provide limited situational equity and justice. The darkness and the labor within these systems remains. Earlier headlines described how Brett Hankison, the ex-Louisville police officer who shot and killed Breonna Taylor, was acquitted. And yet another March Associated Press article describes how "[n]o charges will be filed against the Chicago police officers who chased and fatally shot 13-year-old Adam Toledo and 22-year-old Anthony Alvarez within days of each other last year, prompting sharp criticism of how the department handles foot pursuits, a prosecutor announced Tuesday" (Burnett and Babwin). While the aforementioned cases that did end in conviction provide some justice, the other acquittals simply reiterate what we know hasn't changed, and that is the deeply embedded systemic inequities when it comes to race, policing, and the US legal system.

Much like the legal system, the institutions of higher education in which we work are founded on, and in many cases continue to function within, practices and policies that are deeply rooted in the darkness of systemic racist structures. It is therefore not surprising that we see the same darkness in incidents of violence against African American and other students and faculty of color, all with similarly uneven patterns of accountability. *The Journal of Blacks in Higher Education* (JBHE) keeps a running tab of events, illustrative of the darkness in institutions of higher education. From the many bomb threats faced by HBCUs after the return from winter break to "Racist Graffiti Found on the Campus of Curry College in Milton, Massachusetts," to the "[p]eople dressed up in Ku Klux Klan outfits [who] were seen in a residential hall at the

University of Utah trying to recruit students for a white supremacist group," violence against African Americans and other people of color has been handled with varying degrees (if any) of justice.[1] These headlines still exist. Even with on-going Diversity and Equity initiatives in higher education, deeply embedded institutionalized systems of inequities remain the same without fundamental disruption and recreation.

Now, turning to a focused reflection on the previous half-century of *Composition Studies*, I have to consider how all academic journals inhabit a space situated in the concentric circles of national racism, racism within racist institutions of higher education, and then in the much smaller contained circle of our discipline. Contributing scholars, editors, and reviewers of academic journals within writing studies struggle to find a way to navigate these spaces in an equitable way. While I could easily note that historically, as a journal, *Composition Studies* has pursued institutionalized means of equity through author representation, diverse subjects, position statements of allyship, scholarly coverage, and content that both illustrates and challenges the existing inequitable structures and practices (both disciplinarily and nationally), I have to question whether, moving forward, these same methods will be effective in justly and equitably representing and navigating the "range of professional practices associated with rhetoric and composition: teaching college writing; theorizing rhetoric and composing; administering writing related programs; preparing the field's future teacher-scholars."[2]

Perhaps, at the specific juncture provided by a fifty-year reflection, questions of what is next may lie in a full recreation of the existing structures that have historically constituted the makeup and goals of academic journals. If, historically, the roles of scholarly publications are to disseminate expert knowledge to other experts in the discipline and to a serve as a platform for researchers to reveal their knowledge to one another, allowing them to contribute to the development and design of the field, then pushing forward may mean reconsidering what a journal is and what it could be. Is it enough to capture what is happening within the discipline's "research" for dissemination to others within—and entering—the discipline without reflectively considering what such a journal might look like if it sought to fully disrupt traditional concepts of knowledge, knowledge dissemination, and audience? What would happen if *Composition Studies*, with such a high disciplinary profile and such exclusive acceptance rates, actively redefined what the roles and possibilities of an academic journal might be? What if concerns around traditional, exclusive concepts of rigor and status were set aside to envision what a new definition of academic journal might look like—beyond representation and timely encounters with larger systemic issues?

As is the case when there is a call for any radical disruption in practices, by a product of institutionalized systems that places values on the perpetuation of existing structures, those objecting may see such a disruption as too radical or ultimately leading to the demise of the journal's recognition and reputation in publication circles and larger scholarly debates. What I am suggesting is that moving forward, *Composition Studies* as a journal lead our disciplinary disruption, pushing through what has been done and reimagining what could be done to address larger national and institutionalized systems of inequities and exclusion.

For *Composition Studies*, pushing through practices seen as traditional to academic journals would be a radical extension of what they have been pushing to do for years and would heed the calls for even more disruptions in publishing practices. We see one such call in the 2021 "Anti-Racist Scholarly Reviewing Practices: A Heuristic for Editors, Reviewers, and Authors,"[3] which in its very creation reviewed and responded to challenges made by Angela Haas in her 2020 ATTW "Call to Action to Redress Anti-Blackness and White Supremacy" and Miriam Williams and Natasha Jones in their 2020 blog post, "A Just Use of Imagination," to address racist, inequitable and exclusionary practices in technical and professional communications. The introduction to "Anti-Racist Scholarly Reviewing Practices" acknowledges the need for journals to lead in the changing nature of publication and disciplinary practices and "invite[s] active feedback, revision, and work to keep [even the guiding document that they have created] up-to-date to account for additional scenarios and perspectives" (2). Grounded in Ibram X. Kendi's concepts of anti-racism in policies and ideas as described in his book *How to be an Anti-Racist* (specifically the first chapter), the authors of the heuristic acknowledge that there is no neutral or non-racist position and present "explicit guidance on anti-racist professional practices in the form of a heuristic for editors, reviewers, and authors involved in academic reviewing" (2). In their heuristic, they say that what editors and reviewers will need to do is to "recognize a range of expertise and encourage citation practices that represent diverse canons, epistemological foundations, and ways of knowing; [r]ecognize, intervene in and/or prevent harmful scholarly work—both in publication processes and in published scholarship; [e]stablish and state clear but flexible contingency plans for review processes that prioritize humanity over production; [m]ake the review process transparent; [v]alue the labor of those involved in the review process; [and…] commit to inclusivity among reviewers and in editorial board makeup" (7-9).

While *Composition Studies* has consciously pushed towards epistemologically inclusive practices when it comes to content, established structures to make review processes clear and transparent, and actively worked to create an inclusive editorial board and set of practices,[4] this 50-year anniversary reflection on what comes next should begin with the guidance of the aforementioned heuristic moving to push through any existing practices that can't be fixed and are beyond revision. Moving forward, *Composition Studies* as a journal can and should continue to and find new ways to push, then breathe then push again, to reinvent what the roles and practices of a journal could be and do in achieving substantive disciplinary change.

Notes

1. These headlines are taken from *The Journal of Blacks in Higher Education* (JBHE). The JBHE, dedicated to the conscientious investigation of the status and prospects for African Americans in higher education, provides racial statistics on an institution-by-institution basis.

2. https://compstudiesjournal.com.

3. To acknowledge the labor involved in this document, I am including the contributing authors. As stated in the document, contributors include Lauren E. Cagle, Michelle F. Eble, Laura Gonzales, Meredith A. Johnson, Nathan R. Johnson, Natasha N. Jones, Liz Lane, Temptaous Mckoy, Kristen R. Moore, Ricky Reynoso, Emma J. Rose, GPat Patterson, Fernando Sánchez, Ann Shivers-McNair, Michele Simmons, Erica M. Stone, Jason Tham, Rebecca Walton, and Miriam F. Williams.

4. Most recently, *Composition Studies* released the "Guide for Anti-Racist Scholarly Reviewing Practices at *Composition Studies*" for editorial board members to review, revise, and ultimately vote on.

Works Cited

"Anti-racist Scholarly Reviewing Practices: A Heuristic for Editors, Reviewers, and Authors." 2021. Retrieved from https://tinyurl.com/reviewheuristic.

Burnett, Sara, and Don Babwin. "No Charges against 2 Chicago Officers in Fatal Shootings." *US News and World Report*, 15 Mar. 2022, https://www.usnews.com/news/us/articles/2022-03-15/no-charges-against-2-chicago-officers-in-fatal-shootings.

Carrega, Christina. "What's Behind the Wave of Convictions for Police and Vigilantes? It's More Than Woke Jurors." *Capital B*, 10 Mar. 2022, https://capitalbnews.org/police-shooting-convictions-floyd-arbery/. Accessed 17 Mar. 2022.

Jones, Natasha N., and Miriam F. Williams. "The Just Use of Imagination: A Call to Action." *Association of Teachers of Technical Writing*, 26 June 2020, https://attw.org/blog/the-just-use-of-imagination-a-call-to-action/.

Kaur, Valarie. *See No Stranger: A Memoir and Manifesto of Revolutionary Love*. One World, 2021.

Kendi, Ibram X. *How to Be an Antiracist*. Bodley Head, 2019.

Speculative Middles and *Composition Studies* at 50

Jennifer Clary-Lemon

When I was asked to reflect on the 50th anniversary of *Composition Studies*, I didn't realize that, really, I'd be reflecting on a relationship that spans nearly half of my life and almost all of my professional life. In 2000, as an MA student at DePaul University, I was an editorial assistant for *CS* under Peter Vandenberg. Because of that experience, I wound up writing my dissertation on the role of scholarly journals in shaping discourses of identity. In 2010, I took on the role of Editor of *CS* before it moved on to Laura Micciche's editorship. As anyone who has ever taken on editorial roles with a journal might know, even when you are finished with the day-to-day job, the journal itself stays on in your psyche—an old friend, a familiar read. As time moves on and new editors make their own choices and new scholarship emerges, it forms itself again in your mind—each new issue a mark on a landscape, much the way a sapling makes its way as a member of a larger family of trees and scrub in a forest. There is never a static moment, frozen in time. We are always in the middle of things.

To that end, this reflection is really a reflection on the tension between old and new, between tree and forest as *CS* makes its way towards 50. It is in these between spaces that I see the real contribution that *CS* makes on the landscape of rhetoric and writing studies. To be in this now, we are both looking back and looking forward. We might consider moments like these, as Springgay and Truman do, the "speculative middles" prompted by an attunement to "activating problems and concepts in the midst of the event" (5), to think of what we know in this in-between as both already planned (as the history of the journal laid out by its archives tells us) and at the same time, exploratory (imagining *CS*'s future). When I think about the speculative middles of *CS*, I am drawn toward thinking about problems: the problems facing this small journal in particular, and the problems facing all of us in the field. The tensions between these problems seem to me to point to what the journal has always done well, as well as pointing attention to where it may continue to intervene to help make all of our working lives, and our teaching lives, better.

When I was doing historiographic archival work for my own dissertation, one of the places that drew my attention to the shape of the field through its journals was through publication of special issues; notably, in most of the field's largest journal publications. This kind of activity privileged identity-based rhetoric and was grouped in the mid-seventies (especially for women), the nineties (particularly for people of color and members of LGBTQ communities), and the early millennium (markedly for class and disability-based rhetorics) (see Clary-Lemon). The special issue was a way to make sense of both pressing issues of the moment as well as to give journals a sense of identity—to show what they themselves considered valuable sites of knowledge. When I turn to the archives of *Composition Studies/FEN*, I see these patterns play out as well, tending to poles of both the familiar and the new. On the one hand, the journal signals what has always been important to its readers with its choice of special issues: namely, the ways that we teach and theorize writing and the contexts by which we sustain new approaches to it. Its first special issue in 1995 was one on doctoral education; the next, almost ten years later, "Composition in the Small College" in 2004. Throughout the millennium, *CS* focused on both looking backwards in history (with a special issue "On 1963" in 2008) and forwards into new programmatic and generic spaces, with issues on the writing major (2007), and later, comics and multimodality (2015). On the other hand, *CS* shows with its special issues its commitment to widening the scope of why writing matters, and for whom: for women (in 2011), for multilingual and translingual writers and teachers (2016), and for all of us concerned with equity and access (2020). When I turn to *CS*'s most recent special issue, "Diversity Is Not Justice: Working Toward Radical Transformation and Racial Equity in the Discipline" (2021), I see a journal that is facing both its past and future, proffering critiques of the field's past and present—particularly its investments in academic "whitestreaming" —and moving towards a more equitable discipline that honors and supports Black and Indigenous faculty and students, notably by providing alternative models of knowledge making (Taczak and Davis 10).

When I look at this small sampling of *punctum* that special issues reveal about this journal, I see the problems and the opportunities that it has always had. The pressure of being a small, independent publishing space when so many other venues for scholarship are being amalgamated into large, for-profit publishing houses means that it has had the freedom to hold its care for writing practices with its care for equity. It remains one of the few of the field's journals dedicated to writing theory and practice; to that end, it has maintained over its lifetime a dedication to invitation—both for new scholars and for those who are more established. Yet *CS*, like most venues for scholarship in the academy, is a place that has for a long time been marked by whiteness and privilege. In its 50$^\text{th}$ year, *CS* might mark a turning point for scholarship that can build on its history, care for its most vulnerable, and infuse a field with answers to speculative middles.

In 1974, Richard Coe wrote an award-winning essay about the future of the discipline, "Rhetoric 2001," for *Composition Studies*. In it, he says, "Western culture especially has a pathological tendency to look only at the parts, to not see the forest for the trees" (9). He critiques logics that ignore the whole, arguing that we can—and must—do better to resist this kind of compartmentalizing when we teach writing. In 2022, nearly 50 years after Coe wrote his futuristic piece for the field, you might say we are still struggling with this same tension. From the speculative middles, perhaps we can see all the parts, forest and trees—commitments to writing and teaching writing, commitments to upending the white academy, commitments to keeping knowledge-spaces not-for-profit—as the whole body of work of the field, rather than discrete parts. As Coe notes, "the organism that 'wins against' its environment becomes extinct" (9). Perhaps, in gathering our commitments together holistically, we can be mindful of those environments that show us the seeds in our hands and the earth under our feet. We might, then, turn our face up to the shade and know better the woods that we navigate.

Works Cited

Clary-Lemon, Jennifer. *The Rhetoric of Identity: Scholarly Journals as Sites of Change, 1939-2004.* 2006. Arizona State University, PhD Dissertation.

Coe, Richard. "Rhetoric 2001." *Freshman English News* vol. 3, no. 1, Spring 1974, pp. 1-13.

Springgay, Stephanie, and Sarah E. Truman. "On the Need for Methods Beyond Proceduralism: Speculative Middles, (In) Tensions, and Response-Ability in Research." *Qualitative Inquiry* vol. 24, no. 3, 2018, pp. 1-12.

Taczak, Kara, and Matt Davis. "From the Editors: 2021, In Words." *Composition Studies*, vol. 49, no. 3, 2021, pp. 8-13.

Anti-Racist Futures for Publishing in Rhetoric and Composition

Christina M. LaVecchia

When I think about where we are (and will be) as a discipline, I think about what and who we publish. For me, this particular story starts with the field's most prominent listerv, once known as the WPA-L, which has had a long history of delivering high volumes of mundane activity into email inboxes (calls for papers, job listings, requests for resources or advice), punctuated by the occasional firestorm of controversy. In spring 2019, a particularly strong conflict erupted in response to Asao Inoue's CCCC chair's address about White language supremacy in writing programs (Flaherty). Exchanges on the listserv soon laid bare the reality that the list had long been a space in which Black, Indigenous, and people of color (BIPOC) in the field did not feel welcome and, moreover, revealed how inequities in the broader field's norms around knowledge creation have contributed to the erasure of diverse ways of knowing and making. That is, the conversation—particularly in the backchannels like #WPAlistservfeministrevolution that spilled out onto Twitter and Facebook—soon centered on the overwhelming Whiteness and male-ness of our field's publications and citations.

I remember watching this conversation play out and feeling a hinge point, a real coalescence of energy around the goal of re-seeing and undoing some of the exclusions of our field's knowledge creation practices. For too long these inequities have been felt by those excluded from the table but underacknowledged, especially by those in power.

A quick search of the *Composition Studies* (*CS*) archive illustrates the point. I performed a search in *CompPile*—where the full *CS* open-access archive is indexed—using the database glossary terms and/or keywords *article-writing, scholarly-article, publish, citation, racism, anti-racism, diversity, African-Am, Latin-Am, Asian-Am, Native-Am*, and *whiteness*. This search turned up a number of articles, course designs, book reviews, and Where We Are essays investigating teaching practices that encouraged difference and countered racism.

Here are a few of my pedagogical findings:

- A course design in 1999, Helen Fox's "Unteaching Racism" (from issue 27.1), helps students to understand how they are shaped by racism and White supremacy, as well as racism's institutionalization.
- A 2016 "Where We Are" forum (from issue 44.2) hosts essays on how HBCUs and their writing programs can fulfill activist functions (e.g., "Creative Disruption and the Potential of Writing at HBCUs" by Alexandria Lockett and Sarah RudeWalker) and devel-

op FYC curricula that counter the privileging of Standard English for academic and professional success (e.g., "HBCUs and Writing Programs: Critical Hip Hop Language Pedagogy and First-Year Student Success" by Brian J. Stone and Shawanda Stewart).
- Two other "Where We Are" fora: "The 'Global Turn' and its Implications for Composition," which focused on transnationalism (in issue 44.1), and "Latinx Compositions and Rhetorics," which focused on Latinx identities and practices and decolonialism (in issue 45.2)
- An article in 2019, Edward Hahn's "Reviewing Writing, Rethinking Whiteness: A Study of Composition's Practical Life" (from issue 46.1), that turns an antiracist lens to the mundane practices associated with reviewing writing in the classroom.
- Two articles that encourage linguistic diversity in composition classrooms, one in 2016, "Teaching for Agency: From Appreciating Diversity to Empowering Student Writers" by Shawna Shapiro, Michelle Coz, Gail Shuck, and Emily Simnitt (from issue 44.1 on Composition's "Global Turn"), and another in 2019, "Encouraging Languages other than English in First-Year Writing Courses: Experiences from Linguistically Diverse Writers" by Alyssa Cavazos (from issue 47.1).

Looking over these findings from my search of the archives, I'm struck by how recent most of these pieces are, almost all of them published in the last six years. These results also suggest that, while we are acknowledging the influences of race on our classrooms, programs, and institutions, our previous work has been limited when it comes to reflecting on our own professional practices.

Indeed, previous to the summer 2021 special issue of *CS* (which focused exclusively on supporting BIPOC faculty in the discipline), I could only locate one *CS* article that directly addresses the institutional racism behind our scholarly knowledge-making: the methodological argument in Aja Y. Martinez's 2014 award-winning article, "A Plea for Critical Race Theory Counterstory: Stock Story versus Counterstory Dialogues Concerning Alejandra's 'Fit' in the Academy" (issue 42.2). Martinez notes the systematic exclusions that Chican@s have experienced from higher ed and argues for the necessity of story for making space for their lived experiences. She writes, "narratives counter to these majoritarian or stock stories, then, provide people of color the opportunity to validate, resonate, and awaken to the realization that we 'haven't become clinically paranoid' in our observations and experiences of racism and discrimination within the institution (Villanueva, "Memoria" 15)" (Martinez 51).

When I served as an editorial assistant for *CS* from 2013 to 2017, we made an intentional effort to include diverse perspectives, bodies, and knowledge-making approaches in the journal. (Along with editor Laura Micciche and my fellow editorial assistants Kelly Blewett and Janine Morris, I reflected back on these experiences and imagined other practices for moving forward in this work in "Editing as Inclusion Activism.") I recall huddling together in front of the journal's booth in the CCCC exhibit hall, discussing which sessions we would be attending that day and how we would encourage presenters doing good work to submit to the journal. Naively, I thought it couldn't be that easy to encourage submissions, but I was wrong. We were shocked at how powerful a simple invitation ("this work sounds interesting, you should consider submitting it to the journal for review") was at bringing in new work.

More editorial teams and journals are now asking, what else can we do to invite folks to the table and help them to feel they belong? We need not only to bring the work in, we need to help it find its way to publication, too. Our editorial team began suggesting deadlines for revise and resubmit manuscripts, to underscore the fact that it was an invitation to send the work back and not a rejection. Laura also developed the role of a *CS* editorial consultant, whose "primary task is to work with authors of color who submit manuscripts of great promise and who wish to receive another level of support before resubmitting their work for review" (Blewett et al.).

Another critical development is *CS*'s recent adoption of a guide for anti-racist scholarly reviewing practices, adapted from the heuristic put forward by a coalition of technical communication journal editors in April 2021. (I should also note that several other journals, special issues, and presses have adopted anti-racist editorial policies based on this same document.) The new *CS* guidelines provide recommendations for reviewers regarding authors' uses of citations (which may purposefully be "non-canonical") and ask reviewers when suggesting work to choose pieces by multiply-marginalized and under-represented scholars. These guidelines recognize capacious approaches and the potential for non-traditional sources like personal experiences, email correspondences, and blog and social media posts. And finally, they outline expectations for proactive and clear communication regarding the review process, state explicitly the expectation that the editorial advisory board be a diverse collection of scholars, and pledge specific improvements to editorial practice.

The imperative to make our publications and discourse more diverse has only grown more urgent amidst broader calls for anti-racist work in our classrooms, curricula, writing programs, and professional organizations. How will *CS* and other journals in rhetoric and composition continue this work 50 years from now?

Works Cited

Anti-racist Scholarly Reviewing Practices: A Heuristic for Editors, Reviewers, and Authors. 2021, tinyurl.com/reviewheuristic. Accessed 19 Mar. 2022.

Blewett, Kelly et al. "Editing as Inclusion Activism." *College English*, vol. 81, no. 4, 2019, pp. 273-96.

Cavazos, Alyssa G. "Encouraging Languages other than English in First-Year Writing Courses: Experiences from Linguistically Diverse Writers." *Composition Studies*, vol. 47, no. 1, 2019, pp. 38-56.

Flaherty, Colleen. "More than Hateful Words." *Inside Higher Ed*, 28 Mar. 2019. www.insidehighered.com/news/2019/03/28/racist-writing-instructors-listserv-post-prompts-debate-about-future-field-and-how#.YjY0vjZJECV.link. Accessed 19 Mar. 2022.

Fox, Helen. "Course Designs: Unteaching Racism." *Composition Studies*, vol. 27, no. 1, 1999, pp. 31-59.

Hahn, Edward. "Reviewing Writing, Rethinking Whiteness: A Study in Composition's Practical Life." *Composition Studies*, vol. 46, no. 1, 2018, pp. 15-33.

Inoue, Asao B. "How Do We Language So People Stop Killing Each Other, Or What Do We Do About White Language Supremacy?" *College Composition And Communication*, vol. 71, no. 2, 2019, pp. 352–69.

Lockett, Alexandria, and Sarah RudeWalker. "Creative Disruption and the Potential of Writing at HBCUs [Where We Are: Historically Black Colleges and Universities and Writing Programs]." *Composition Studies*, vol. 44, no. 2, 2016, pp. 172-78.

Martinez, Aja Y. "A Plea for Critical Race Theory Counterstory: Stock Story versus Counterstory Dialogues Concerning Alejandra's 'Fit' in the Academy." *Composition Studies*, vol. 42, no. 2, 2014, pp. 33-55.

Shapiro, Shawna, Michelle Coz, Gail Shuck, and Emily Simnitt. "Teaching for Agency: From Appreciating Diversity to Empowering Student Writers." *Composition Studies*, vol. 44, no. 1, 2016, pp. 31-52.

Stone, Brian J., and Shawanda Stewart. "HBCUs and Writing Programs: Critical Hip Hop Language Pedagogy and First-Year Student Success." *Composition Studies*, vol. 44, no. 2, 2016, pp. 183-86.

"Where We Are: Latinx Compositions and Rhetorics." *Composition Studies*, vol. 45, no. 2, 2017, pp. 210-36.

"Where We Are: The 'Global Turn' and its Implications for Composition." *Composition Studies*, vol. 44, no. 1, 2016, pp. 127-50.

On the Future of Writing about Teaching

Carrie S. Leverenz

The history of *Composition Studies* is in many ways my history. In 1981, when *Composition Studies* was still *Freshman English News*, I began an MA in English. Not far into my course work, I found myself unengaged by my seminars on the Romantic Poets and Bibliographic Methods but excited by teaching composition. The only scholarly article on teaching I remember reading in my practicum was an early piece by Kenneth Bruffee on peer response. I longed for more. Without realizing it, I wanted what Gary Tate hoped for when he founded *Freshman English News* in 1972: "A broadening of our sense of what is possible [when teaching composition], an extension of our vision, [that] might well occur when we know how others have tried and succeeded, how still others have tried and failed" (1).

By 1992, when *Freshman English News* became *Composition Studies* under the editorship of Christina Murphy, I was in my third year of a PhD program in Rhetoric and Composition. After completing my MA, I had been lucky to secure a series of temporary teaching appointments at a small liberal arts college, and my love of teaching led me to pursue a PhD. In grad school, I learned that the field of composition involved much more than teaching first-year writing. The courses I took—History of Rhetoric, Gender and Writing, the Rhetoric of Human Science, Basic Writing—signified the breadth of this field. The newly named *Composition Studies/Freshman English News* sought to capture this breadth by "exploring the issues that define the fields of rhetoric and composition, rhetorical theory, cultural criticism, and composition pedagogy" (Murphy 2). The journal continues to make representing the breadth of the field an important part of its mission.

When my TCU colleague Ann George and I took over editing *Composition Studies* in 2003, the journal was already publishing on a range of subjects befitting its more capacious name. We had no plans to change the mission of the journal, but we did affirm in our first editors' note that *Composition Studies* would remain "a journal where both of these qualities of writing instruction—as a noble service and as an engaging intellectual activity—are exemplified and explored" (15). In the interview Ann and I did with Tate for our inaugural issue, he expressed his desire for more of what *Freshman English News* had once aimed to do: "There's a lot of really important, intellectually sound talk about teaching writing and what composition study should be, but we don't really see, very much, the teaching of writing in action, in the classroom, inside the office" (18).

In the early aughts, there were at least two reasons for Tate to worry about the status of writing about teaching in a field whose founding preoccupation was how to teach writing. First was the debate sometimes termed the "theory wars" between scholars interested in theorizing about writing beyond the classroom and those who continued focusing within it. Some of this debate took place in the pages of *Composition Studies*. For example, the lead article in the last issue of *Freshman English News* before its name change was a piece by Gary A. Olson titled "The Role of Theory in Composition Scholarship." In it, Olson argued that "while pedagogical theory is one form of scholarship, there is room for other kinds of theoretical, speculative scholarship" (5). In a subsequent *Composition Studies* article, "The Death of Composition as an Intellectual Discipline," Olson defended his theoretical work from attacks by composition scholars like Wendy Bishop who, in a 1999 *CCC* article, derided the language of theory and called for a return to more teaching-centered scholarship. Interestingly, Olson's argument for the value of theory did not appear in the lead spot but instead followed James Sledd's "Return to Service," a piece that clearly comes down on the side of teaching over theory: "I make no apologies for undignified concern with maligned Freshman English, a course whose careful teaching is infinitely more important than the further development of 'composition theory'" (11). A look at recent issues of *Composition Studies*, which continue to feature the course designs launched under the editorship of Peter Vandenberg, who took over the journal in 1996, and the roll-out in 2021 of the companion *FEN Blog*, whose name reminds readers of the journal's origins as *Freshman English News*, make clear that whatever debates we're having about who we are as a discipline, we are still teachers of writing who want to hear from other teachers about "what is possible" so that we can "extend our vision." This is especially important for those of us who are white, CIS-gendered, able-bodied, neurotypical. As the editors of the *FEN blog* describe it, "the blog promises to expand what stories are told in the field and who tells them" ("Welcome").

A second threat to writing about teaching actually grew out of a deep respect for that writing. In a *CCC* article published in 1998, Paul Anderson argued that writing about students and their texts should be considered human subjects research. This meant that most writing about what happened in a classroom would require approval from an Institutional Review Board. CCCC made this position official in 2003, with its "Guidelines for the Ethical Conduct of Research in Composition Studies" (the same semester Ann and I edited our first issue of *Composition Studies*). One of the key ethical considerations in human subjects research is informed consent: people involved in research should understand what is being studied, including the risks and benefits, before voluntarily consenting to participate. Few of us would quarrel with the idea that we should ask students for permission to use their work, but the new guidelines did produce some negative effects. Because every IRB is shaped by its local research culture, its response to proposals seeking approval for writing about teaching can vary from refusal to recognize this writing as research to rejection on the grounds that all writing about students is unethical. Even when an IRB does review such proposals, it can take weeks or months to receive approval, complicating a teacher's ability to write about a particular class.

How might these threats affect the future of writing about teaching in composition studies? I'll address the second threat first. Given the limited time graduate students have to complete their dissertations, having to navigate an IRB before starting research may seem too costly a route to pursue. We should not be surprised, then, that Benjamin Miller, who classified recent Rhetoric and Composition dissertations by research method using the categories created by Steven North, found that only 13% of the 2,711 dissertations he plotted were Practitioner studies (159). Scholars on the tenure track may also find it unfeasible to pursue IRB approval for a classroom study that, once conducted, may take several more years to write and publish. Recent revisions in IRB regulations and a subsequent update in the CCCC Guidelines have addressed some of these quandaries, but it is still challenging to write about an unanticipated insight that occurs during the semester or even after the class has concluded, since IRB approval cannot be granted after the fact. As a field, we need to continue to involve ourselves in debates about the ethical pursuit of writing about teaching, including staying up-to-date on our local IRB processes so that we can encourage and support graduate students who want to study their own teaching. And those of us well into our careers should pursue such studies ourselves, which might mean returning to the composition classroom where, at least for me, I'm reminded of how much more I want to know about teaching writing well.

As for the first threat, I think Seth Kahn has it right when he points out all the ways in which our disciplinary discourse devalues teaching, and by extension, writing about teaching. For example, we regularly talk about teaching as something one can be "released" from (600). And graduate students often learn from their mentors that the "best" jobs are those with less teaching and more support for research (592). Those who aren't offered tenure-track, research-oriented jobs can feel like failures, while those who actually want teaching-intensive jobs may be seen as "settling." That needs to change. In these pandemic-influenced times, institutions may be shutting down low-enrolled majors and even departments, but they are not (yet) shutting down writing programs. And the always evolving nature of writing means that whatever we once knew about teaching writing needs to evolve as well. We need to know more about teaching from different cultural positions, to increasingly diverse students, in a political context where disinformation flourishes and alternate facts abound. Students need what we have to teach.

Second, changes in the job market for Rhetoric and Composition PhDs mean the first job for many will be a teaching-focused position, often non-tenure track. In my survey of RhetComp job seekers over the last decade, many on the job market lamented that search committees were more interested in what they could teach than in their research. What if their teaching and research were more closely related? I'm not saying that all research in composition needs to be about teaching—I agree with Olson that the field should have room for research and theory about other writing-related concerns—but I also think graduate programs that fail to teach students how to write (and publish) about their teaching fail to prepare them for the careers they may actually have. If all of us could see our classrooms as sites of knowledge-making about writing, know how to plan teaching-related research, be able to deal with the vagaries of our local IRBs, and be aware of available outlets for sharing what we learn, perhaps fewer of us would feel torn between being the researcher we *want* to be and the teacher we *have* to be. I hope that *Composition Studies* will continue to be one of those outlets, a place to publish not only about the field but about the work those in the field spend most of our time doing.

Works Cited

Anderson, Paul V. "Simple Gifts: Ethical Issues in the Conduct of Person-Based Composition Research." *College Composition and Communication*, vol. 49, no. 1, 1998, pp. 63-89.

CCCC Guidelines for the Ethical Conduct of Research in Composition Studies. CCCC, 2003, rev. 2015, https://cccc.ncte.org/cccc/resources/positions/ethical-conduct

George, Ann, and Carrie Leverenz. "A Conversation with Gary Tate." *Composition Studies,* vol. 31, no. 2, 2003, pp. 17-26.

—. "Editor's Note." *Composition Studies*, vol. 31, no. 2, 2003, pp. 15-16.

Kahn, Seth. "We Value Teaching Too Much to Keep Devaluing It." *College English*, vol. 82, no. 6, 2020, pp. 591-611.

Miller, Benjamin. "Mapping the Methods of Composition/Rhetoric Dissertations: A 'Landscape Plotted and Pieced.'" *College Composition and Communication*, vol. 66, no. 1, 2014, pp. 145-176.

Murphy, Christina. "Editorial Policy," *Composition Studies,* vol. 20, no. 2, 1992, pp. 2.

North, Steven M.. *The Making of Knowledge in Composition: Portrait of an Emerging Field*. Heinemann, 1987.

Olson, Gary A. "The Role of Theory in Composition Scholarship." *Freshman English News*, vol. 19, no. 3, 1991, pp. 4-5.

—. "The Death of Composition as an Intellectual Discipline." *Composition Studies,* vol. 28, no.2, 2000, pp. 33-42.

Sledd, James. "Return to Service." *Composition Studies*, vol. 28, no. 2, 2000, pp. 11-32.
Tate, Gary. "From the Editor." *Freshman English News*, vol. 1, no. 1, 1972, p. 1.
"Welcome to FEN Blog!" *Composition Studies,* 28 February 2021, https://compstudiesjournal.com/2021/02/28/welcome-to-fen-blog/. Accessed 17 March 2022.

Where We've Been and Where We Might Go

Bob Mayberry

In 1972, when Gary Tate launched *Freshman English News* (hereafter *FEN*)—the original name of what became *Composition Studies*—he provided the nascent discipline of composition with a forum for conversation. He would be pleased to see how far both this forum and the discipline have come. To prepare this article, I looked back over the issues I edited from 1981-1985 and discovered an interesting bookends effect.

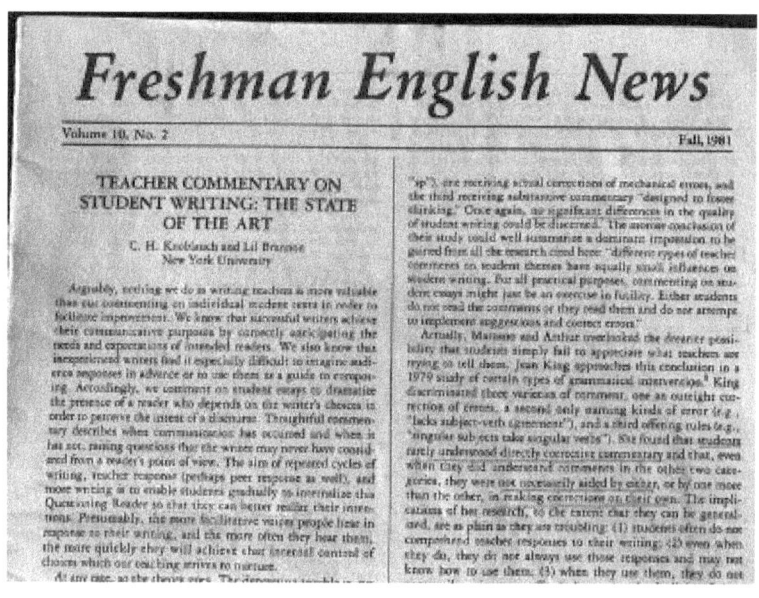

Figure 1.

In fall of 1981, Gary appointed me "Acting Editor" for my first issue, Volume 10, Number 2. The lead article, as shown in Figure 1, is by C.H. Knoblauch and Lil Brannon, an excerpt from their book *Rhetorical Traditions and the Teaching of Writing*, which would be published by Boynton/Cook three years later. The subject is, as the title makes clear, "Teacher Commentary on Student Writing," and the focus is on the abundant research suggesting that teacher comments have little or no effect on the quality of student writing. In the 70s and early 80s, traditional practice, as Knoblauch and Brannon make clear, was for teachers to make comments and corrections on student papers, return them and move on to the next assignment. Revision was not yet standard practice.

So one way we can understand how far we have come as a discipline since *FEN* was launched is to recognize how pervasive revision practices have become in our discipline. When I started teaching freshman comp in 1972 as an ill-prepared teaching assistant, revision was rarely mentioned. It certainly wasn't built into the composition curriculum the way it so often is today. I spent a decade as a teaching assistant in three different graduate programs under the tutelage of four very different composition directors and only the last one I encountered, in the final years of my doctoral work, expected us to build multiple drafts and revisions into our curricula. None of the dozens of textbooks I was assigned or sought out in those years made revision a central activity in the writing class. But that was all changing.

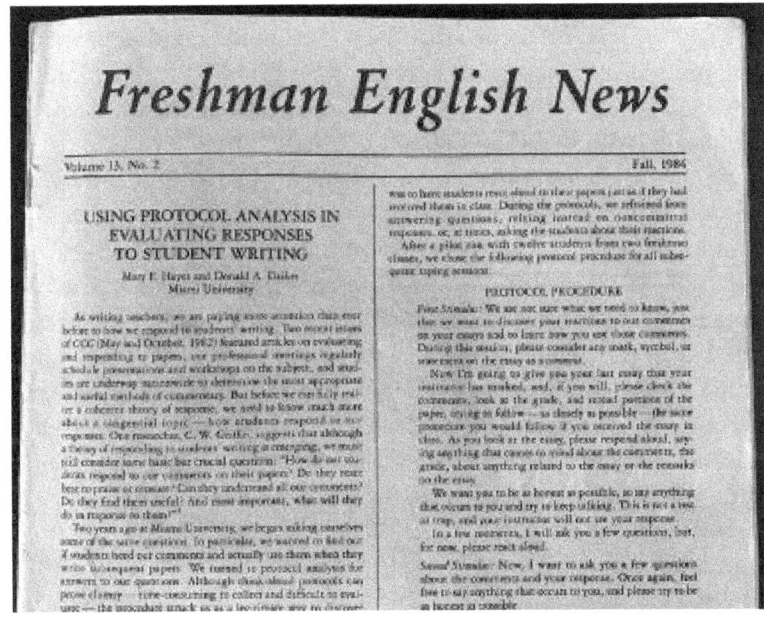

Figure 2.

Knoblauch and Brannon were on the cutting edge of that particular trial balloon, to paraphrase Marshall McLuhan, and *FEN* was perhaps the first journal to include articles critiquing standard practice and suggest the crucial role of revision in the student learning process. It's no surprise that three years after the Knoblauch and Brannon article, the subject of teacher commentary took centerstage again in *FEN*.

The fall 1984 issue, Volume 13, Number 2 (see Figure 2), leads with an article by Mary Hayes and Donald Daiker, "Using Protocol Analysis in Evaluating Responses to Student Writing," which cites Knoblauch and Brannon's work as the starting point for Hayes and Daiker's efforts to understand how students respond to written feedback from teachers. They conclude that personal conferences with students "remain one of the best ways" for teachers and students to communicate (Hayes & Daiker 4). And they assume, in their protocol, that students are expected or required to revise their initial drafts. That they can assume revision is part of most composition curricula is a clear marker of changes in the profession.

The degree of change is further indicated by the final article in the issue, Richard Jenseth's review of the publication of Knoblauch and Brannon's book in 1984. Jenseth notes that Knoblauch and Brannon's sixth chapter is devoted entirely to revision practices, distinguishing between "failed ideas" (like correcting papers) and a growing body of "facilitative" responses that initiate a dialog between teacher and student on "what a writer has actually said and why she has said it," rather than on what the writer should do to improve the paper. The latter type of comments, Knoblauch and Brannon argue, impose the teacher's agenda on the writing and "limits the student's role to 'copy editor,'" which makes serious revision unlikely (Jenseth 23).

These two articles, both referencing research launched in *FEN* three years earlier, give us a useful gauge in measuring how the discipline was changing. Revision was becoming a common expectation in the discipline, and teacher commentary was shifting from correction to conversation with the writer. (Coincidentally, while the Knoblauch and Brannon article was in the first issue I edited, the Hayes and Daiker article and the Jenseth review were published in the final *FEN* issue I worked on. Those two issues of *FEN* and the issue of teacher commentary shaped an early period of my career. I subsequently published several articles on responding to student writing, including a chapter in my memoir, *Unteaching: A Writing Teacher's Odyssey*. So the issues surrounding teacher commentary and these three articles in *FEN* were central to my work throughout my career.)

The disciplinary shift from single draft to multiple drafts has not been an easy one, especially given the increased size of composition classrooms and the heavy demands on composition instructors. In the early 90s, I taught in an English department where the tenured faculty, none of whom taught composition, dictated much of the freshman composition curriculum and specifically banned revision and student-teacher conferences! (My article about the experience, "Opening Doors," was published in *Composition Studies* in 1995.) Outrageous as that seems, my experience is not unique. There are still schools and departments and composition programs where progressive pedagogy has been restricted or outright prohibited. Our discipline's evolution from traditional to progressive practices, from product to process pedagogies, has been bumpy and remains incomplete.

A few years ago, while attending the Conference on College Composition and Communication, I arranged to meet a friend and former colleague for lunch at a nearby restaurant. It was filled with academics, of course, but what struck me was how many were sitting at a table, sipping their preferred beverage, while marking student papers. I was stunned. I had given up marking papers years before and assumed that most other composition teachers had done the same. Apparently not. When my friend arrived, he apologized for being late. His excuse? He'd been marking student papers!

We had a lengthy, if highly charged, discussion about the practice. He knew all the research and all the articles against marking papers, but, he said, "my chair expects it." I wondered: How many of those sitting around us were going through the motions of a debunked practice just to please a superior? Why haven't we liberated ourselves from the expectations and demands of non-compositionists? Those questions still haunt me, even in retirement.

When I look through current issues of *Composition Studies* and see how far we've come as a discipline since Gary Tate launched *Freshman English News*, my sense of pride in our discipline is tempered by an awareness that while we may agree in theory on the better practices in our field, we sometimes remain crippled by our need or desire to please administrators ignorant of current research. As Victor Villanueva pointed out in a recent *Composition Studies* article, "Tradition and Change," it is a "deficit presumption" to assume student writers lack something which we professionals must provide. That presumption drives our collective impulse to correct essays and direct revision, both of which leave us rewriting the essays, not the students. In spite of decades of scholarship, that presumption, Villanueva reminds us, remains.

When Gary Tate launched *Freshman English News*, there was no discipline called composition. He gave us a medium for conversation just as our field of study was emerging. The transition from *Freshman English News* to *Composition Studies* over two decades (1972-92) parallels the development of the discipline. We have much to be proud of, but we've left many of our colleagues behind. While the issue of teacher feedback and written comments on essays has largely disappeared from *Composition Studies* articles, that is not because everyone has adopted better practices.

Some are restricted from doing so by uninformed administrators, some by antiquated pedagogies imposed on them, some by ignorance of current scholarship, and some simply because changing old habits can be exhausting. We all have a responsibility to inform colleagues about the scholarship in the field and invite, persuade, or cajole them into adopting the best practices our research has identified.

That, it seems to me, would be a fulfillment of Gary Tate's dream and an important, dynamic role for a journal to take up on its fiftieth birthday.

Works Cited

Hayes, Mary, and Donald Daiker. "Using Protocol Analysis in Evaluating Responses to Student Writing." *Freshman English News,* vol. 13, no. 2, 1984, pp.1-4, 10.

Jenseth, Richard. "Review." *Freshman English News*, vol. 13, no. 2, 1981, pp. 22-24.

Knoblauch, C.H., and Lil Brannon. "Teacher Commentary on Student Writing: The State of the Art." *Freshman English News*, vol. 10, no. 2, 1981, pp. 1-4.

Mayberry, Bob. *Unteaching: A Writing Teacher's Odyssey.* Create Space, 2017.

Villanueva, Victor. "Tradition and Change." *Composition Studies*, vol. 49, no. 1, 2021, pp. 156–159.

Fragile Material

Laura R. Micciche

When I signed on to edit this journal in 2013, I didn't realize that I had also agreed to be head archivist of forty-one years of publishing history. Not even when I received the thirty or so cardboard boxes shipped by previous editor Jennifer Clary-Lemon from the University of Winnipeg in Canada to the English department office at the University of Cincinnati in Ohio.

No, my first thought was how to move these towering boxes to my office. After retrieving a rolling cart from a supply closet, I loaded as many boxes as I could while still being able to push the cart down the hall. Three trips later, I had unloaded the entire boxed history of *Composition Studies* in my suddenly cramped office.

As I opened the boxes and poked around, I began to feel uneasy. Shouldn't this material be in a library somewhere, not in a second-floor office of the charming but shabby McMicken Hall? Inside was a complete print archive. I found a photocopy of the first issue, when the journal was called *Freshman English News*. A three-columned newsletter published in 1972 by founding editor Gary Tate at Texas Christian University, it looked like something I might have produced in my Desktop Publishing class in 1987. I later read on the journal's website that the inaugural issue was "pasted together on [Tate's] dining room table and distributed for free" ("History"). The more I explored the contents of those boxes, the more I could see the professionalization of the field in the format of the journal itself. It began as a stapled series of 8.5" x 11" pieces of paper and over time became a bound 6" x 9" journal with cardstock covers, and later glossy covers, most in off-white or beige. Simultaneously, the journal morphed from being a site for teacher exchange to one that hosts a broad range of scholarly and pedagogical work in writing studies.

Browsing the stuff in those boxes, I could see, too, how the logo for the journal name was refined from a neat cursive line to the current design: "composition" in lower case, and "STUDIES" just underneath in all caps. About the creation of that refined logo, Peter Vandenberg, editor from 1996 to 2003, described in an email to me how he and his assistant (and future editor) Clary-Lemon fiddled to get it right: "I will never forget the fumbling around with new-to-us design software that Jen and I did to get that 'p' in *composition* to line up with and breach the 'u' in *studies* (which we worried about for quite a while for the obvious reasons)."

Vandenberg told me that when he assumed the editorship in 1996, he drove from Chicago to Fort Worth to pick up the entire archive and then drove it back across the country to his home institution, DePaul University. Wanting to ensure that the journal would be safely stored and made accessible to future readers, he donated a complete set of issues to his university's library. As it turned out, that set never made it to the stacks or anywhere else. It was likely thrown away when the librarian's office was cleaned out upon death or retirement, Peter didn't know which.

Luckily, that wasn't the only set of issues. The boxes I inherited included the full print archive, yes, but also copious evidence of how the journal was made over time and where it had traveled. Among my discoveries: personal correspondence between editors and authors, receipts for bills long since paid, three-ring binders overflowing with correspondence from subscription companies like EBSCO and JSTOR, microfilm reels in acid-free storage boxes, promotional pens from Texas Christian University, a vintage-looking stapler, and an embossed stamp bearing the journal's name. Traces of editors surfaced in handwritten post-it notes and copies of typewritten letters on institutional stationery addressed to subscribers and contributors.

Unsure what to do with this slice of the field's history, I cleared six shelves of a bookcase in my office to house the print archive of the journal. The binders and other random materials were stacked willy-nilly on top of a filing cabinet. During my six-year tenure as editor, I rarely accessed content in this clunky archive, instead completing most of my work digitally. But I did handle the physical journal during post-production. Dave Blakesley at Parlor Press sent me hard copies for contributors twice a year. I packaged each contributor's copy in a mailing envelope, printed and applied address labels, and carried stacks of envelopes to the outgoing mail station in my departmental office.

Taking sample journals, pens, stickers, and subscription forms to the Conference on College Composition and Communication (CCCC) each year was the other instance when I dealt with the literal weight of the journal. When CCCC was a flight away, I packed journal supplies in an extra suitcase; when it was driving distance, everything went into my backseat; when both were impractical, I mailed boxes of supplies to the site in advance of the conference, after which I then repackaged and shipped everything back to myself. Some of these expenses were covered by my department; sometimes I absorbed the cost, having forgotten to get receipts. I never asked assistants to do these tasks, which I considered too menial, bordering on insulting, but in hindsight I could have used a hand.

In my role as editor, I joined a long line of caretakers who have preserved the physical history of *Composition Studies* by overseeing the archive's journeys from Fort Worth to Chicago in 1996, back to Forth Worth in 2003, on to Winnipeg in 2010, to Cincinnati in 2013, and then back to Fort Worth in

2019 (more about that below). Must be dumb luck that not a single box was lost or destroyed in these many moves across state and country borders.

Understanding that luck runs out and preservation requires intention and planning, I arranged, with Brad Lucas at TCU, a stable home for *Composition Studies*' archive. That's where it will stay for use by future researchers and historians, no longer leading a peripatetic existence as editorial teams change every three to six years. More to the point, original paper copies are finite. If issues go missing, one version of the history of the field does too. Print copies embody more than readable content; their tactility, born of a specific material, technological moment, is unreproducible in digital form.

What's probably obvious in this story is the outsized role that individuals have played over this journal's history. Also, there's a rag-tag quality to the work behind the scenes, as there likely is for many independent journals. Idiosyncrasy and autonomy are precisely what make indy journals exciting—they can innovate and respond to what's going on in the culture and the profession with a nimbleness not always available to journals beholden to parent organizations. *Composition Studies* is demonstrating that right now through the FEN Blog, where contributors write about "the ways that writing and literacy education meet the needs of the moment and contribute to pluralistic, democratic public discourse" ("FEN Blog").

The freshness of indy journals comes with a share of risk. How will our histories be preserved? Who will drive across the country to pick up an archive? How long can non-revenue-generating projects that we need for connection, growth, and career stability survive? What happens when caretakers don't have the resources to pay for web presence, travel to conferences, mailing expenses?

While answers to some of these questions might be to forsake print, it's no secret that digital publishing is also resource hungry. Matters of sustainability and preservation loom large in the life of any journal, regardless of medium. For example, the field's longest continuously publishing online peer-reviewed journal, *Kairos: A Journal of Rhetoric, Technology, and Pedagogy*, recently created a voluntary membership model that asks readers to help cover increasing server expenses—costs traditionally covered by the senior editorial staff out of their own pockets (the journal's open-access status is unaffected by membership) ("Kairos"). The short-lived *CCC Online*, which published one issue in 2012—the content of which has remained inaccessible almost since then—is also proof that sustainability is not limited to print (or independent) journals ("CCC Online"). To some extent, all knowledge-making ventures are vulnerable to time, money, space, human resources, and the limits of good intentions.

So, let's not take for granted the significance of this 50th anniversary of an independent journal that began on a kitchen table. Originally a forum for first year writing teachers at two-year and four-year colleges to share their experiences, the journal has grown with the field and shows no signs of slowing down. Let's think about how to support the sponsors of knowledge-making that we depend on for community and career advancement, among other things. What human, institutional, and organizational resources are necessary for another 50 years of continuous publishing?

Like other publication venues, *Composition Studies* might look from the outside to be more stable than it really is, less dependent on individuals than it really is. The growth of our field and our personal livelihood rely on having the means to share our work. This sharing is frequently contingent on the good will, energy, and uncompensated labor of people behind the scenes who make this very fragile enterprise a reality for the field at large.

Works Cited

"CCC Online Issue 1.1: January 2012." *CCC Online,* https://cccc.ncte.org/cccc/ccconline/v1-1. Accessed 9 May 2022.

"FEN Blog." *Composition Studies*, https://compstudiesjournal.com/blog /. Accessed 9 May 2022.

"History | Composition Studies." *Composition Studies*, https://compstudiesjournal.com/history/history. Accessed 9 May 2022.

"Kairos: A Journal of Rhetoric, Technology, and Pedagogy Is Creating Open-Access, Peer-Reviewed Scholarly Multimedia." *Patreon*, https://www.patreon.com/kairosrtp. Accessed 9 May 2022.

Vandenberg, Peter. "RE: Question about CS." Received by Laura Micciche, 10 March 2022. Email.

Book Reviews

Self+Culture+Writing: Autoethnography for/as Writing Studies edited by Rebecca L. Jackson and Jackie Grutsch McKinney. Utah State University Press, 2021. 230 pp.

Reviewed by Bryna Siegel Finer, Indiana University of Pennsylvania.

While ethnography and autoethnography are subjects often covered in qualitative research manuals and mostly in social sciences, *Self+Culture+Writing: Autoethnography for/as Writing Studies* is, to my knowledge, the first book entirely devoted to autoethnography (literally translated to self+culture+writing) in the discipline of writing studies. It is essential reading if one is interested not only in writing autoethnography but in learning more about how this research method is grounded epistemologically in writing studies as a field. Divided into three parts with a thorough critical introduction, the book aims to "define and explain autoethnography as both a method of inquiry and a genre of writing . . . [showcasing] autoethnography as both a research process and product" (3). In other words, the book contains models of the genre as well as writing about autoethnography both as a research method and as a teaching tool.

As a researcher who writes autoethnography and a teacher who assigns the genre, I was keenly interested in seeing how the editors would position it in writing studies. The critical introduction serves as a guide to the form's evolution, providing both history and several definitions of autoethnography, focusing primarily on analytic and evocative autoethnography. The history is comprehensive, including explorations of other narrative genres, such as autobiographies and other self-reflexive work. Most important for the framing of the book, they define writing studies autoethnography as a form in which "the author writes from personal experiences within writing/writing studies"; "the author uses an inductive, qualitative approach for project design, data collection, and analysis"; "the author writes in conversation with other texts"; and "the author writes back or intervenes in a cultural narrative or conversation" (11). The key element that distinguishes this form from other autoethnographies is the first criterion: writing from within writing/writing studies. This includes "personal experiences with(in) the discipline or practices related to language and representation, literacy, writing, teaching writing, studying writing/writers, being a writer; and/or other related experiences at the heart of the study" (11). It is easy to see how the sample autoethnographies and other work in the book fall under this definition.

Part 1 contains six autoethnographies, each demonstrating a different way of melding research, personal narrative, and cultural analysis or critique. For instance, in "Her Own Voice: Coming Out in Academia with Bipolar Disorder," Tiffany Rainey provides a personal narrative interspersed with scholarly contextualization in a vignette-style piece; she calls on other rhetoricians to write about their experiences with mental health and/or disability stigma and to use autoethnography as their research method. In Chapter 2, Shereen Inayatulla writes what she calls a "vulnerable auto*myth*nography," which employs "autobiography, literacy narrative, myth, and embroidered memories" (45). Inayatulla's writing is nearly all personal narrative—it's self-professed goal is storytelling, with very little scholarly intervention. Her piece is a good example of autoethnography's investigation of brown, queer, Muslim cultural practices. Like Rainey, Inayatulla's autoethnography "centers the body as a site of knowledge production" (45). Rebecca Hallman Martini, in Chapter 3, neatly weaves scholarship into narrative in her chapter, "When Things Fall Apart," which she classifies as an evocative autoethnography. She "uses personal experience to understand the intersections of labor conditions, mental health, and activism among graduate students in writing studies" (58). For Martini, examining the intersection of personal and academic opens space for broader understandings of the discipline of Writing Studies. This holds true for the remaining chapters in the section. Readers will find an autoethnographic study of a student in Leslie Akts' piece, a collaborative autoethnography written by Elena Garcia and her father, and another autoethnographic teaching project in Chapter 6 by Soyeon Lee. While diverse in their presentation of information, all of them write from within writing studies and fulfill the criteria for writing studies autoethnography as defined by the editors in their introduction.

In Part 2, readers encounter five essays that make arguments for teaching autoethnography in a variety of contexts, all writing studies related. In Chapter 7, we learn about an assignment in a two-year college in Kristen Higgins, Anthony Wanke, and Marcie Sims' essay. They argue that teaching autoethnography to their students is social justice work in its pedagogy and assessment, and they appreciate how it "emphasizes creativity, self-study, and narrative techniques [that] becom[e] a tool for our students to explore their identities in tension with the cultural narratives that contribute to the self or perception of the self" (117). In Chapter 8, Amanda Sladek also teaches an autoethnographic assignment to marginalized students: multilingual writers. The literacy autoethnography she teaches allows students "to explore their communities through their own lenses and using their own Englishes" (126). Chapter 9 describes a graduate student autoethnography. Written by Sue Doe and her students Kira Marshall-McKelvey, Ross Atkinson, Caleb Gonzalez, Lilly Halboth, and Jennifer Owen, it describes an autoethnographic approach the goal of which is to "represent and empower voices of graduate students who worked alongside faculty members and informed that faculty member of the experiences of those on the margins (and beginnings) of disciplinary identity development" (136). William Duffy, in Chapter 10, provides a discussion of autoethnography to tell the stories of the discipline. Lastly, in this section, Trixie Smith contributes a "collage essay" (159) describing how autoethnography has been used by the National Writing Project.

Arguably, the most compelling section is the last, where readers get a chance to see autoethnography "extended" to places where we, perhaps, have not experienced it before. These include black women's slave narratives and other writing as autoethnography in Louis Maraj's chapter. He argues that the way these women analyze culture means they were writing autoethnography and that attention should be called to these texts where "intersections with culture laid the groundwork for a Black and Black feminist tradition of autoethnography in the fields of rhetoric, writing, and literacy studies" (176). Importantly, Maraj is interested in how these autoethnographies demonstrate the blurry line between creative and analytical (176). In Chapter 13, "Writing With Not About: Constellating Stories in Autoethnography," John Gagnon calls upon a "native/Indigenous paradigm" (188). He posits a cultural studies theory of constellating or constellational autoethnography, that which focuses on "presently describing encounters, the dynamics of those encounters, and attending to the other forces at work that manifest in each encounter" (189). Like native or Indigenous writing, Gagnon's constellating autoethnography demonstrates that "stories are what we are" (191). Autum Laws, in Chapter 14, also pushes autoethnography to new territory, as she uses disability, Chicana, and queer lenses to argue for "models of disability autoethnographies that resist traditional writing techniques" and "resist the dominant narratives in writing studies" that are traditionally "white-supremacist and heteronormative" (200). In the last chapter, readers are brought into the multi-modal realm when Alison Cardinal, Melissa Atienza, and Aliyah Jones reflect on experiences, affordances, and constraints of using participatory video as a research method. They describe "the power of participatory video as an autoethnographic method to cocreate knowledge" about literacy (211).

According to the editors, while there are many ways into autoethnography, no book exists that defines autoethnography in writing studies as a discipline, until now. The book explores autoethnography from a variety of perspectives, in a diversity of places, and from a wide range of voices. *Self+Culture+Writing* serves as a resource manual to the genre, an argument for why we need autoethnographies in writing studies, and an example of how they make meaning in the discipline.

Indiana, PA

Working in the Archives: Practical Research Methods for Rhetoric and Composition, edited by Alexis E. Ramsey, Wendy B Sharer, Barbara L'Eplattenier, and Lisa Mastrangelo. Southern Illinois UP, 2010. 336 p.

Reviewed by Lynée Lewis Gaillet, Georgia State University

As a 1980s graduate student at Texas Christian University (TCU), the inaugural home of *Composition Studies* (*CS*), I developed interests in archival research and the history of rhetoric and composition (RC) while studying with leading lights Jim Corder, Winifred Horner, and Gary Tate. At TCU, I was strongly influenced by foundational works in this emerging field, particularly Winifred Bryan Horner's *The Present State of Scholarship in Historical and Contemporary Rhetoric* (first edition 1984), Gary Tate and Edward P. J. Corbett's *The Writing Teachers' Sourcebook* (second edition 1988), and Nan Johnson's *Nineteenth-Century Rhetoric in North America* (1991). I had the pleasure of reviewing Johnson's important work in the spring of 1992 when the journal *Freshman English News* got a new name and look, adding *CS* to the title. However, the 2010 publication of *Working in the Archives* (*WitA*) concretized the trajectory of my career by giving a face and credence to the kinds of research and teaching I had been doing since entering graduate school. In providing practical methods to undergird archival investigations, this collection's essays, penned by experienced archival researchers, de-mystify primary research for students and scholars new to this research method, inspiring novel applications of archival investigation. Adding to researcher narratives found in Gesa Kirsch and Liz Rohan's *Beyond the Archives: Research as a Lived Process* (2008), *WitA* made archival research personal and approachable, suggesting avenues of investigation that included pedagogy, interdisciplinary scholarship, and efforts to unsettle collections. Contributors to *WitA* not only invite readers to join ongoing scholarly conversations, but also provide the necessary tools, vocabulary, and encouragement to speak up.

RC as a field has long advocated interdisciplinary investigation, but historically researchers proverbially stayed in their own (comfortable) lanes, except for occasional cross-departmental work within humanities and social science departments. In the classroom, for example, Bonnie Stone Sunstein and Elizabeth Chiseri-Strater's textbook *Fieldworking: Reading and Writing Research* (1st edition 1996) famously offered instructors a platform for combining observation, mapping, and community primary research methods with writing instruction. Many of us interested in teaching composition with archives began with this text, supplementing Sunstein and Chiseri-Strater's excellent ethnographic heuristics with exercises requiring examination of ephemera and artifacts. However, the 2010 publication of *WitA* (although not a traditional textbook) introduced RC instructors to jargon and expert information easily adapted into classroom exercises focused specifically on archives. In *WitA*, Marshall's "Looking for Letters" and Zinkham's "Finding and Researching Photographs" addressed artifact analysis; Morris and Rose's "Invisible Hands" and Lucas and Strain's "Keep the Conversation Going" inspired teachers to design course projects including finding aids and oral histories; and Gaillet's "Archival Survival" and Yakel's "Searching and Seeking in the Deep Web" offered advice for visiting brick and mortar archives and accessing digital collections. *WitA*'s practical essays spawned interests in teaching with archives and provided adaptable materials for doing so throughout the vertical curriculum (see subsequent pedagogical scholarship including Beuhl, Chute, and Fields; Comer, Harker, and McCorkle; Enoch and VanHaitsma; Gaillet and Eble; Graban and Hayden; Greer and Grobman; Hayden; VanHaitsma).

WitA also asked researchers to look outside their own narrow disciplinary interests to expand understandings of archival investigation, foreshadowing later essays by special collection librarians who remind us that archival research (a niche methodology within RC) is actually the domain of trained colleagues. Information Specialist Michelle Caswell, for example, laments that "humanities scholarship [rarely engages in] conversation with ideas, debates, and lineages in archival studies" (para. 4). *WitA* made inroads into interdisciplinary acknowledgement and cooperation, visible in Morris and Rose's library science/RC scholarly collaboration and through inclusion of essays by Yakel (Professor of Information and Preservation of Archives) and Zinkham (Curator for Library of Congress). Current RC researchers note the importance of special collection scholarship and have begun citing archivist scholars (particularly when attempting to unsettle archives, discussing community archiving practices, or when investigating pedagogy/information technology). However, important pieces by RC/special collection collaborators such as Morris and Rose's "Invisible Hands: Recognizing Archivists' Work to Make Records Accessible" or Amy Lueck and Nadia Nasr's "Frameworks for Collaboration: Articulating Information Literacy and Writing Goals in the Archives" aren't commonplace in RC scholarship. Coauthoring with special collection librarians can extend *WitA* contributor's notions of "Archival Research as a Social Practice" (Lerner) in overt and meaningful ways. As a field, humanities scholars need to accept Caswell's challenge not only to acknowledge and co-investigate with our interdisciplinary colleagues but also to coauthor with them; RC archivist researchers and teachers (who have a long history of relying upon the expertise of archival librarians both to guide our scholarship and mentor students) are uniquely poised to engage in this mutually-beneficial collaborative work.

Partnering with archivists also enriches RC's efforts to unsettle archives—decolonize and repatriate materials, recognize community and ground up archives, and resist entrenched collection practices and spaces—by expanding archival researchers' knowledge of ethical practices alongside practical methods. Embedded in *WitA*'s how-to essays (e.g., essays by Glenn and Enoch; Ritter; Graban; Bergmann) are principles that move us towards elements of contemporary practices of unsettling archives, now evidenced in cutting-edge scholarship like the 2021 double special issue of *Across the Disciplines*, "Unsettling Archival Research across the Disciplines: Engaging Critical, Communal, and Digital Archives," and the forthcoming 2022 collection *Unsettling Archival Research: Engaging Critical, Communal, and Digital Archives*. This scholarship overtly promotes "important cross-disciplinary conversation by bringing archivists, librarians, and information scientists into dialogue with rhetorical scholars doing archival work" (Kirsch, Smith, Allen, and García 2021) and provides models for engaging in collaborative, necessary, and game-changing primary research that addresses both historical investigation and current pressing social justice issues. Contemporary unsettling scholarship extends discussions of positionality, serendipity, archival responsibility, digital investigation, primary methods, and the need to research outside narrowly defined repositories that *WitA* contributors explore alongside practical methods. *WitA's* longevity and enduring relevance lies in its warm invitation to take up the mantle of archival research, sage advice that encourages readers to confidently and skillfully approach academic and cultural topics aligned with personal interests, and open discussions concerning the inherent possibilities and challenges within this (sometimes mysterious) methodology.

Like *WitA,* the design and mission of *CS* also invites readers to discover the possibilities within writing studies for themselves and to reinterpret/recalibrate scholarly conversations. Over the years, my students (now professors and academic professionals in their own right) have published course designs, book reviews, and articles in the pages of *CS,* a journal that welcomes intergenerational exchanges and collaborations (e.g., "Where We Are" in issue 49.1). I am grateful to the editors and contributors (past and present) of this award-winning, independent journal for introducing me to the field all those years ago and helping to shape my career as a researcher, administrator, and teacher in innumerable ways. Happy Birthday, *Composition Studies*!

Works Cited

Buehl, Jonathan, Tamar Chute, and Ann Fields. "Training in the Archives: Archival Research as Professional Development." *College Composition and Communication*, vol. 64, no. 2, 2012, pp. 274–305.

Caswell, Michelle. "'The archive' is not an archives: acknowledging the intellectual contributions of archival studies." *Reconstruction: Studies in Contemporary Culture*, vol. 16, no. 1, spring 2016. Gale Academic OneFile, link.gale.com/apps/

doc/A484096647/AONE?u=anon~7439ab59&sid=googleScholar&xid=7c0c3081. Accessed 4 Feb. 2022.

Comer, Kathryn, Michael Harker, and Ben McCorkle, eds. *The Archive as Classroom: Pedagogical Approaches to the Digital Archive of Literacy Narratives*. Utah State UP, 2019.

Enoch, Jessica, and Pamela VanHaitsma. "Archival Literacy: Reading the Rhetoric of Digital Archives in the Undergraduate Classroom." *College Composition and Communication*, vol. 67, no. 2, 2015, pp. 216–42.

Gaillet, Lynée Lewis, and Michelle F. Eble. *Primary Research and Writing: People, Places and Spaces*. Routledge, 2016.

Graban, Tarez Samra, and Wendy Hayden. *Teaching through the Archives: Text, Collaboration, and Activism*. Southern Illinois UP, 2022.

Greer, Jane, and Laurie Grobman. *Pedagogies of Public Memory: Teaching Writing and Rhetoric at Museums, Memorials, and Archives*. Routledge, 2015.

Horner, Winifred Bryan. *The Present State of Scholarship in Historical and Contemporary Rhetoric*. 1st ed., U of Missouri P, 1984.

Hayden, Wendy. "And Gladly Teach: The Archival Turn's Pedagogical Turn." *College English*, vol. 80, no. 2, 2017, pp. 133–58.

Johnson, Nan. *Nineteenth-Century Rhetoric in North America*. Southern Illinois UP, 1991.

Kirsch, Gesa, and Liz Rohan, eds. *Beyond the Archives: Research as a Lived Process*. Southern Illinois UP, 2008.

Kirsch, Gesa, Walker Smith, Caitlin Burns Allen, and Romeo García, eds. "Unsettling Archival Research across the Disciplines: Engaging Critical, Communal, and Digital Archives," special issue of *Across the Disciplines* vol. 18, no. 1/2, 2021. https://wac.colostate.edu/atd/special/archives/. Accessed 10 Feb 2022.

Kirsch, Gesa, Walker Smith, Caitlin Burns Allen, and Romeo García, eds. *Unsettling Archival Research: Engaging Critical, Communal, and Digital Archives*. Southern Illinois UP, forthcoming.

Lueck, Amy, and Nasr, Nadia. "Frameworks for Collaboration: Articulating Information Literacy and Writing Goals in the Archives." *Pedagogy*, vol. 19, no. 1, 2019, pp. 176–184.

Sunstein, Bonnie Stone, and Elizabeth Chiseri-Strater. *Fieldworking: Reading and Writing Research*. 1st ed., Prentice Hall, 1996.

Tate, Gary, and Edward P. J. Corbett, eds. *The Writing Teacher's Sourcebook*. Oxford UP, 1988.

VanHaitsma, Pamela. "New Pedagogical Engagements with Archives: Student Inquiry and Composing in Digital Spaces." *College English*, vol. 78, no. 1, 2015, pp. 34–55.

VanHaitsma, Pamela. "Digital LGBTQ Archives as Sites of Public Memory and Pedagogy." *Rhetoric and Public Affairs*, vol. 22, no. 2, 2019, pp. 253-280.

Postprocess Postmortem, by Kristopher Lotier. The WAC Clearinghouse/University Press of Colorado, 2021. 220 pp.

Reviewed by Jason Tham, Texas Tech University

> Before there was *postprocess*—a word, a name—there were some seeds: scattered ideas, tenets, and principles that hadn't yet been bound together in a conceptual package. (Lotier 4)

As an ancient axiom from the analects of Confucius goes, the beginning of wisdom is to call things by their right names (必也正名乎). Modern education has similarly cast in its foundation the tendency to organize and categorize information. By labeling affinity subjects with distinctive names, scholars participate in knowledge making, teaching, and continued learning. In this special 50th anniversary celebration edition of *Composition Studies*, I have elected to review a book that looks back at a period when the term postprocess was made popular by writing teachers and researchers who were seeking The Next Big Thing in composition during a time when everything else did the same—at the turn of the millennium. Kristopher Lotier's *Postprocess Postmortem*, though sounding morbid, is apt for an occasion such as this special edition because postprocess theory was supposedly introduced to respond to the eminent process era that took off in 1972, in large part due to Donald Murray's essay in *College Composition and Communication*, "Teach Writing as a Process, Not Product." That was the year *Freshman English News* (the previous name of *Composition Studies*) was founded. Early contents in *FEN* included commentaries and reports on process methods in composition pedagogy. Lotier's historiography begins at this era and takes readers on a ride into the new century while performing a rhetorical autopsy on the purported demise of postprocess after 2008 (Heard 283; *Beyond Postprocess*).

In his introductory chapter, Lotier sets out to chart the origins and trajectories of postprocess theory in order to situate it within the larger discourse of composition pedagogy inthe American tradition. In this first chapter, he details his historiographic research method for tracing the lineage of postprocess. Readers may appreciate his description of the revisionist, zoom-in-zoom-out technique in outlining historical timelines and emergence of ideas, a method that resembles a mashup of rhetorical circulation and citation analysis. After qualifying his methodology, Lotier effectively summarizes the key discussions that will be featured in the following chapters. Then, 18 pages in, he finally gets to the historical origins and distinctions between post-process (hyphenated) and postprocess (unhyphenated) that he has been teasing from the beginning of the book. I'll leave it to the readers to enjoy the thrill by finding

Lotier's interpretation here on their own. At any rate, one can expect to read about the progressive "theory wars" (18) that have caused great debates among cognitive, expressivist, social, and constructivist theorists in the late 80s and through the early 2000s.

Into the second chapter, Lotier discusses the paradigm-formation and movement/theory-building phenomena in writing studies enthusiastically. An important highlight in this chapter is the author's take on the field's criticisms on postprocess theory, including that of Bruce McComiskey (*Teaching*), Helen Foster (*Networked*), Richard Fulkerson ("Of Pre- and Post-process"), and John Whicker ("Narratives"), all of whom Lotier calls out specifically. While Lotier agrees with Lisa Ede's argument for "healthy suspicions" toward disciplinary taxonomies, he reminds readers that Ede, too, said that taxonomies are important for organizing thinking (*Situating*). So, Lotier hopes that critics would give postprocess a fair chance to advance field knowledge, rather than simply dismissing it. In the remainder of the chapter, Lotier synthesizes the scholarship surrounding Thomas Kent's *Paralogic Rhetoric*, a fundamental literature that informs Lotier's overall thesis. In closing the chapter, he presents Kent's approach to talking about disciplinary formations, i.e., vocabularies, as a way to characterize postprocess. Except for its relevance to naming and organizing theory, however, I do not feel strongly about the usefulness of the notion of vocabulary for the purposes of defending postprocess.

Chapters 3 and 4 take readers into the heart of the book in terms of serious postmortem as Lotier dissects a broad-based effort in the 1980s and 90s that sought to reintegrate theories of reading with writing theories. Lotier finds that such effort has resulted in the displacement of process theory, and in turn formulated a critical core premise of postprocess—writing is interpretive. Additionally, through his onerous unpacking of Martin Nystrand and Louise Wetherbee Phelps' works, Lotier has identified two other premises that have been commonly accepted as threshold concepts for writing—writing is public and writing is situated. Together, these premises complicate process theory. Here, Lotier makes a detour northward; he calls attention to three scholars from a Canadian university—Russell Hunt, James Reither, and Douglas Vipond—whose collective (and collaborative) works have been deemed by Anthony Paré ("Toward") as the foundation of postprocess pedagogy. In tracing this "alternate genealogy of postprocess writing and pedagogy" (Lotier 92), he takes readers down a historic journey through stories that have been largely contained by geographical borders and the close-knit community called Inkshed (a newsletter turned conference turned academic press), thus making chapter 4 one of the two most enthralling chapters for me—the other being the opening chapter.

From Canada, Lotier returns to Kent's scholarship in chapter 5 to further explicate the development of postprocess from Writing in the Disciplines

(WID) and technical/professional communication viewpoints. Interestingly, the chapter opens with Sid Dobrin's critique of Kent's paralogic hermeneutics (*Postcomposition*; *Constructing*) as unfitting for teaching writing due to the pedagogical imperatives imparted on postprocess, hence limiting its applicability to the project of composition studies as we know it. Lotier quite masterfully weaves together the ripple effects of Dobrin's influence in the ultimate transformation of composition into writing studies, with support from field advocate Charles Bazerman. Lotier then turns to WID and non-first-year-writing contexts where postprocess has also extended effects. For a technical communication scholar like myself, this part of the book sparks joy as Lotier shares insights about the influence of Kent's work on his colleagues in professional communication (e.g., Nancy Roundy Blyler; Rebecca Burnett; Charles Kostelnick; David Russell; and Charlotte Thralls), albeit all of them were at that time working at the same institution; that is, Iowa State University.

In chapter 6, Lotier uses his previously published article of the same title, "Around 1986," to anchor postprocess in invention-related discourses that were somewhat revitalized by Marilyn Cooper's essay, "The Ecology of Writing." This revitalization is perhaps most evident in how Cooper was taken up by socio-epistemic rhetoricians and then most recently new-materialist theorists, who, per Lotier's observation, hold opposite ideas about discourse. In this telling case that could only be shown by time, Lotier demonstrates how concepts evolve based on their uptakes and applications. Through the lens of inventional rhetoric, Lotier hints at the possible cause of death for postprocess—readers construct meanings of texts as much as authors do. And since meanings are never static, as they change over time, postprocess may have suffered from its vague, abstract, and open nature, resulting in inconsistent uptakes and contentions against its applicability in modern pedagogies. Of course, this is my own reading of the case. Readers may find more in-depth deliberations on the tension between postprocess and invention before the end of this chapter.

Closing the book, Lotier ironically offers an invitation to leave matters at the open, suggesting that postprocess isn't really dead-dead. Within these final pages, Lotier ignites hope. Postprocess is not just a period or a theory to convince educators of a specific way of teaching writing. Rather, postprocess is writing that shows greater awareness of contexts, including time, place, audience, and many more factors that composition teachers often invoke—an "intensification" (Lotier 187) of what process paradigm offers but with intentions to boost its dynamism. I do like the way Lotier puts it, that postprocess suggests a "need to study and teach writing in the myriad places where it arises" (189-190). Always-already, writing is situated; writing is public; writing is interpretive. Whether we acknowledge it or not, many of us who teach writing are subscribed to such tenets. Where I hoped the conclusion would lead is a next step—perhaps a transprocess trajectory that could take us into a third-space where process intersects with agency, positionality, ethics, and justice. Post—whether after, beyond, or free of—process signals change. Our current climate demands that change socially, professionally, personally, and globally. Transformative and transformational composition may be a diacritic extrication for our humane future(s).

As we commemorate the 50th year of the founding of *Composition Studies*, Lotier's *Postprocess Postmortem* serves as a reminder about the lively dynamics of our field, as well as a captivating account of where we have come from and where we may be going. For one, I hope we are headed into a more equitable space of publishing where knowledge isn't guarded behind paywalls, thus my selection of Lotier's open-access book for a review in this special edition. As readers may concur, *Postprocess Postmortem* provides a critical yet generous critique of composition history. It is appropriate for graduate seminars in composition theory and pedagogy practicum, and its methods can be useful to students and scholars alike who are interested in historiography and fieldwide citations research. For me, this was an unputdownable read, thanks in part to the luxury of a winter break and work-free days. Earnestly, Lotier reminds me that change is the only constant; our field and our journal are *externalized* (to borrow Lotier's emphasis) by what we actively pursue in the present, just as the *pre* and *post* prefixes could only be externalized by—yes, you guessed it right—process.

Lubbock, Texas

Works Cited

Cooper, Marilyn. "The Ecology of Writing." *College English,* vol. 48, no. 4, 1986, pp. 364-375.
Dobrin, Sidney. *Constructing Knowledges: The Politics of Theory-Building and Pedagogy in Composition*. SUNY Press, 1997.
---. *Postcomposition*. Southern Illinois UP, 2011.
Dobrin, Sidney, J.A Rice, and Michael Vastola, editors. *Beyond Postprocess*. Utah State UP, 2011.
Ede, Lisa. *Situating Composition: Composition Studies and the Politics of Location*. Southern Illinois UP, 2004.
Foster, Helen. *Networked Process: Dissolving Boundaries of Process and Post-Process*. Parlor Press, 2007.
Fulkerson, Richard. "Of Pre- and Post-Process: Reviews and Reminations." *Composition Studies,* vol. 29, no. 2, Fall 2001, pp. 93-119.
Heard, Matthew. "What Should We Do with Postprocess Theory." *Pedagogy: Critical Approaches to Teaching Literature, Language, Composition, and Culture,* vol. 8, no. 2, 2008, pp. 283-304.

Kent, Thomas. *Paralogic Rhetoric: A Theory of Communicative Interaction*. Bucknell UP, 1993.
McComiskey, Bruce. *Teaching Composition as a Social Process*. Utah State UP, 2000.
Murray, Donald. "Teach Writing as a Process, Not Product." *Cross-Talk in Comp Theory: A Reader*. 3rd ed., edited by Victor Villanueva and Kristin L. Arola. NCTE, 2011, pp, 3-6.
Paré, Anthony. "Toward a Post-Process Pedagogy; or, What's a Theory Got to Do with It?" *English Quarterly*, vol. 26, no. 2, Winter 1994, pp. 4-9.
Whicker, John. "Narratives, Metaphors, and Power-Moves: The History, Meanings, and Implications of 'Post-Process.'" *JAC*, vol. 31, nos. 3/4, 2011, pp. 497-531.

Contributors

Chris Anson is Distinguished University Professor and Director of the Campus Writing and Speaking Program at North Carolina State University. He has published extensively in writing studies and has spoken and consulted widely across the U.S. and in several dozen other countries. He is Past Chair of CCCC and Past President of the CWPA. More at www.ansonica.net.

Anthony Atkins is Associate Professor of English at UNC Wilmington. He recently directed the Conference on Applied Learning in Higher Education, and co-guest edited the latest issue of *The Journal of Applied Learning in Higher Education*.

Anis Bawarshi is Professor of English at the University of Washington, where he specializes in the study and teaching of writing, rhetorical genre theory, writing program administration, and research on knowledge transfer. He is coeditor of the book series *Reference Guides to Rhetoric and Composition*, and recently co-edited *Genre and the Performance of Publics* (with Mary Jo Reiff).

Ronisha Browdy is Assistant Professor in the English Department at Florida State University, where she teaches courses in rhetoric, writing, and cultural rhetorics. Her primary research centralizes Black women's naming practices as acts of resistance and self-empowerment in both private and public spaces.

Sheila Carter-Tod is the Executive Director of Writing and Associate Professor of English at the University of Denver. She has directed the Composition Program and Curricular and Pedagogical Development in the College Access Collaborative both at Virginia Tech. She has chaired the NCTE's Racism and Bias committee and held leadership roles on CCCC and CWPA's executive boards and committees. She has published works in *College Composition and Communication, Enculturation, Composition Studies, Council of Journal of Writing Program Administration,* and others. Her research/teaching/service/outreach focuses on writing program administration, race and rhetorics, composition theory, and writing pedagogy.

Yvette Chairez is a PhD candidate in English at the University of Texas at San Antonio, where her research focuses on visual and cultural rhetorics, sociolinguistics, performance studies, and the digital humanities, especially as they pertain to the representations of the actual lived experiences of mothers and Latina women.

Jennifer Clary-Lemon is Associate Professor at the University of Waterloo. She is the author of *Planting the Anthropocene: Rhetorics of Natureculture*, and her work has appeared in *Rhetoric Review, Discourse and Society, enculturation*, and *College Composition and Communication*, among others. Her research interests include rhetorics of the environment, new material rhetorics, critical discourse studies, and research methods.

Victor Del Hierro is Assistant Professor of Digital Rhetoric and Technical Communication in the English department at the University of Florida.

Sid Dobrin is Professor and Chair of the Department of English at the University of Florida. He is the Founding Director of the Trace Innovation Initiative, an interdisciplinary research hub focused on intersections of writing studies, digital media studies, and ecocriticism. He is the author and editor of numerous books and articles.

Jay T. Dolmage is committed to disability rights in scholarship, service, and teaching. His work brings together rhetoric, writing, disability studies, and critical pedagogy. His first book, entitled *Disability Rhetoric*, was published with Syracuse University Press in 2014. A*cademic Ableism: Disability and Higher Education* was published with Michigan University Press in 2017 and is available in an open-access version online. *Disabled Upon Arrival: Eugenics, Immigration, and the Construction of Race and Disability* was published in 2018 with Ohio State University Press. He is the Founding Editor of the Canadian *Journal of Disability Studies*.

Peter Elbow is Professor of English Emeritus at UMass Amherst. He directed the Writing Program there and at SUNY Stony Brook and taught also at M.I.T., Franconia College, and Evergreen State College. He has published 8 books and 100 essays. He emphasized interdisciplinary teaching and the democratization of writing.

Jessica Enoch is Professor of English and Director of the Academic Writing Program at the University of Maryland. Her recent publications include *Domestic Occupations: Spatial Rhetorics and Women's Work*; *Mestiza Rhetorics: An Anthology of Mexicana Activism in the Spanish-Language Press, 1887-1922* (co-edited with Cristina Ramírez), *Women at Work: Rhetorics of Gender and Labor* (co-edited with David Gold), and *Retellings: Opportunities for Feminist Research in Rhetoric and Composition Studies* (co-edited with Jordynn Jack).

Douglas Eyman is Director of Writing and Rhetoric Programs at George Mason University, where he teaches courses in digital rhetoric and technical communication. Eyman is the senior editor and publisher of *Kairos: A Journal of Rhetoric, Technology, and Pedagogy*.

Bryna Siegel Finer is the Director of Undergraduate Writing Programs at Indiana University of Pennsylvania. Her scholarship has appeared in *Rhetoric Review*, *Teaching English in the Two-Year College*, and elsewhere. She is the co-editor of two collections: *Writing Program Architecture* and *Women's Health Advocacy*.

Lynée Lewis Gaillet, Distinguished University Professor of English at Georgia State University, is author of numerous works addressing writing program administration, composition/rhetoric history and pedagogy, publishing matters, mentoring, and archival research methods. She served as Book Review Editor of *Composition Studies*, and over the years her contributions to the journal have included book reviews, course designs, articles, and an interview.

Victoria Ramirez Gentry is a PhD student at The University of Texas at San Antonio (UTSA). Her dissertation focuses on the hybridity of multiethnic, Latinx identities. She teaches technical writing and lives in San Antonio with her husband, their son, and their two rescue dogs.

Cheryl Glenn is Distinguished Professor of English and Women's Studies, Director of the Program in Writing and Rhetoric, and co-founder of Penn State's Center for Democratic Deliberation. She has earned numerous research, scholarship, teaching, and mentoring awards and has delivered lectures and workshops across North America, Europe, Asia, the Middle East, and Africa. In 2015, she received an honorary doctorate from Orebro University in Sweden for her rhetorical scholarship and influence. In 2019, she received the Conference on College Composition and Communication (CCCC) Exemplar Award. Glenn's scholarly work focuses on histories of women's rhetorics and writing practices, feminist theories and practices, inclusionary rhetorical practices and theories, and contexts and processes for the teaching of writing.

Laura Gonzales is Assistant Professor of Digital Writing and Cultural Rhetorics in the Department of English at the University of Florida.

Alexandra Hidalgo is an award-winning Venezuelan filmmaker, writer, and editor, whose documentaries have been official selections for film festivals in 15 countries and been screened at universities around the United States. Her videos and writing have been featured on *The Hollywood Reporter, IndieWire, NPR*, and *The Criterion Collection*. Her video book *Cámara Retórica: A Feminist Filmmaking Methodology for Rhetoric and Composition* received the *Computers and Composition* Distinguished Book Award. She is Associate Professor and the Crow Chair of English at the University of Pittsburgh.

Sue Hum is Associate Professor of English at the University of Texas at San Antonio. She specializes in visual rhetoric, antiracist pedagogy, and writing enriched curricula. She is co-principal investigator of over $1,800,000 in funded projects from the National Science Foundation, the United States Department of Agriculture, and the Burroughs Wellcome Fund. She is author of *Persuading with Numbers: A Primer for Engaging Quantitative Information* (Kona, 2017) and co-editor of *Open Words: Access and English Studies*, available through WAC Clearinghouse.

Dale Jacobs is the author of *Graphic Encounters: Comics and the Sponsorship of Multimodal Literacy* (Bloomsbury Academic, 2013). His essays on comics have appeared in journals such as *Inks, English Journal, CCC, Biography, Journal of Teaching Writing*, and *Studies in Comics*. His hybrid creative nonfiction/academic book, *On Comics and Grief: The 1976 Project*, is forthcoming from Wilfred Laurier University Press.

Christina M. LaVecchia is a Research Fellow in the Knowledge and Evaluation Research (KER) Unit at Mayo Clinic, where she researches patient-clinician communication and care that fits patients' values and preferences. Her other work focuses on writing pedagogies, invention, digital literacies, and professional practices. Currently she is co-editing a volume on revision practices (*Revising Moves: Sharing and Narrating Revision in Action*).

Rebecca Lorimer Leonard is Associate Professor of English at the University of Massachusetts Amherst, where she teaches undergraduate and graduate courses on language diversity, literacy studies, and research methods. She has published in *College English, Journal of Language, Identity, & Education, Journal of Second Language Writing*, and *Research in the Teaching of English*, among others.

Carrie S. Leverenz is Professor of English at TCU where she teaches writing from first-year to graduate level. At TCU, she served for 11 years as Director of Composition and for 10 years as Director of the New Media Writing Studio (now CDeX). Her current work focuses on writing about teaching.

Aja Y. Martinez is Associate Professor of English at University of North Texas. Her scholarship, published nationally and internationally, makes a compelling case for counterstory as methodology through the well-established framework of critical race theory (CRT). She is author of the award-winning book *Counterstory: The Rhetoric and Writing of Critical Race Theory*, and her writing has appeared in *College English*, *Composition Studies*, *Peitho*, and *Rhetoric Review*.

Bob Mayberry taught at TCU and edited *Freshman English News* from 1980-83, then turned the journal over to Christina Murphy to join the Iowa Playwrights Workshop. After that, he directed composition programs at UNLV, Alaska Southeast, Grand Valley State, and Cal State Channel Islands. His book *UnTeaching* recounts those experiences.

Cruz Medina is Associate Professor of Rhetoric and Composition at Santa Clara University. Cruz served as NCTE/CCCC Latinx Caucus co-chair from 2017-2021. He has been Bread Loaf School of English faculty since 2016. His recent monograph project applies decolonial methods and CRT to a volunteer English program with predominantly Indigenous Guatemalan students.

Laura R. Micciche, editor of this journal from 2013 to 2019, is co-editor, with Chris Carter of the *WPA Book Series* published by Parlor Press. She teaches and writes about feminist writing pedagogy and theory, composing practices, editing and ethics, and style. Her recent publications include *Failure Pedagogies*, co-edited with Allison Carr; *Acknowledging Writing Partners*; and the co-written "Editing as Inclusion Activism," published in *College English*.

Esther Milu is Assistant Professor at the University of Central Florida. Her scholarship centers on multilingual pedagogies, translingual writing, Black immigrant and transnational literacies, and decolonial rhetorics. Previous work has appeared in *Research in the Teaching of English*, *College English*, and *College Composition and Communication*.

Staci M. Perryman-Clark is Professor of English and African American studies and the director of the Institute for Intercultural and Anthropological Studies, housed within the College of Arts and Sciences, at Western Michigan University. Perryman-Clark currently serves as the assistant chair of the Conference on College Composition and Communication. She is a 2008 recipient of the CCCC Scholars for the Dream Travel Award and a 2020 recipient of the Council of Writing Program Administrators Best Book Award.

Louise Wetherbee Phelps, Emeritus Professor at Syracuse University, is currently appointed as Scholar-in-Residence and Adjunct Professor of Rhetoric and Writing at Old Dominion University, where she has taught and mentored doctoral students since 2009. Her current research focuses on literacy and aging, writing over the life-span, and cross-generational relations.

Mary Jo Reiff, Professor of English at the University of Kansas, teaches courses in rhetoric-composition theory, research, and pedagogy. She has published articles and chapters on audience theory, writing knowledge transfer, public rhetoric, and rhetorical genre studies.

Hannah J. Rule is Associate Professor of English in Composition and Rhetoric at the University of South Carolina, where she teaches courses in first-year writing, writing and embodiment, survey of composition studies, and the teaching of writing. Recent projects include her 2019 monograph, *Situating Writing Processes* (UP of Colorado/WAC Clearinghouse).

Jason Tham is on the faculty in the technical communication and rhetoric program in the Department of English at Texas Tech University. He is the book review editor for *Composition Studies*.

Alexis Sabryn Walston is a PhD candidate in Language, Writing, and Rhetoric at the University of Maryland. Her research focuses on the rhetorical power of appearance, women's rhetorics, rhetorical theory, and composition pedagogy.

PURSUE A DEGREE IN

RHETORIC

- DIGITAL MEDIA
- CULTURAL STUDIES
- CRITICAL THEORY
- PEDAGOGY & PRACTICE
- SOCIAL JUSTICE
- EMERGING TECHNOLOGIES
- VISUAL CULTURE
- MULTILINGUAL WRITING
- CIVIC ENGAGEMENT
- SOCIAL MEDIA

INDIANA UNIVERSITY

LEARN MORE AT **ENGLISH.INDIANA.EDU**

COLLEGE OF ARTS + SCIENCES
DEPARTMENT OF ENGLISH

RHETORIC AND COMPOSITION AT UNCG

R&C FACULTY
- Heather Brook Adams
- Risa Applegarth
- Nancy Myers
- Steve Yarbrough

The superb faculty and the community of fellow graduate students makes this program stand out, in my opinion. I can't think of anywhere else where I'd want to be studying.
-Current Student

Potential research and teaching areas
Rhetorical Theory | History of Rhetoric
Writing Studies | Literacy | Pedagogy
Feminist Rhetoric | Feminist Historiography
Public Advocacy | Disability Rhetorics
Multimodal Composing | Queer Rhetorics
Qualitative Methods | Archival Methods
Rhetoric of Science | Environmental Rhetoric
Technical and Professional Communication

WHY UNCG?
✓ Strong and supportive community
✓ Wide range of teaching opportunities
✓ Deep mentoring

With thriving graduate programs in rhetoric and composition, literature, and creative writing + strong cross-disciplinary partnerships, UNCG has long served as a home and training ground for outstanding teacher-scholars. We invite you to learn more about our flexible, accessible program.

RECENT COURSE OFFERINGS
Theorizing from the Body
Rhetoric of Health and Medicine
Political Rhetoric
Leading a Writer's Life
Women's Rhetoric and Feminist Pedagogy
Spatial and Material Rhetoric
Genre Theory
Equipment for Living: Rhetoric and Writing Theory Outside the Academy

RANKED #3 IN PHD PROGRAMS IN NC

FOR INFORMATION OR TO APPLY ONLINE, VISIT ENGLISH.UNCG.EDU

Florida State University
Rhetoric and Composition MA and PhD

Find out more!

Graduate students here can count on two things: a healthy sense of rigor, but also a sense of ongoing mentoring and support - Dr. Tarez Samra Graban

We're a program that will challenge what you think you know, and have you add on to that and grow - Dr. Rhea Estelle Lathan

At Florida State, graduate students can look forward to opportunity- to engage in scholarship, to teach upper division courses, to discover if they like administration, to see where their professional identity might take them - Dr. Kristie S. Fleckenstein

✓ Strong foundations in histories and theories of rhetoric and composition

✓ Emphasis on intersectionality and diversity across the curriculum, university, and community

✓ Commitment to fostering curricular, pedagogical, and disciplinary expertise

✓ Vibrant community to support all stages of graduate work

Rhetoric & Composition PhD Program

Professional Opportunities

- Positions available to GTAs: Pedagogy and Outreach Coordinator; Special Projects/Assessment Coordinator; English Composition Program Mentors; Academic Writing Center positions
- Travel funds
- Teach a wide range of courses
- Certificates in Professional Writing and Women's Gender & Sexuality Studies

Resources

- Russel K. Durst Distinguished Lecture Series
- Lucy Schultz Archive of 19th century textbooks & handbooks
- Pat Belanoff Summer Research Award
- Taft research support for summer, dissertation, & special projects

Program Special Features: Competitive stipends; 1/1 teaching assignment; urban setting with opportunities for community-engaged research; small cohort & strong mentoring; job market class for academic & nonacademic positions

Faculty

Chris Carter, writing theory, visual & cultural rhetorics, activist rhetorics, film & media studies

Christina LaVecchia (starting spring 2023), writing pedagogy, invention, rhetorics of health & medicine, WAC

Laura R. Micciche, composing practices, feminist rhetorics, graduate writing pedagogy, WPA

Samantha NeCamp, Appalachian literacies, adult literacies, language differences

Contact: Laura Micciche, micciclr@ucmail.uc.edu | Web: https://tinyurl.com/2jr87bsb

2023 CCCC Chicago Convention

FEBRUARY 15–18 | CHICAGO, IL

HTTPS://CCCC.NCTE.ORG/CCCC/CONV

DOING HOPE IN DESPERATE TIMES

CCCC STUDIES IN WRITING & RHETORIC SERIES

Counterstory
by Aja Martinez

Materiality and Writing Studies
by Holly Hassel and Cassandra Phillips

Available at the CCCC Convention and Online Now at
https://store.ncte.org/studies-writing-and-rhetoric

PARLOR PRESS
EQUIPMENT FOR LIVING

Now with Parlor Press!

Studies in Rhetorics and Feminism
  Series Editors: Cheryl Glenn and Shirley Wilson Logan

Emerging Conversations in the Global Humanities
  Series Editor: Victor E. Taylor

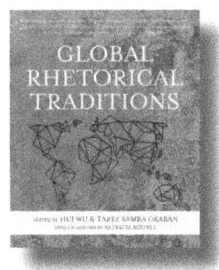

New Releases

Global Rhetorical Traditions, edited by Hui Wu and Tarez Samra Graban

Rhetorical Listening in Action: A Concept-Tacticc Approach by Krista Ratcliffe and Kyle Jensen

A Rhetoric of Becoming: USAmerican Women in Qatar by Nancy Small

Emotions and Affect in Writing Centers edited by Janine Morris and Kelly Concannon

MLA Mina Shaughnessy Prize and CCCC Best Book Award 2021!

Creole Composition: Academic Writing and Rhetoric in the Anglophone Caribbean, edited by Vivette Milson-Whyte, Raymond Oenbring, and Brianne Jaquette

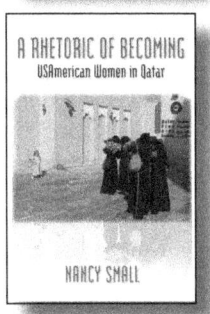

Check Out Our New Website!
Discounts, blog, open access titles, instant downloads, and more.

www.parlorpress.com

Composition Studies **Discount:** Use CS20 at checkout to receive a 20% discount on all titles not on sale through August 1, 2022.

www.ingramcontent.com/pod-product-compliance
Lightning Source LLC
Chambersburg PA
CBHW031320160426
43196CB00007B/596